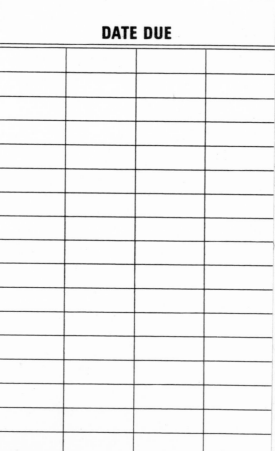

## DATE DUE

| | | | |
|---|---|---|---|
| | | | |
| | | | |
| | | | |
| | | | |
| | | | |
| | | | |
| | | | |
| | | | |
| | | | |
| | | | |
| | | | |
| | | | |
| | | | |
| | | | |
| | | | |
| | | | |

# OTTAWA
# WATERWAY

# ROBERT LEGGET,

O.C.

# OTTAWA
# WATERWAY

## GATEWAY TO A
## CONTINENT

UNIVERSITY OF TORONTO PRESS

TORONTO AND BUFFALO

© University of Toronto Press 1975
Toronto and Buffalo
Printed in Canada

**Library of Congress Cataloging in Publication Data**

Legget, Robert Ferguson.
  Ottawa waterway.

  Bibliography: p.
  Includes index.
    1. Ottawa River, Ont. and Que. – History.   2. Ottawa Valley,
  Ont. and Que. – History.    1. Title. F1054.09L43    971.3′8    75-6780
  ISBN 0-8020-2189-1

Hommage

à

Sieur Samuel de Champlain

de Brouage

Fondateur du Canada

Explorateur de la Rivière

des Outaouais

Great and Good Man

# CONTENTS

# MAPS AND DIAGRAMS

# ILLUSTRATIONS

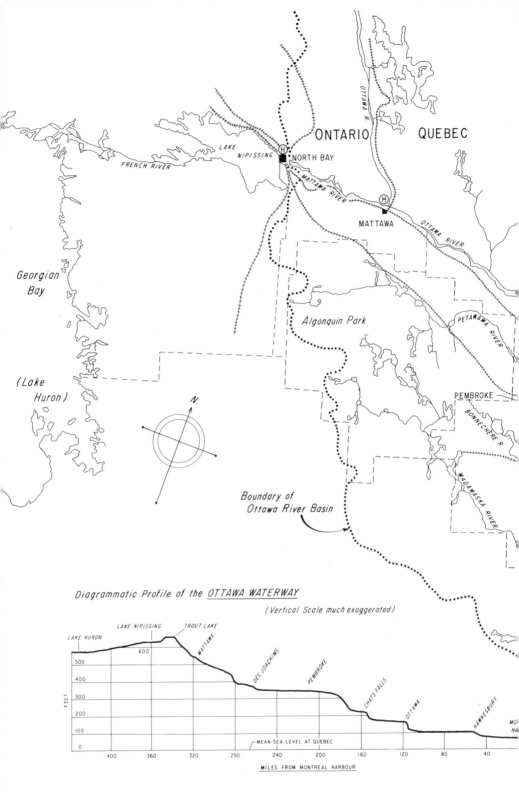

ONTARIO QUEBEC

OTTAWA R.

LAKE NIPISSING

FRENCH RIVER

NORTH BAY

MATTAWA RIVER

MATTAWA

OTTAWA RIVER

Georgian
Bay

Algonquin Park

PETAWAWA RIVER

(Lake
Huron)

PEMBROKE

BONNECHERE R.

N

MADAWASKA RIVER

Boundary of
Ottawa River Basin

Diagrammatic Profile of the OTTAWA WATERWAY

(Vertical Scale much exaggerated)

LAKE NIPISSING    TROUT LAKE

LAKE HURON

MATTAWA

DES JOACHIMS

PEMBROKE

CHATS FALLS

OTTAWA

HAWKESBURY

MO
HA

600

500

400

FEET

300

200

100

0

MEAN SEA LEVEL AT QUEBEC

400    360    320    250    240    200    160    120    80    40

MILES FROM MONTREAL HARBOUR

J.D.S.

# OTTAWA
# WATERWAY

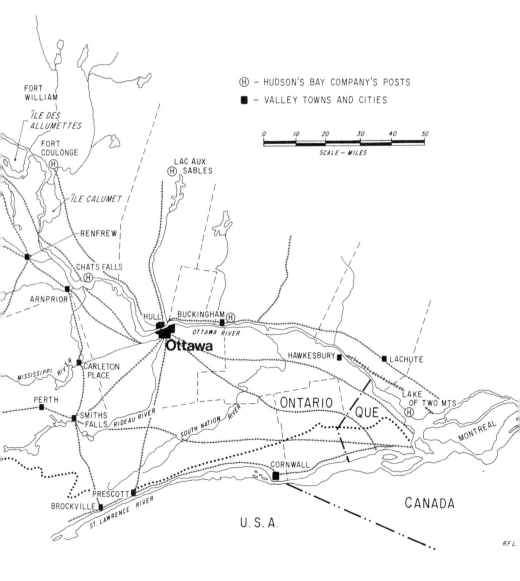

Ⓗ – HUDSON'S BAY COMPANY'S POSTS

■ – VALLEY TOWNS AND CITIES

SCALE – MILES

0   10   20   30   40   50

FORT
WILLIAM

ÎLE DES
ALLUMETTES

FORT
COULONGE
Ⓗ

ÎLE CALUMET

LAC AUX
Ⓗ SABLES

RENFREW

CHATS FALLS
Ⓗ

ARNPRIOR

HULL   BUCKINGHAM Ⓗ

OTTAWA RIVER

Ottawa

HAWKESBURY   LACHUTE

MISSISSIPPI RIVER

CARLETON
PLACE

PERTH

LAKE
OF TWO MTS
Ⓗ

ONTARIO   QUE

SMITHS
FALLS   RIDEAU RIVER

SOUTH NATION RIVER

MONTREAL

CORNWALL

PRESCOTT

BROCKVILLE

ST. LAWRENCE RIVER

CANADA

U.S.A.

R.F.L.

'Jadis la rivière des Outaouais constituait la ligne de partage entre le Haut et le Bas-Canada, entre les gens d'expression française et les gens d'expression anglaise. Après la Confédération, ce site a été choisi pour symboliser l'union de tous les Canadiens. C'était là, pour Lester Pearson, une notion capitale; pour lui, l'Outaouais n'était pas une ligne de démarcation, mais un trait d'union.'

Her Majesty Queen Elizabeth II of Canada, speaking at the opening of the Lester B. Pearson Building in Ottawa on 1 August, 1973.

(The Ottawa River once was the dividing line between Upper and Lower Canada, between the people of French and English language. After Confederation this site was chosen to symbolize the union of all Canadians. To Lester Pearson that was a prime notion; for him, the Ottawa River was not a dividing line but a hyphen.)

# ONE

# The Waterway

'It is the Grand River that you mean; for by this and no other name will they recognize and designate it.' So spoke a man of the Ottawa a century ago about the river-men. It was *la Grande Rivière* of Jacques Cartier, *la Grande Rivière du Nord* to those who followed him. It is still a grand river today even though almost all of its myriad rapids have been tamed and harnessed for the 'use and convenience of man.' Greatest tributary of the River St Lawrence, with an average flow greater than that of all the rivers of England and Wales combined, its links with adjacent rivers gave access to the Northern Sea, the Pacific Ocean, and the Mississippi. In the earliest days of Canada, it was truly the gateway to the continent.

On its waters journeyed Jolliet to the Mississippi, Mackenzie on his way to the Arctic Sea and then to the Pacific, Franklin towards his great survey of the Arctic coast of Canada. After the War of 1812, it was for several decades the vital link in the defence of British North America, its canal system a matter of concern to the Duke of Wellington for the latter half of his long life. Down its rapids came the timbers that helped to build many of the last wooden ships of the British navy. On the white steamships that once sailed its placid waters between the rapids travelled visiting royalty, governors general and their suites, and Sir John A. Macdonald and his companions on their way to the conferences that led to the formation of Canada as an independent nation. If there is one river in North America to which John Burns's telling epithet of 'liquid history' applies, it is the Ottawa. And if 'history is as useless and necessary as poetry or music,' the story of the Ottawa should be a vital part of this country's cultural heritage.

The Ottawa has been well called the River of Canada. It was in use as a route to the west well before the St Lawrence; it still provides the shortest water route to the Great Lakes. Rising 155 miles due north of the capital city of Ottawa, it flows first to the west, then southwards through Lake Temiskaming to its junction with the Mattawa River, which comes from the west. Then the Ottawa turns east, its 308-mile course to Montreal being that best known to Canadians of today, as also of yesterday, for this was the principal part of what we will call the Ottawa Waterway. By using the Mattawa River, portaging to Lake Nipissing, sailing along its southern shore and then down the French River, travellers reached Georgian Bay and so gained access to all the upper Great Lakes. This 430-mile water route served for well over two centuries as the main-line of the journey to the north, the west, and (to a lesser degree) the midwest – and this despite its many rapids, necessitating arduous portages. Today, these same rapids are tamed in great water-power plants, almost four and one-half million horsepower being now generated on the Ottawa River and its tributaries.

The Indians had used this waterway from time immemorial, as they had also the portage from Lac des Quinze, beyond the head of Lake Temiskaming, to Lake Abitibi. Further travel down the Abitibi River brought them to the shores of James Bay. Indians guided the two young emissaries of Champlain whom he sent up the Ottawa in 1611–12, in advance of his own first journey in 1613 from Lachine to Allumette Island near Pembroke. His second journey in 1615 took him along the whole waterway to the Indian settlements on Georgian Bay. His example, and the written records that he prepared and published, gave impetus to steadily increasing use of the river by explorers, by dedicated Récollet and Jesuit priests, and by adventurous young Frenchmen who, with the Indians, laid the foundations of the fur trade. Jean Nicollet was one of the first of the explorers; that his baggage included a robe of Chinese damask (which he wore for his encounter with distant Indians) showed how the dream of reaching the China Sea lay behind these early journeys into the unknown. The starting point for all journeys up the Ottawa was named La Chine – derisively in all probability– a reminder to this day of those vain hopes.

The priests founded their missions, notably in Huronia, and travelled widely, assisted by young Frenchmen and friendly Indians without whose aid their efforts to bring Christianity to *les sauvages* could not have been effective. Exploration and trading for furs were inevitably associated with these early journeys. The intrusions aroused the ire of the Iroquois to the south and led to several decades of bloody conflict, during which some of the Jesuit missionaries were tortured and put to death by the Indians. The new town of Montreal was the objective of major Indian attacks, one being repulsed on the Ottawa by Dollard des Ormeaux and a group of young companions, another partly succeeding through what is still known as the Lachine Massacre.

Closing of the Ottawa route for some years in mid-century because of Indian hostilities did not stop the trading in furs. Indians came to Trois Rivières by journeying up the Gatineau River and across its portage to the St Maurice River; French traders used the same route but in reverse. The more adventurous, however, still used the Ottawa despite all alarms, a notable shipment of valuable furs being brought down in 1660 by Groseilliers and Radisson, perhaps the best known of all the fur traders of that time. It was the seizure of this entire load of furs by the French governor, who had not given permission for the journey, that led eventually to the foundation in 1670 of the Company of Adventurers of England Trading into Hudson's Bay.

Voyages of exploration continued, always associated in some way with the fur trade, the demand for beaver fur for hat-making reaching remarkable proportions. Political developments in the colonies to the south and the presence of the Hudson's Bay Company as a rival in the north directed extension of the fur trade to the west, where La Vérendrye and his sons made notable journeys on the prairies in the 1730s. The trade continued and, indeed, expanded following the transfer of power to Great Britain in 1763, after a brief hiatus linked with the Pontiac uprising. British merchants, following the British army into Montreal and Quebec, were soon co-operating closely with those French fur merchants who chose not to return to their native France, this sharing of experience being one of the happier aspects of those troubled years. As the fur trade became better known, it attracted Scotsmen, who eventually came to play such a large part in it that their names are even today prominent in Montreal – in McGill University and McTavish Street, for example.

As the lines of communication grew longer, the need for organization became clear and so began that succession of associations of fur-trading partners known as the North West Company. To these doughty men, W.S. Wallace has paid this tribute: 'These men were hardy, courageous, shrewd, and proud. They spent a good part of their lives travelling incredible distances in birch bark canoes, shooting rapids, or navigating inland seas. They suffered hunger and starvation. They were robbed and murdered by the Indians, and sometimes by one another. They fell the victim of smallpox, syphilis, and rum. Yet they conquered half a continent, and they built a commercial empire, the like of which North America at least has never seen.' And their journeys all started up the Ottawa Waterway. The long lines of communication finally proved too burdensome and the Nor'Westers amalgamated with the Hudson's Bay Company in 1821. Thereafter, furs from the north and west, and incoming supplies, were transported by way of Hudson Bay; but the Ottawa was far from finished as a water route.

The waterways and major coastlines of Canada had by this time been well explored. Much of the interior was still unknown, but the foundations of Canada had been established by the fur traders. Harold A. Innis has put this well in *The Fur Trade in Canada*:

By 1821, the Northwest Company had built up an organization which extended from the Atlantic to the Pacific. The foundations of the present Dominion of Canada had been securely laid. The boundaries of the trade were changed slightly in later periods, but primarily the territory over which the Northwest Company had organized its trade was the territory which later became the Dominion. The work of the French traders and explorers and of the English who built upon foundations laid down by them was complete. ... The Northwest Company was the forerunner of confederation, and it was built on the work of the French *voyageur*, the contributions of the Indian, especially the canoe, Indian corn and pemmican, and the organizing ability of Anglo-American merchants.

Fortunately for the combined Company, and for Canada, the Company's fortunes were guided for the next forty years by one who was, perhaps, the greatest of all the men of the Ottawa, Sir George Simpson. Known as 'the Little Emperor,' he made his headquarters at Lachine and set out from there each spring by canoe up the Ottawa, to make his annual tour of inspection and attend the council meeting at Norway House. His canoe journeys became almost legendary in his lifetime, but he saw also the start of real settlement in the Ottawa Valley – the beginnings and remarkable growth of steamship traffic on the Ottawa and the commencement of railway construction in the valley, with all of which he was associated. When he died in August 1860, he had just welcomed to his home the Prince of Wales, who had visited Canada to open the Victoria railway bridge in Montreal and to lay the foundation stone of the new Parliament Buildings at Ottawa, rising on a magnificent site within view of the great Chaudière Falls.

These mid-century years saw the Ottawa River probably at its busiest. Great rafts of squared timbers slowly went down to the St Lawrence for shipment to the markets of Europe. Barges by the hundreds, loaded with sawn lumber, were towed down to the markets of Montreal, eastern Canada, and the United States. Many tugs enlivened the river, but they were dominated by the fleets of fine white steamships that had been developed for passenger service – from Lachine to Carillon, Grenville to Ottawa, Aylmer to Quyon and on to Portage du Fort, thence to Pembroke. At one time smaller steamers served the upper river all the way to Mattawa. One vessel was licensed in Ottawa to carry 1,100 passengers. And there were still canoes on the river, the Ottawa Waterway being used as a through route to and from the west certainly as late as 1869 and probably even in later years, although the construction of railways up the valley (reaching North Bay in 1882) brought to an end official use of the river. After that, canoe travellers made the long journey mainly for pleasure.

The two sections of the lower river had since 1834 been linked between Carillon and Grenville by the three small Ottawa river canals. These were constructed by the British government as a part of defence measures for protection against possible attack from the United States. Kingston was the great fortress of the time, guarding the exit from Lake Ontario. During the War of 1812, all supplies and reinforcements from Montreal had to be brought to Kingston through the turbulent international section of the St Lawrence. The supply brigades were never ambushed, but an alternative route from Montreal to Kingston was desired in order to obviate possibility of a break in the supply line in the event of further hostilities. The Ottawa River, the Rideau River and Lakes, and the Cataraqui River provided such a route but they had to be canalized where rapids existed, to permit the passage of small naval craft and of barges loaded with supplies. This was the origin of the Rideau Canal, built between 1826 and 1832 but unavailable as part of the through route until the Ottawa River canals were completed in 1834. They had been started as early as 1819, but were built (by the Royal Staff Corps, not by the Royal Engineers) under somewhat severe limitations of funds and resources.

Throughout the century Whitehall continued to be concerned about measures necessary for the protection, first of the colonies of the Canadas, later of united Canada. Repeated suggestions were made for the canalization of the Ottawa in order to provide direct access to the Great Lakes for British naval vessels. As late as 1865, the admiral commanding at Halifax and the general commanding the British forces in Canada made a traverse of the entire waterway from Georgian Bay to Montreal, by canoe, in order to judge for themselves the possibility of converting it into a fully canalized route.

Defence authorities were not alone, however, in wanting to see the Ottawa Waterway become a full-scale ship canal all the way from Montreal to Georgian Bay. During the years, many surveys were made and plans prepared. After exhaustive studies, the Department of Public Works, Canada, presented in 1908 a magnificent report on the whole project, the total cost being estimated at $100 million. The system would have been three hundred miles shorter than the route now provided by the St Lawrence Seaway, and all of it would have been in Canada. If Sir Wilfrid Laurier had won the 1911 election, it would probably have been built; for so he had promised. He was defeated and the dream faded, but would not die. The big 'if' – how would eastern Canada have developed if the Georgian Bay Ship Canal had been built? – remains a tantalizing conjecture in Canadian history.

These are the main strands that are woven together in the story of the Ottawa Waterway that follows. Some parts of the story are well known; some have been forgotten. The link provided by the still turbulent little Mattawa River in connecting the Ottawa River with Lake Nipissing, the French River, Georgian Bay, and the Great Lakes, is perhaps not always appreciated today. These streams and lakes constituted one of the great waterways of North America, and indeed still do. The Ottawa River itself remains a majestic stream that dominates the unfolding scene. From the top of the Peace Tower in the city of Ottawa, at the heart of Canada, one can follow the river in its broad sweep from Lac Deschenes in the west around to where it begins its quiet sixty-mile flow towards the east. Standing on this spot, a Canadian may well resolve to do his or her part to ensure that for those who come after, the Ottawa will continue to be the Grand River of Canada.

# TWO

# The Setting

One hundred and fifty-five miles due north of the city of Ottawa there is a lake with the musical name of Capimitchigama. It is one of a myriad of lakes to be seen from the air on a clear day in this typical Shield country, country that seems to be more water than land. The areas between the lakes are lush green in high summer, betraying the muskeg that makes all summer travel other than by water or air next to impossible. Lake Capimitchigama is a long and narrow body of water, oriented almost due NE-SW as are so many of the lakes in this area. Its distinction is that it is now recognized as the source of the Ottawa River.

So impenetrable is this wild area, so flat the terrain and so widespread the water coverage, that it was only with the advent of modern survey methods, aided by aerial photography, that the source of the Ottawa could be determined. Its general location was known from the earliest days of bush travel up the Gatineau Valley but only in recent years has it been possible accurately to delineate the watershed between the Ottawa and St Maurice rivers. So interlaced are the streams and lakes of this wilderness area that within less than ten miles from Lake Capimitchigama streams will be found flowing to the south feeding the Gatineau River. Only thirty miles away are the streams that flow into the St Maurice drainage basin. This is indeed a meeting-place of waters.

The stream that leaves Lake Capimitchigama as the embryonic Ottawa River flows west on a winding course before it reaches the head of Lake Temiskaming almost exactly on the interprovincial boundary between Ontario and Quebec. Originally it had the usual characteristic of northern Canadian waters, rapids alternating with quiet lakes, and dropped almost 500 feet between Capimitchigama and Lake Temiskaming. This long boundary lake carries the flow of the Ottawa River almost due south. After leaving Temiskaming, the river veers somewhat to the east but with a course mainly south for 90 miles, dropping in level again another 100 feet. Then at Mattawa it takes another turn, this time to the east, and becomes the familiar Ottawa River, flowing down the Ottawa Valley past the valley towns and the capital city of Ottawa, and eventually joining the St Lawrence River at the Island of Montreal. Its total length is about 700 miles; its total drop in level no less than 1,100 feet, of which over 400 feet is in the last section flowing east.

There are few major rivers of the world that turn back on themselves to such a degree as the Ottawa, which finishes its course in exactly the opposite direction to that which it follows for the first third. Its drainage area of 57,000 square miles is considerably larger than England and Wales together; its average flow is expressed by engineers as about 70,000 cubic feet of water per second. This average flow of the Ottawa River is said to be greater than that of all the rivers of England and Wales put together. When one remembers that the Ottawa is still only a tributary of the St Lawrence, its magnitude becomes all the more impressive.

The flow of the Ottawa derives from the fall of rain and snow all over its catchment area. This is recorded in about 100 rain gauges up and down the valley, snow depths being measured by observers who follow regular routes through the bush during the winter. Precipitation in a year varies from some 20 inches at the source of the river to about 30 near Montreal, the average being about 25 inches. This is a typical figure for temperate climates. Snowfall averages some 90 inches over the same area, this being the equivalent of about 9 of the 25 inches of total precipitation. Half of this rain and snow runs off the land to form the river flow, the remainder being either evaporated into the atmosphere or absorbed in the ground, from which some of it may seep back as springs into the streams and lakes that feed the main river.

The 'catchment area' is the area over which the rain and snow are caught to flow into the Ottawa River either directly or down its tributary streams. There are many of the latter; the pattern they form in the catchment area, which can be seen to be roughly oval in shape, is not unlike the fine veins in a leaf. In the general map of the catchment area (page 12), notice that at three points the edge of the basin comes very close to other bodies of water. Most surprising is the proximity of the Ottawa River catchment area to the bank of the St Lawrence River between Brockville and Prescott. This physiographic feature is curious, since the bank of the St Lawrence does not rise steeply from the water level as might be expected. The whole region is so flat-lying that it is almost by chance that the headwaters of the South Nation River flow northward to the Ottawa rather than the few miles south into the St Lawrence. At the western edge of the basin, the boundary comes very close to Lake Nipissing, and in the north to Lake Abitibi. These features are more understandable since lakes are often found in the headwaters of rivers, Capimitchigama on the Ottawa being but one of many examples. The proximity of the two large lakes mentioned to head-water streams of the Ottawa is significant, since each provides a canoe route that can be followed after coming up the Ottawa, thus giving access to other rivers flowing west and north.

In the upper reaches of the river we find the Winneway River coming in to Lac Simard and so to Lac des Quinze from the south, and a number of smaller rivers from the north, all with lovely names of Indian origin – Camachigama, Capitachoutane, Chococouane, and Kinojevis – names which almost demand to be set to music. Into Lake Temiskaming come the Blanche River from the north, the Montreal and Matabitchouan from the west, the Kipawa and the Gordon from the east. The Mattawa enters from the west just as the Ottawa makes its final turn to the east. Thereafter, on the north shore we have the Dumoine, the Noire, and the Coulonge flowing down from their rocky sources; and from the south, the Petawawa, the Bonnechère, the Madawaska, and the Mississippi, the latter in no way resembling its great namesake to the south. The Madawaska is the largest and longest of the south bank tributaries; some 200 miles long, it drops about 1,000 feet from its source to its confluence with the Ottawa. At Ottawa the Rideau River comes in across the flat plains from the south, and further downstream, the South Nation from its source close to the St Lawrence. From the north descend the Gatineau, the largest tributary of the Ottawa, the Lièvre (another important river), the Petite Nation, the Rouge, and the Nord. These main feeders of the Ottawa are supplemented by numerous smaller streams, all contributing their share to the great volume of water discharged into the St Lawrence River below the Lake of Two Mountains.

There are still Canadians who do not realize that the metropolis of Montreal is located on an island, an island so large that it is easy to forget this fact as one moves about the streets of the great city. Even some of those who do know the Island of Montreal well find it difficult to appreciate that the junction of the Ottawa and the St Lawrence is not a simple confluence of two great rivers. The Ottawa brings its waters to the main

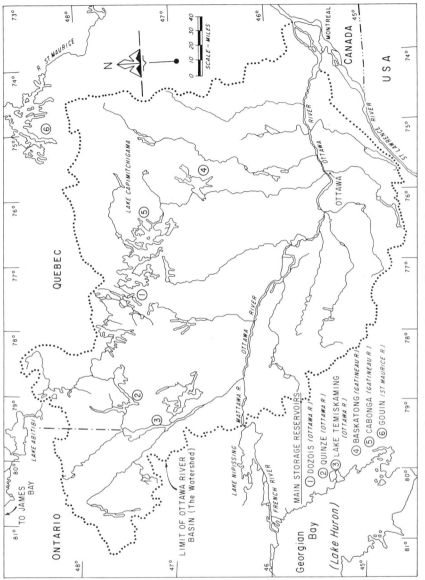

Catchment area, or basin, of the Ottawa River showing links with other river systems.

stream through four separate channels. Two of these are the outlets from the Lake of Two Mountains into Lake St Louis, one at Ste Anne de Bellevue and the other at Vaudreuil, noticeable as one crosses either the road or the railway bridges at these locations on any journey between the city of Montreal and the south bank of the Ottawa. The third outlet, the Back River or Rivière des Prairies, forms the Island of Montreal; and the fourth forms the less well known Île Jésu, today the location of the growing city of Laval. A small drop in water level occurs between the Lake of Two Mountains and Lake St Louis, never more than five feet and usually less than this but still an impediment to navigation. Below Lake St Louis come the great Lachine Rapids, the natural barrier that impeded all early explorers and led to the founding of Montreal at its foot. The same drop in level that creates the Lachine Rapids was taken up in the two rivers to the north of Montreal by a series of rapids with a total drop of almost fifty feet before they combined at Bout de l'Île just before entering the enlarged St Lawrence River.

The Lachine Rapids remain to this day untamed and so can still be seen in their original glory, as can also the swift water at Ste Anne's and Vaudreuil, especially at the time of high water in the late spring. The beautiful rapids on the two 'back' rivers have long since disappeared through the construction of dams. In the early nineteenth century there was some controversy whether the main navigation route from the Ottawa to the St Lawrence should be by way of Ste Anne's or down the Back River. Today the solution that has been followed, with the navigation lock at Ste Anne de Bellevue, seems obvious; but serious consideration was once given to the alternate route.

The flow from the Ottawa is not divided equally between the four outlets. Before the river was controlled, the larger part of the total discharge probably went down the channels at Ste Anne's and Vaudreuil. Today, however, the two back rivers are controlled by dams, one of which includes a large water-power station, through which flows about 50 per cent of the water of the Ottawa. About 10 per cent is discharged past the dam in the Rivière des Mille Îles, so that approximately 40 per cent of the total flow now goes down the two rapids still seen by all who approach the Island of Montreal from the west. This water combines with that of the St Lawrence itself, which comes into Lake St Louis from the west. Even from the shore, one can see the difference between the two streams; and from the air, approaching Montreal's international airport, a sharp line dividing the two is noticeable – the Ottawa water brown with sediment, the St Lawrence water clearer, its sediment removed during its flow down the Coteau

The Island of Montreal and the waterways around it.

Rapids and before passing through the great Beauharnois powerhouse. Lake St Louis, therefore, is not a mixing basin for the two streams, but once the combined flow of the two rivers has gone through the Lachine Rapids, the mixing is indeed complete.

All who are blessed with any sense of history must find it a moving sight to watch the water tumbling down the swift stretch of river at Lachine, knowing that they are looking at almost the same scene viewed by Champlain three and a half centuries ago. So also with the rapids at Ste Anne's and Vaudreuil, although here the qualification implied by 'almost' is more marked. The general appearance of the rapids is just the same but the maximum flow at the time of the spring floods today is not quite as high as it used to be, nor does the flow become quite as low as formerly at the end of summer. The change has been effected by the construction of major storage reservoirs in the headwaters of the Ottawa and of some of its tributaries, especially the Gatineau River. These great man-made lakes are rarely seen since they are so inaccessible. They are used in logging operations, but, apart from the lumber crews, only an occasional fisherman or canoeist sees them. No regularly scheduled airplane flights cross the area, and so they continue their silent service almost unknown.

Reservoirs have been used to regulate the flow of rivers for a long time; some minor attempts were made on tributaries of the Ottawa many years ago. It was, however, the report of engineers of the Department of Public Works in 1909 that first directed governmental attention to the advantages that such regulation would have for the Ottawa River, notably (at that time) for the early water-power plants at the Chaudière Falls at Ottawa. Three of the main regulating dams were therefore constructed between 1911 and 1914 by the government of Canada. One was above the Quinze Rapids, upstream from Lake Temiskaming, raising the level of Quinze Lake and Lac Simard. The most important was the dam across the outlet from Lake Temiskaming, close to the town of the same name, which has ever since controlled the level of the lake. The third was on the small Kipawa River, where a relatively small dam controlled an unusually large body of water. Each dam, equipped with floodgates to allow regulated quantities of water to pass, provides a means of increasing low-water flow and reducing floods. This is achieved by allowing the level in the reservoir to drop before the spring floods start, so that the peak of the flood can fill up the reservoir while normal river flow continues down the river.

Two other great storage reservoirs were built in 1927 and 1929 by the Gatineau Power Company in the headwaters of the Gatineau River; they are now part of the Hydro Quebec system. Through critically located dam sites, it was possible to create in the Baskatong and Cabonga reservoirs – the latter close to the source of the Ottawa River, and the former about one hundred miles north of the city of Ottawa – two of the largest man-made storage lakes in Canada. The last major storage project was completed in 1948 by the formation of the Dozois Reservoir immediately to the west of Cabonga Lake, as it is now known. There are many smaller regulating dams on the tributaries of the Ottawa, and the great water-power plants on the river provide some degree of regulation. It has been, however, the operation of the main storage reservoirs that has effected the changes in the annual cycle of the flow of the Ottawa River. This has brought economic

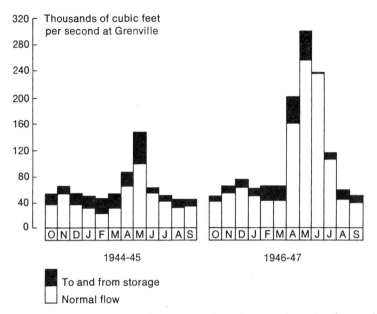

Hydrographs illustrating variation in the flow of the Ottawa River, despite regulating reservoirs.

advantage to power generation, but the spectacular floods of springtimes long ago are seen no more.

It may be helpful to give a very general idea of how the river's flow varies throughout the year. On this page are two of what engineers call hydrographs. The vertical bar against each month indicates its volume of flow. The general pattern for the flow of the Ottawa is always the same – a steady decrease with the coming of winter, February often having the lowest of the year, and then a very sudden increase as the spring flood occurs in April or May. Hydrographs for two successive years show that, despite the regulating dams, there can still be a great difference from one year to the next because of varying rainfall or of changes in the rate at which the snow melts in the spring. The ratio of the maximum flow to the minimum is important. In 1870 this ratio was about ten to one, but in 1930 it had been reduced to only five to one, low flow having been increased and spring floods decreased by the balancing effect of the reservoirs.

Some readers may be surprised to see any flow at all indicated for months in the depths of winter when most of the river is covered with ice. But beneath the ice the flow goes on. Power stations on the river continue to operate, even though the power they generate in winter months may be less than they produce in the spring. In mid-winter one can look at a station's tailrace and see the water boiling up after its passage through the turbines, flowing off downstream until its velocity is reduced sufficiently for the ice to form, when the water disappears beneath its cover.

The great rapids of earlier days did not freeze in winter, though their spray made beautiful ice patterns. Turbulence of this kind can cause the formation of an unusual form of needle-ice, generally known as *frazil*. If this gets into water intakes, it can cause serious trouble. Frazil was responsible for one of the most unusual natural phenomena on the river, great ice humps that used to rise every winter almost forty feet above the normal river level in a narrow section just below Greece's Point, some seven miles downstream from Hawkesbury. They were noticed and recorded as early as 1686 by Chevalier de Troyes, and thereafter by many winter travellers along the Ottawa. They were brought to the attention of the National Research Council in 1962 by Miss Helen Lambart, an interested resident of the area, and were studied, measured, and recorded before the water level of the river was raised by the building of the Carillon Dam, which destroyed this unusual feature for all time. A narrow gorge in the river bed, 301 feet deep and about 1,500 feet long, was then discovered; the slow passage of water through this had allowed the frazil, formed within the Long Sault, to accumulate beneath the ice cover, creating the humps which always attracted so much local interest.

Before man had started to build dams across it and span it with bridges, the Ottawa must have been one of the wildest rivers in North America. Some of its rapids became almost world famous, and its majestic smooth-flowing stretches were renowned for their beauty far beyond the borders of Canada. Even today, despite all that man has done, it is possible to get a few glimpses of the great river as it used to be. The Lake of Two Mountains itself is but little changed, apart from the buildings around its shores; it is still a singularly lovely body of water on which to sail. The reaches of the river immediately below the city of Ottawa are not too different from what the early explorers saw, if one can only shut one's eyes to what men have built beside them.

Lac Deschenes is still the same beautiful stretch of smooth water that must have been such a relief for early travellers. The river at Pembroke is the same as it was in the earliest times apart, as usual, from the works of man along the banks. One has not to go too far above Pembroke, however, to see, especially looking to the north shore, scenes that are identical with those of three centuries ago. And if one can, in imagination, forget the road and railway bridges at Mattawa, here the junction of the two rivers is still the quiet and lovely spot that was a vital turning-point in canoe journeys up and down the Ottawa throughout more than two hundred years.

There are available for all to read brief accounts by early travellers up the river; but a more telling description and one that will show us what it was like little more than six generations ago is that given by one of the great Canadian engineers of the last century. The language of the engineer today is sometimes described as a 'blueprint and a grunt,' but in earlier days engineers in this country and elsewhere were often eloquent in their speeches and quite endearing in their writing. I can think of no better words with which to describe the river as it used to be than those used by Thomas Coltrin Keefer in a lecture that he gave in Montreal in January 1854.

Keefer was the younger of two notable brothers who were among the greatest of the early engineers of Canada. Both contributed much to the development of the Ottawa River. One can easily visualize Keefer's youthful enthusiasm for the river as one reads his words today, especially those which prepared his city audience for their journey up the wild waters of the Ottawa:

The requisites for an examination of the Ottawa are:– a strong constitution, and a still stronger digestion, – the stomach of a locomotive and the appetite of a saw-mill, – abilities to ride without a saddle, – to walk after as well as before dinner, – to paddle a bark canoe, run a rapid, and swim when your canoe is swamped in a 'Cellar,' or riddled on a rock. You must be able to eat salt pork and petrified biscuit, and drink tea which would peel the tongue of a buffalo; or if you can get far enough away, and are something of a vegetarian, you may try *tripe de roche* [edible lichen] with Labrador tea for an alternative. If you 'tho' hating punch and prelacy,' are yet like...
*the Puritan divine, Who followed after Timothy and took a little wine*, it must be high wines, 40 o.p., condensed for convenience in portaging, and in colour and in character veritable blue ruin ... If you would sleep on a sweltering night in June, nothing short of chloroform will render a novice insensible to the melody of those swamp serenaders, the mosquitoes, or the tactics of their bloodthirsty ally, the black fly, who noiselessly fastens upon your jugular while the mosquito is bragging in your face. Two remedies are at your service, either of which some persons will be found captious enough to consider worse than the disease. The first cure is the one applied to hams – smoke yourself until your eyes are like burned holes in a blanket, and until you have creosote enough in your mouth to cure a toothache. The second is to smear all your assailable parts with Canadian balsam, until

after a night's tossing in your blanket, you have wool enough on your face and hands to make you look as well as feel, – decidedly sheepish. But do not consider me as desiring in the slightest degree to damp the ardour of any enthusiastic Tourist up the Ottawa.

There were a few steamboats in service on the Ottawa by the year in which this lecture was given, but the trip up the river made in imagination by the Montreal audience that night was by canoe, with vivid descriptions of all the joys of travelling with a keen crew of *voyageurs*. 'Sylvan cookery' was even described, including such delights as the best way to roast a partridge over a wood fire. Thomas Keefer saw the great Long Sault, but was able to bypass the turbulent five miles, as well as the smaller rapids downstream again at Chute à Blondeau and Carillon, by using the Ottawa River canals, simple as they were and slow of passage. This twelve-mile stretch of rough water, however, was really the worst impediment that all travellers up the Ottawa before 1834 had to face. There were portage trails around the three rapids from the earliest days of the French régime, but these did not obviate the struggle to get canoes and other craft up the swift water by either poling or hauling.

Let us read what these rapids were like in the seventeenth century. They were mentioned in almost all of the early records, but in none more graphically than in the journal of the Chevalier de Troyes, who went up the Ottawa in the early spring of 1686. He left what is now Ste Anne de Bellevue with his fleet of thirty-five canoes as early as 30 March, with ice still on the lake strong enough, at first, to support the oxen used for hauling some of the baggage. After camping on Carillon Island and meeting Sieur de la Forest, who had also started early in the season, on a journey to Illinois with three canoes, de Troyes reached the foot of the Long Sault on the 3rd of April.

All that day I walked with a naked sword in my hand, using it to test the thin ice which had formed the previous night. As the day wore on, I found myself in a spot where the ice sagged for ten feet all around me. I marched on with confidence, however, trusting in the thick ice that I believed would be found underneath. But the frequent use of my sword made me realize my error as well as the danger I was in. I, therefore, left the river which was the shortest route and continued along the bank ... At the foot of the Long Sault Rapids, we saw the remains of the old fort where seventeen Frenchmen [under Dollard des Ormeaux], during the old wars of the Iroquois, fought off seven hundred of those savages ... We were at the foot of a rapids that

never freezes, and where it is necessary to line and pole the canoe upstream. Since St Germaine [his chief scout], whom I had sent to recon-
noitre the portage through the woods, told me it was impossible, I resolved
to go up the rapids as if it were a full summer, that is, in water up to the waist
... Although the trail was very bad, the river was even worse ... There, it
was necessary to load and unload the canoes continuously because of ice
jams which covered a quarter of a league of the river. Crevasses in the ice
were so wide that we had to build bridges to get our canoes, supplies, and
munitions across ... During the portage over the ice, however, we had two
canoes smashed and one of the canoeists swam ashore despite the extreme
cold. When he came to camp to tell me of this accident, he also told me of a
quarrel that had broken out among some of the people in the smashed
canoes. They really wished to kill one another ... On their arrival in camp
[with the assistant adjutant], I punished them by confiscating the rest of
their brandy. For each barrel confiscated, I made them carry a sack of
Indian corn which they were forbidden to eat ... On the fourteenth, Easter
Sunday, we made our devotions at a high mass which we sang with all the
solemnity that the weather and place would allow. All morning there was a
very strong north wind ... The fifteenth of April, I broke camp after mass
and left by land with Father Silvie and the men who were not needed to
handle the canoes. I took this course not only because of the difficulty of
the rapids, but also because of the excessive cold. The frigid weather,
however, did not prevent those who were ordered to bring up the canoes
from working in water up to their waists, and sometimes up to their necks,
in order to pull the canoes. In the terribly swift water, it is impossible to
pole them ... [and, after relating several accidents] Only a few men joined
me because of the great number of canoes which were smashed. Apart from
the fact that it was necessary to repair the damaged canoes, it was clearly
impossible for the men to withstand such great fatigue any longer. It is easy
to judge this by the fact that it took them from six in the morning till six in
the evening to cover about a league and a half. The men were soaked to the
skin and spent more time in the water than in the canoes.

Two hundred years after de Troyes made this hazardous journey and
with the Long Sault safely behind him, Thomas Keefer continued his
imaginary journey up the Ottawa in 1854. From the head of the Long Sault,
he had smooth sailing for the sixty miles up to the next great river barrier,
the falls of the Chaudière, the site of the early settlements of Hull, first, and
then of Bytown, now Ottawa.

Arriving at Bytown, the traveller is at once struck with the total change of scene. Waterfalls, cascades, rapids, and whirlpools, bold cliffs overlooking square miles of variegated forest, and picturesque islands revealing here and there a placid pool, or shiny thread of intermediate water, charm and rivet the beholder; whilst works of art of no mean order, happily as well as usefully situated, give life and vigour to the scene. The most interesting, because the most unique, of the passing scenes is the descent of the timber in the latter part of May through the slides, which are artificial rapids under due control.

And this is what the Chaudière used to look like, little more than one hundred years ago; how difficult it is to visualize this scene today! There was no dallying at even such a settlement as Bytown, and so the imaginary journey continued to Chaudière Lake, which

extends upwards about thirty miles when it is terminated by the Chats Rapids – a crescent-like dam of primitive rock stretching across the Ottawa nearly three miles in extent – over which the river breaks at high water in more than thirty independent *chûtes* of every conceivable form; some divided by large rocks, others arched over by the leaning forest trees under which the white foam of the rapid plays in lively contrast to the dark green foliage above, the whole presenting a scene of picturesque beauty to which the oldest *voyageurs* are not insensible. The Chats falls and rapids, three miles in length, unite the Chaudière and Chats Lakes, the latter fifty feet above the former.

Chaudière Lake is the name used in some of these earlier records for what is today known as Lac Deschenes. Chats Lake is today very much the same as it was when Thomas Keefer had a stirring adventure at the Chenaux Rapids, although it is now a few feet higher and the rapids have disappeared under the higher water levels caused by a great modern hydro-electric power dam.

In running that rapid during a heavy snowstorm in a late November afternoon, my canoe was sunk, my bowsman drowned, and the rest of the party – rescued from a rock, upon which we should have frozen in a few hours, by a boat sent from the little steamer (the first on the Lake) which had anchored under the islands – were made welcome and thankful guests of her kind-hearted captain. The loss of life by drowning on the Ottawa is often frightful. In a prosperous year, about ten thousand men are afloat on loose timber, or in frail canoes, and as many as eighty lives have been lost in a single spring. The strongest swimmer has in broken water no more chance than a child. Some of the eddies in high water become whirlpools, tearing a bark canoe into shreds and engulfing every soul in it.

After the Chenaux Rapids the river is navigable for six miles to Portage du Fort. A few miles farther on comes a feature seen nowhere else on the Ottawa – the main stream splits into two separate channels around Calumet Island (see sketch map, page 24). Here the river drops more than a hundred feet, producing rapids and the Calumet Falls. A seven-mile portage took our travellers around these obstructions. Embarking again at the head of the Calumet Falls, they soon entered Coulonge Lake, a beautiful sheet of water nearly encircled by an amphitheatre of hills. Forty miles from the Grand Calumet, at Culbute, the canoes were lifted over a wall of rock, were loaded again, and proceeded for forty miles of uninterrupted navigation.

At last the *voyageurs* came to Fort William, at the mouth of the 'Deep River,' a remarkable reach of the Ottawa where rafts with a hundred fathoms of chain have been unable to find anchorage. In Keefer's words:

About a mile in width, with high but sloping and well wooded banks on the south, and a bold naked chain of rocks rising 600 to 800 feet over the water on the north shore, it is so straight that a cannon ball, if projected with sufficient force, would follow the ice for the whole distance of five-and-twenty miles. One remarkable cliff, the Oiseaux rock, rises a bare, perpendicular and apparently overhanging wall, nearly eight hundred feet in height, returning a magnificent echo to the canoe song of the passing *voyageurs*. Upon the outermost point of the highest peak stands a solitary dwarf pine which, diminished by the great height, appears by the moon's misty light not unlike the short but substantial figure of an Esquimaux maiden; and tradition or imagination has attached to the spot a story of the Squaw's leap; how that an Indian woman took advantage of the impetus afforded (by heavy bodies falling freely through a given space) the more speedily to rejoin the object of her affections on the happy hunting grounds of the bright Spirit Land.

The travellers continued up the Ottawa, and the imaginary journey ended:

Twelve miles above the Matteawan, after ascending three rapids with thirty feet fall, we enter the Seven-League Lake which is separated by the Long Sault rapid (falling forty-eight ft.) from Lake Temiskaming, a navigable sheet of water sixty-seven miles in length, varying from six miles to one-fourth of a mile in width. Beyond this lake, the Ottawa is unsurveyed.

This, then, was the Ottawa as it was seen by travellers in the middle of the nineteenth century and as it had been from time immemorial. Its course, however, had been carved out ages before white men, or even Indians, saw it, by geological forces that established the landscape. There is a great difference between the section of the river coming up from Montreal as far as the Chats Rapids and that portion that lies upstream of this great rock barrier. In the 150 miles from Montreal to the head of Lac Deschenes, there occurred only the small rapids at Ste Anne's, the Long Sault and Carillon Rapids at Hawkesbury, and the Chaudière Falls at Ottawa to impede easy sailing on the long stretches of smooth water. Once past Chats Falls, however, there were rapids innumerable all the way up to the source, apart from the long stretch of smooth water provided by Lake Temiskaming. It requires only a glance at a geological map of the Ottawa area to see that geology is responsible for this remarkable difference. Below Chats Falls, the Ottawa River runs through the flat plain of the Ottawa lowland, as it is called by physiographers, whereas above the falls it is a channel underlain generally by the rocks of the Precambrian Shield, that vast area of the oldest known bedrock that makes up so large a part of northern Canada.

Much of the vast expanse of sands and clays in the valley extending beyond Pembroke, up the St Lawrence almost as far as Kingston, and down the St Lawrence until way past Gaspé, was deposited long ago when all this vast region lay beneath the sea. This former inroad of the ocean is called by scientists the Champlain Sea. The level of the Champlain Sea was higher than the level of the Atlantic Ocean today; but, of more importance, the level of the land surface was lower than it is now. This was the result of the glaciation that covered all of eastern Canada and much of the northeastern United States (as far south as New York) in the Pleistocene era. Geologists have been able to determine, through a study of glacial soils and in other ways, how the Pleistocene ice slowly and repeatedly advanced from the north until it was finally halted. It then retreated some distance, only to advance again with some new change in climatic conditions.

The last of these advances of the ice is known as the Wisconsin Glaciation, since the ice then extended generally as far as the southern boundary of that state, earlier glaciation having reached as far south as St Louis,

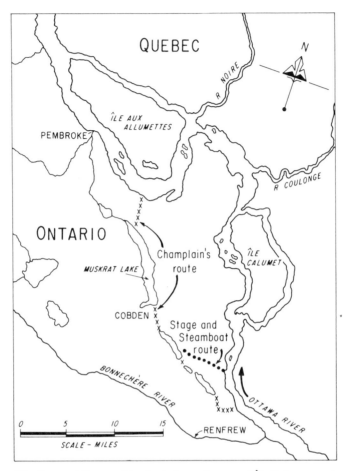

The Ottawa River and its dual channels around Île Calumet and Île aux Allumettes.

Missouri. The last glaciation reached its maximum extent about 16,000 years ago and then started its slow retreat. Even this was not a regular process since minor readvances occurred. By 12,000 years ago the ice front had retreated to an east-west line running along the north side of the present Ottawa Valley, but it still blocked the great lake, named Algonquin, that had been formed by glacial melt waters over rather more than the area now occupied by Lake Huron and Georgian Bay. Far to the east the recession of the ice had permitted the earlier Atlantic Ocean to come flooding up the St Lawrence Valley as the Champlain Sea.

About 11,200 years ago the waters of Lake Algonquin, being at a higher level than those of the Champlain Sea, broke through the land barrier that had just been exposed by the retreating ice and started flowing eastwards into the Sea instead of by way of the Great Lakes route through what we know today as Niagara. The breakthrough occurred at a location now known as Fossmill, a small place about twenty-five miles south of North Bay. A large flow of glacial melt water began from Lake Algonquin, whose water level slowly fell. The ice, however, went on receding to the north, eventually passing the location now occupied by the city of North Bay. This opened up another outlet for the waters of Lake Algonquin, its level now lowered so that the beginning of Lake Nipissing had become separated from it.

In this way there was formed the natural river channel from Lake Nipissing along what is now the Rivière des Vases and then down the valley of the Mattawa River into the Ottawa. This became the route followed by so many travellers in Canada, coming up from Montreal to gain access into the Great Lakes, then separating in various directions for discoveries to the south, the west, and the north. And this natural waterway was formed as a result of the recession of the ice just about 10,000 years ago. Probably about 4,000 years ago Lake Nipissing began to drain down the French River; drainage of the lakes into the Mississippi basin then came to an end, until artificially opened up again in recent years through the Chicago Drainage Canal; and all outflow from the Great Lakes came over Niagara Falls into Lake Ontario and so down the St Lawrence to the sea, as it does today. But the old glacial river channels remained, obscured from immediate recognition by the inevitable processes of surface erosion and change, and now they are covered by vegetation where they are not in use as modern waterways.

It is not often that Pleistocene geology is so directly and obviously the cause of the formation of a natural water route between adjacent watersheds, but another prime example is to be found further north, also in the

Ottawa basin. The ice continued its retreat to the north. The Great Lakes began to take on the form we know today, although they were still at higher elevations than now. Other glacial melt-water lakes formed close to the ice front, one of these being known as Lake Barlow. The clay deposited on its bottom now makes the clay belt of northern Ontario such good agricultural land. As the ice still receded to the north, smaller Lake Ojibway was formed in what is now the basin of the Abitibi River. It could not drain to the north, as does the Abitibi, because of the ice, and so it drained to the south into the catchment area of the Ottawa River, providing yet another glacial river channel. In the course of time, with rising of the land, the direction of this drainage was reversed and the present drainage basin of the Abitibi River was established. The old route of discharge from Lake Ojibway remained, however, and it provided the second waterway outlet from the Ottawa basin, this time to James Bay, for early travellers who came up the Ottawa, through Lake Temiskaming, and on over the height of land, down to Arctic waters. This channel was formed about 8,000 years ago.

There must be few major rivers of the world the course of which is so obviously dependent on local geology as is that of the Ottawa. What little has been said may enable those interested to recognize, for example, the many evidences of old courses used by the Ottawa River but now dry land, to be seen all the way down the valley below Pembroke. Travellers by air, upon leaving Uplands Airport in Ottawa, can, when the air is clear, see vivid signs of these old watercourses just as they leave Ottawa – La Mer Bleue to the east and the minor valley containing Constance Lake to the west. It is almost unique to find a bog and fen still in its natural state – certainly of such wide extent (6,300 acres) as La Mer Bleue – adjacent to a major city; and it is good to think that its preservation is now reasonably well assured.

Sand deposits will be more understandable when the great outflows of glacial rivers are recalled. Such deposits are found in several parts of the valley in addition to the Petawawa area, a good example being the Sandpits at Uplands in Ottawa. And the landslides that occur periodically in the valley, especially in the Ottawa region, as a consequence of man's activities, would not be regarded as 'Acts of God' or things of mystery, as is sometimes suggested in the less well informed press reports, if the unusual nature of the Leda Clay were kept in mind. (Leda is the name generally given to the sensitive clay deposited at the bottom of the Champlain Sea.)

This general picture has long been known, having been appreciated and developed by the earliest geologists to visit the valley. When it is recalled that they could travel only by canoe up the river and its tributaries, since

One of Sir William Logan's typical field sketches of scenes on the Ottawa River.

the unbroken forests that came to the water's edge made travel on land nearly impossible, the accuracy of observations made almost entirely from the water is truly remarkable.

The founder and first Director of the Geological Survey of Canada was Sir William Logan. After practical experience in the coal mines of South Wales, where he learned his geology the hard way, he came to Canada by official invitation to study its geology, starting from scratch and for a time working entirely on his own. His activity was as astounding as the accuracy and significance of his observations, his first geological map in Canada (1856) being still valid in general pattern. At the end of June 1845, Logan embarked on a journey up the Ottawa that took him to the upper reaches of Lake Temiskaming. His carefully kept field notes, in leatherbound notebooks, are now one of the treasures of the Public Archives. They were written in pencil as he travelled but always carefully inked in at night, and illustrated with sketches that are a delight to the eye.

In his second official report of the Survey, the *Report of Progress for the Year 1845–46*, published in Montreal in 1847, Logan wrote:

Supplying ourselves with provisions, we were enabled to forward them up the Ottawa first by steam propellers to Bytown, and thence by steamboats plying on the Lakes Chaudière and Chats, with the assistance of wagon conveyance established at the portages as far as the Falls of the Calumet, a distance of about 175 miles. Four Indians were hired at Caughnawaga and, with the aid of the gentlemen in charge of the Hudson's Bay posts, at Lachine and the Lake of Two Mountains, we obtained a couple of excellent birchbark canoes.

At Bytown, Logan arranged with Mr McDermott, the Provincial Surveyor, for a record of barometric pressure to be kept so that he could later correct his own barometric observations up the Ottawa; he also studied some of the geological features of the area around the village.

After being kindly received at the Falls of the Calumet by a Mr Nagle, in charge of the timber slide that had just been constructed there, they got to Pembroke and made a short excursion up the Muskrat River. At Fort William, they were warmly received by the Hudson's Bay Company Factor, Mr Brown, admired the great long stretch of Deep River, portaged the Joachim Falls and reached the mouth of Bennett's Brook 'about five miles further up the River. This constituted the highest point to which the Ottawa had been surveyed.'

Then the hard work of the journey commenced, since Logan had decided not only to record the geology of the banks, but to survey the river as accurately as he could. For this purpose, he used a Rochon's micrometer telescope for measuring distances, a theodolite for bearings, and a good levelling instrument and staff for elevations, all instruments being carried in their canoes and portaged, together with supplies and geological specimens, at all major rapids.

The measurements of the day were plotted in our tents at night, by which means we were always prepared by the inspection of our map the better to understand the geological relations of separate parts ... This part of our survey occupied seven weeks and, notwithstanding the weather was of the most unfavourable description for upwards of one-half of our time, there having been scarcely a day without rain; we were enabled to add to the topographical delineation of the country 150 miles of the main trunk of the Ottawa to the head of Lake Temiskeamang ... and about fifty miles on the chain of lakes constituting the Mattawa or Little River (a tributary falling in on the right bank seventeen leagues from our starting point).

It was October before they went up the Mattawa and here they 'met with a great many small rapids and [took] the levels of them all; very difficult going, the Bush is so thick on the Bank that it is almost impassable.' The slight change in language is an indication that this last quotation is from Logan's field notes.

The party rested on Sundays, but in view of the lateness of the season, they did travel back down the Mattawa on a Sunday, 12 October and 'camped at Lake Gallant [on the Monday] being very wet and fatigued.' They went as far as Lake Nipissing, the levels they took showing that 'the highest point of land is only 24′6″ above the water and that a tamarask swamp ... would make it difficult to bring the Lake Nipissing down the Ottawa.' This is an observation of unusual interest, both geologically and also in view of later plans for the canalization of the entire Ottawa route. The night of 15 October was 'very cold' with the first frost of the season, but on reaching the junction of the Mattawa with the Ottawa late in the day, they did not turn downstream but went north to continue their survey up to and in Lake Temiskaming. On the 29th, they camped at the famous Hudson's Bay Company Post at the Narrows. Logan found 'the view from Post Temiskaming the most beautiful I ever saw.'

They encountered a tremendous gale from the south on the 31st and made no headway that day, but they carried on the next day and reached the head of the lake. They had a little snow on the morning of 7 November, wind from the north on the 8th, so strong that it was impossible to take any bearings, and on the 9th it was 'rather inclined to freeze in the morning [with] the wind from the north. Beautiful sunshine in the morning. Embarked and proceeded down the Lake; arrived at Post Temiskaming at 1 o'clock p.m., remained there overnight, changed our two canoes for one.' Only then did they set off on their long journey downstream to Montreal, which they completed safely. The records of the survey work done were passed on to Joseph Bouchette for inclusion in the new edition of his topographical map of Canada. The geological observations provided part of the base for Logan's later reports, especially for his remarkable book, *The Geology of Canada*, published in 1863.

This, then, was the Ottawa waterway as it existed in 1846. Its main section was the easterly flowing part of the Ottawa River for 308 miles upstream from Montreal, with major rapids at Carillon-Grenville (miles 48 to 60), the Chaudière (mile 117), and Chats Falls (mile 150) and thereafter at numerous locations along the river, the section known as Deep River (mile 226 to 254) being the only remaining stretch of quiet water until the mouth of the Mattawa River was reached. The total rise in elevation from the St Lawrence River at Montreal was 473 feet. By continuing up the Ottawa along its southward flowing section, through Lake Temiskaming and then through Quinze Lake, a portage could be reached that led into the Abitibi River, with its Arctic-oriented watershed giving access to James Bay. This route was used by some early travellers, but the principal extension of the main stream of the Ottawa was to continue west up the little Mattawa River, through its forty miles of turbulent waters and quiet connecting lakes, rising another 168 feet to Trout Lake at a summit elevation of 666.95 feet above mean sea level. Four miles only separated the upper end of Trout Lake from Lake Nipissing, four miles that could be crossed by means of difficult portages and the minute River Vase. Thirty miles of clear sailing then followed across Lake Nipissing and into the quiet headwaters of the French River; then came rapids again along the remaining 48 miles of this still untamed and wild river, leading finally into Lake Huron, with a drop in level of 86 feet. From the harbour of Montreal to the mouth of the French River in Lake Huron is a total distance of 430.76 miles.

This was the Ottawa Waterway, gateway to the continent.

# THREE

# Canoes on the Ottawa

The Ottawa is truly Champlain's river. Although he was not the first white man to sail on its waters and see its beauties, the two who preceded him were his emissaries. Etienne Brulé was first up the Ottawa, probably in 1610, certainly reaching Georgian Bay in 1611 and so being the first white man also to see Lake Huron. Champlain next sent Nicolas de Vignau to live with the Indians in 1611. Vignau returned to Paris in 1612 and told Champlain that he had been to the 'Northern Sea,' presumably Hudson Bay, named only some years later after Henry Hudson, who was set adrift there by his mutinous crew in this same year, 1611. Vignau kept no written records, so far as is known, as Champlain did when he started his own pioneer journey up the Ottawa in 1613. It was his regular practice to record all his journeys, and he published the resulting journals.

Born about 1570 in Brouage, a small fishing port in Brittany, Champlain paid his first visit to Canada in 1603. When he died at Quebec on Christmas Day 1635, after crossing the Atlantic no less than twenty-three times in his efforts to get New France established, he knew that the settlement he had founded would continue. There are an increasing number of good books about Champlain in both French and English, in addition to several editions of his own *Voyages*, all of which make clear that the two journeys up the Ottawa were the climax of his explorations, since he did not leave Quebec again on any long journeys after his return on 11 July 1616. One of the best of all introductions to his Ottawa River journeys is also one of the latest volumes about Champlain, the record of a retracing (mainly by air!) of all his explorations in North America, by Samuel Eliot Morison, the noted sailor and historian. It is, however, to Champlain's own works that the interested student of the Ottawa will wish to turn, since all that we can do here is to summarize his two notable journeys.

It was during his first visit to Canada in 1603 that Champlain sailed a pinnace from Tadoussac, with some friendly Montagnais Indians, up the St Lawrence as far as the site of Montreal. He was repeating Jacques Cartier's journey of 1535 but found almost nothing left of the Indian establishments Cartier had seen. He learned that he could not use ships' boats for any journeys beyond the great rapids, now called Lachine but named by him the Sault St Louis, but would have to use Indian guides and Indian birch-bark canoes. From the Montagnais he got some idea of the journey up the Ottawa and of Lakes Ontario and Erie, but gained the impression that the latter were salt. It was not until 1611 that he was able to come again up the St Lawrence, now with a desire to extend the trade in furs that had already been well established at Tadoussac and to find out more about the Ottawa. It was on 13 June that, near Lachine, he finally met with a group of Hurons and Algonquins, accompanied by Etienne Brulé, who was then well able to speak their language, a great advantage since Champlain himself never did manage to learn the Indian tongues. Together, Champlain and Brulé planned a journey up the Ottawa, and the establishment of some trading posts, for the year following.

After the meeting, the Indians gave Champlain what must have been one of his most thrilling experiences – a trip down the Lachine Rapids (in which one of his young men and an Indian had just been drowned, while they were waiting for the meeting), his own canoe being escorted by seven others. He took furs back with him down-river and thus started the fur trading from the Ottawa region that was to prove so profitable. Back again in France, he published in 1613 one of the best of his volumes, which contained his remarkable 1612 map, quite the best map of northeastern North America issued up to that time. It showed the Ottawa River and its connecting lakes clearly, although somewhat inaccurately.

His sixth *Voyage* started at Honfleur on 6 March 1613. He took about six weeks for the journey to Tadoussac, from which he again set out for Quebec in a shallop, going on to Montreal where a small party of Algonquin Indians agreed to guide him up the Ottawa in return for his promise to lead them in warfare the next year. On 27 May his journey up the Ottawa started, with a portage round the Lachine Rapids. He had two canoes and travelled with four French companions, an Indian guide, and an interpreter. They followed the route that we now know, experiencing great difficulty in mounting the Long Sault. Champlain's account of how his canoe turned broadside in the swift water, the pull almost tearing off one of his hands, is a most graphic piece of writing despite all his customary restraint.

They met fifteen canoes full of Algonquins coming down-stream and so added another steersman and guide. At the Chaudière they stopped for the regular Indian ceremony at the falls, portaged Chats Falls, but left the main river in order to use the Muskrat route with all its difficulties, not the least of which were the mosquitoes, lamented in this first account of a journey up the Ottawa as they have been in practically every other account ever written. It was on this part of the route, close to the village of Cobden, that Champlain may have lost his astrolabe. One such as he used was certainly found here in 1867, and after various vicissitudes came into the possession of the New York Historical Society, where it is known as 'Champlain's Astrolabe.' Kindly loaned, on occasion, for display in Canada, this small copper surveying instrument is our only physical link with these great and historic journeys. One can but hope that some day it may be returned to this country to occupy the honoured place it should have among Canada's national treasures. Even if Champlain did not himself lose it in 1613, it may still be his, since in his will he left his compass and copper astrolabe to a Père Lalémant, an adventurous priest, who could well have lost it later on the Muskrat route.

Near the site of Pembroke, they met Tessouat, an old Indian chief whom Champlain had first met in 1603; he received them kindly and conducted them to his headquarters on Morrison Island. Champlain tried to get the chief to lend him canoes and guide him to Lake Nipissing or even to Hudson Bay, of which he had heard from Vignau. Then occurred the well-known dramatic scene when, appalled by the violent reaction of the Indians, Vignau retracted all that he had previously told Champlain about his journeys, saying that he had not seen any other lake. Admiral Morison and others are inclined to believe that Vignau followed the easiest course in this retraction and that he had really either seen Hudson Bay or heard directly from the Indians about it, since the Indians had apparently seen at least one survivor from Henry Hudson's expedition. The reaction of the Indians was natural since they occupied a strategic position at Allumette Lake, intercepting all traffic going downstream and acting as middlemen, to use a polite expression to describe a practice not unlike that of some of the robber barons of European history. They would certainly not want to have their preserves interfered with. Champlain must have sensed this for he gave up all idea of proceeding further and retraced his journey to the Lachine Rapids, which he reached by 17 June, the mere three weeks taken for the round trip being remarkable even today.

He returned to France, reaching St Malo on 26 September, and was soon involved in arrangements for a new company to further the growth of New France. This took so much time that it was not until 24 April 1615 that he was able to sail again from Honfleur. Accompanying him now were four Récollet friars from the monastery at Brouage, who hoped to convert the Indians. Père Le Caron was so anxious to start his work that he pushed on up the St Lawrence ahead of Champlain and up the Ottawa, intending to spend a winter with the Indians. He was the first of a band of heroic priests the record of whose exploits forms one of the shining parts of early Canadian history. The other friars celebrated the first Mass at Montreal on Midsummer Day and shortly thereafter Champlain was off up the Ottawa again.

Accompanied by two French companions and ten Indians, with a great deal of warlike equipment to assist the Hurons in attacking the Iroquois, they followed the same route as before to Lake Allumette but then went on into the unknown. The labour of carrying all the equipment over the many portages in the upper reaches of the main Ottawa can be imagined. The baggage must have included an astrolabe, since Champlain recorded the latitude of the Mattawa River junction as 46°N, only 18' less than the correct value. On the way to Lake Huron he met three hundred Algonquin warriors whom he recorded as Outaouais. Their chief told him that they regularly came to this place to gather and dry blueberries for winter use.

This 1615 journey of Champlain was the third known traverse of the entire Ottawa Waterway by a white man, following Brûlé and Father Le Caron. It is vividly described in yet another of Champlain's published volumes and shown in his famous 1616 map, a portion of which is reproduced on page 51 of this volume. The relative accuracy of his delineation of the Ottawa and Lakes Nipissing and Huron, based only on his one round journey along this route, is truly remarkable. His return down the Ottawa did not come until May and June of the following year, his safe arrival at Quebec on 11 July being duly celebrated by a service of thanksgiving. He had fulfilled his promise and accompanied the Hurons on the long journey down the route now followed by the Trent Canal, across Lake Ontario and into Iroquois country. The ensuing fight with the Onondagas almost took his life since he was wounded in the leg and knee, but his courage and example were not enough to rally the Hurons, and retreat was necessary.

This was the worst journey the great explorer ever had to make; for six days he was carried in a basket on the back of an Indian, who must indeed have been a man of might. Champlain was not permitted to return directly to Quebec – even if, as is probable, he had heard of the shorter St Lawrence route – but had to return and winter with the Hurons in their poor quarters on Georgian Bay. Naturally he studied their way of life, and recorded it, but his patience must have been sorely tried by 20 May when he was able to leave for the long journey up the French River, across Lake Nipissing, and then down the Mattawa, Ottawa, and St Lawrence rivers to the relative comfort of his Habitation at Quebec.

Although Champlain himself never went up the Ottawa Waterway again, his was the example that opened the way for the steadily increasing use of this route to the west, his written records serving as guides for many of those who followed. On his 1615 voyage across the Atlantic, he must have told Father Joseph Le Caron much about his first journey up the great river, since the impatient Récollet priest had already left the island of Montreal for the west when Champlain reached there towards the end of June. Father Le Caron had accompanied some of the Indians who had come down the Ottawa, as was their custom early in the year; twelve other Frenchmen, all well armed, had also gone with him. From fragments of his letters, we know something of the experiences of this saintly priest on this second voyage of a white man along the complete route of the Ottawa Waterway.

It would be hard to tell you how tired I was with paddling all day, with all my strength, among the Indians; wading the rivers a hundred times or more, through the mud and over the sharp rocks that cut my feet; carrying the canoe and luggage through the woods to avoid the rapids and frightful cataracts; and half starved all the while, for we had nothing to eat but a little *sagamite*, a sort of porridge of water and pounded maize, of which they gave us a small allowance every morning and night. But I must needs tell you what abundant consolation I found under all my troubles; for when one sees so many infidels needing nothing but a drop of water to make them children of God, one feels an inexpressible ardour to labour for their conversion, and sacrifice to it one's repose and life.

It was to take far more than 'a drop of water' to convert the Indians as Père Le Caron so devoutly hoped, but deep-seated faith such as that reflected in even this brief extract supported these first Christian missionaries of Canada through experiences of almost incredible severity. Père Gabriel Sagard was another of the early Récollet priests to use the Ottawa route and he left a written record of some of his experiences. He also went barefoot 'in imitation of our Seraphic father, Saint Francis,' and relates:

We often came upon rocks, mudholes, and fallen trees, which we had to scramble over, and sometimes we must force our way with head and hands through dense woods and thickets, without road or path. When the time came, my Indians looked for a good place to pass the night ... others looked for two flat stones to bruise the Indian corn, of which they make sagamite.

The filthiness of the preparation of this dish and its inadequate nutritional quality, even though bits of fish were sometimes thrown in, were but the least of the good father's worries; another was the perennial problem of the woods:

One must always keep a smiling, modest, contented face and now and then sing a hymn, both for his own consolation and to please and edify the savages ... [but] if I had not kept my face wrapped in a cloth, I am almost sure they [the mosquitoes] would have blinded me, so pestiferous and poisonous are the bites of these little demons ... I confess that this is the worst martyrdom I suffered in this country; hunger, thirst, weariness, and fever are nothing to it.

Unfortunately, martyrdom for some of his successors was to be a far more fearsome thing than anything he experienced before he returned to France in 1624.

Always few in number, the Récollets asked for assistance from the Jesuit Order. The Jesuit *Relations* give some idea of the many journeys up and down the Ottawa Waterway made by the Jesuit priests and their helpers in serving the mission to the Hurons. Père Le Moyne, for example, left Quebec in July 1638 with the usual Indian guides but for some reason they abandoned him at a remote spot on the Ottawa, leaving him with one other in the forest. He managed to keep alive, remaining near the river bank. By fortunate chance, Père Du Peron came up the river two weeks later, also with Indian guides who treated him quite well. They saw Le Moyne, and Du Peron, after some bribing of his Indians, was able to rescue him and take him all the way to the mission.

The mission continued for about ten more years; by 1649 there were eighteen Jesuit priests in Huronia with over forty French supporting staff, but the end was near. The Iroquois were on the war path, determined to destroy the Hurons and Algonquins; the white men with them suffered the same fate. Brébeuf and Lalémant were both murdered in 1649. Father Ragueneau had the sad task of closing the mission in 1650, leading all the remaining Frenchmen and about three hundred Hurons down the Ottawa to Quebec.

Even before this tragic end to all the original hopes of the Récollets and

Jesuits for the establishment of a permanent mission to the Indians, exploration of the lands beyond those seen by Champlain had started. Jean Nicollet was one of the pioneers. He arrived in Canada in 1618, and was immediately asked by Champlain to go up the Ottawa to Allumette Island in order to consolidate the fine liaison already established with the Algonquins. He stayed there two years. He learned the languages of the Hurons and Algonquins and was so well accepted that he spent a total of nine years living with them, including the years of the English occupation of Quebec.

It was again almost certainly in response to a request from Champlain that he went up the Ottawa in 1633, being joined by Père Le Jeune, in order to explore the country beyond Lake Nipissing (which he now knew well) and to pacify Indians living on what is now known as Green Bay. In keeping with the thinking of the times, his aim was to find the China Sea which, according to the Indians, was not far from Green Bay. Accordingly, Nicollet included in his limited baggage a 'robe of Chinese damask embroidered with birds and flowers.' Escorted by seven Hurons, he found his way past the future site of Michilimackinac and into Lake Michigan, then down to the foot of Green Bay. He wore the Chinese robe for his first contact with the Winnebagoes, striking them with terror by his gaudy array, but eventually he had to admit he had not reached the China Sea, for which this attire was better suited. He did explore the Fox River and reached a point only three days' sail from the Wisconsin River, being therefore the first white man to come close to the headwaters of the Mississippi. He returned to Quebec in the autumn of 1634 but was accidentally drowned in 1642.

For a time, furs were still brought down to Trois Rivières and Quebec by Hurons who went up the Gatineau and portaged to the St Maurice River in a long detour to avoid that part of the Ottawa by then under firm control of the Mohawks. Early traders used the same route in coming to the upper River, notably Nicholas Gatineau *dit* Duplessis of Trois Rivières who in 1650 came down the river that now bears his name. Heroic priests made attempts at peace making. There was a brief truce in 1654 when a large convoy of canoes did get through to Quebec with a load of furs, but the attacks were renewed.

With the Hurons dispersed, the Iroquois decided to launch a full-scale attack on the fledgling settlement of Montreal. News reached Quebec that five hundred Indians were camped below Montreal, with four hundred more ready to come down the Ottawa to join them. This was in April 1660, a notable point in the early history of Canada since it was then that Adam Dollard des Ormeaux with sixteen young companions set out from Montreal to go up the Ottawa. After a short but sharp encounter on Nun's

Island, they reached the foot of the Long Sault on Saturday 1 May. Iroquois scouts were seen on the Sunday and later that same day two hundred fully armed warriors swept down the rapids while Dollard and his men were eating in the open. They managed to get back to their little stockaded fort, and then began the siege that practically every Canadian schoolboy knows about – lasting eight or nine days before Dollard and all his companions had been either killed or captured. How many of the hundreds of Iroquois were killed we do not know, all available reports being naturally indirect. The full effect of this courageous stand will long be debated but there is no doubt that it proved to be a turning point in the struggle with the Indians for control of the Ottawa. Exact location of the fort defended by Dollard and his men was determined almost with certainty by Dr G.R. Rigby, Miss Helen Lambart, and their associates from the Argenteuil County Historical Society, as at the foot of the old Carillon portage on the north shore just downstream of Île Persévérance. It is now, alas, submerged beneath the water impounded by the Carillon Dam.

Only a short time after Dollard's stand at Carillon there came down the Ottawa another flotilla of canoes conveying a large number of Indians led by Médard Chouart des Groseilliers and his younger brother-in-law, Pierre-Esprit Radisson, with a very large load of furs. The immense load of furs brought economic relief to the tiny colony in 1660, even though its seizure by the governor, with the resultant defection of Radisson and Groseilliers to the British, was to have such devastating long-term effects on the future of New France.

Great changes had taken place in France by this time, changes that were soon to be reflected in the fortunes of New France. Following Mazarin's death, Louis XIV became absolute ruler in 1661, his great reign lasting until 1715. Within two years, a new form of government was decided upon for the little colony on the St Lawrence, with dual appointments of governor and intendant, aided by a council, an arrangement that was to continue satisfactorily until 1763. Jean Talon was the first intendant to arrive in Canada; the first man appointed had failed to take up his post. Talon served as intendant from 1665 to 1668 and again from 1670 to 1672. The years of his tenure of office are regarded by many as among the finest in the history of New France. His energy was prodigious. Although he does not appear to have sailed up the Ottawa, he knew about the river and even suggested that its rapids should be controlled, since they 'interfere to such an extent with the Indians' travelling by water, that sometimes they are discouraged from coming down to us to bring us their pelts.' He lost little time in directing others to take this route, however, and to explore the unknown territories to the west. A Jesuit mission was established at Michilimackinac in 1670, to be followed by a fort built in 1679, under the next régime.

On 3 September 1670, Talon appointed Simon-François Daumont de Saint-Lusson as a deputy commissioner 'to seek out the copper mine in the country of the Ottawas, the Nez-Percés, and the Illinois, and of other nations discovered or to be discovered in North America in the region of Lake Superior or Freshwater Sea.' Clearly intended as a response to British explorations of Hudson Bay, and a reflection of the use being made of information brought back to Quebec by earlier travellers, this instruction led to Saint-Lusson leaving on a journey up the Ottawa in October of the same year, accompanied by the interpreter Nicolas Perrot. He wintered at Manitoulin Island but went on to Sault Ste Marie where, in June 1671, he convened a great meeting at which fourteen Indian nations were represented. In the name of the King, Saint-Lusson took possession of an area that really amounted to all the land from James Bay to the Gulf of Mexico and westwards to the Rocky Mountains. Père Claude Allouez, one of the greatest of the Jesuit travelling missionaries, who had first come up the Ottawa in 1665, preached an eloquent sermon to the great gathering in the Indian tongues which he had learned.

In the fall of 1669 Talon dispatched Adrien Jolliet and Jean Peré to investigate a copper mine, and to look for 'an easier route than the usual one' down the Ottawa River, to make easier the transport of the ore that Talon hoped to receive. Jolliet and Peré did not find the mine but did as they were asked about the route and, with Indian aid, found the route through Lake Huron, Lake St Clair, Lake Erie, the Niagara River, and so to Lake Ontario and the St Lawrence. This opened up what was to become the St Lawrence route to the Great Lakes, easier to travel than the Ottawa route since fewer rapids had to be breasted but more than three hundred miles longer.

When camped near Hamilton, Ontario, Jolliet and Peré by fortunate chance met René-Robert Cavelier de la Salle and his party, including the Sulpicians Dollier de Casson and Bréhant de Galinée, who had left Montreal in July 1669 and after great difficulty surmounted the rapids on the St Lawrence River, reaching Lake Ontario on 2 August. It is impossible to determine now where La Salle travelled after leaving the two Sulpicians to travel on their own. It is probable that he did explore parts of the Ohio River and Nicolas Perrot recorded that he met him in the early summer of 1670 hunting on the Ottawa River near Chats Falls.

In 1685 news reached the little French colony that the British had set up permanent posts on Hudson Bay, following the establishment of the Honourable Company, and had added insult to injury by carrying off a considerable shipment of beaver pelts intended for Quebec. This would not do. Governor Brisay de Denonville, one of the other great administrators of New France, charged the Chevalier de Troyes, a captain in the Piémont regiment who had arrived at Quebec in August 1685 to lead an expedition to rout the British from the bay and to capture those he could, especially any associated with Pierre Radisson, whose treachery was regarded seriously. De Troyes had the good fortune to have as his three senior officers the brothers Le Moyne – Jacques, Pierre, and Paul – with Pierre Allemand, an experienced pilot, and Père Silvy, both of whom had already been to Hudson Bay previously, but by sea. The company consisted of thirty soldiers and seventy militiamen, the full troop being divided into three sections, travelling in over thirty canoes.

They left Montreal on 20 March while the ice was still on the Ottawa, with what hazards in the early part of their journey we have already seen. With improvement in the weather their progress improved; they reached the junction at Mattawa on 10 May but here they left the accustomed route to the west, turning north up the Ottawa and into Lake Temiskaming, then following the route to the portage into the Abitibi River, finally reaching James Bay on 20 June. Without difficulty they captured three British forts – Monsipi (Moose Factory), Rupert (Charles), and Albany, and all without losing a man. Pierre Le Moyne remained in charge of the forts but de Troyes with the main body of the troop returned safely to Quebec by the beginning of October, having lost only three men, by drowning and exposure. In many ways this was one of the most remarkable journeys up and down the Ottawa Waterway, fortunately recorded graphically and even wittily for us by the Chevalier himself. Although essentially a military expedition, and a very successful one, it was prompted by the competition for beaver pelts, having been financed in large part by the Compagnie du Nord, which then held the monopoly for this vital trade.

Competition came from the British not only on the great Bay but also in New York and Albany. To add to the complex picture that developed so early in the fur trade, Louis de Buade de Frontenac, who was governor of New France 1672–82 (and again, 1689–98) had established Fort Frontenac (Kingston) in 1673 as a fur-trading post, and encouraged La Salle and others to entice the Indians to bring their furs down the St Lawrence, instead of down the Ottawa. Talon was deeply involved in the fur trade, having given his young relative François-Marie Perrot the governorship of Montreal, a position that Perrot used to gain possession of the large island at the mouth of the Ottawa that now bears his name. Here he established a fur-trading post, the operation of which was yet another example of the robber baron procedure, to the discomfiture of the Montreal merchants. His conduct was so questionable that Frontenac had him arrested and imprisoned, but Perrot was able to resume his brigandage and continue it until 1683. The Indians were still bringing their furs down the Ottawa so that the strategic location of Île Perrot can readily be appreciated. At about the same time, Frontenac granted to Jacques Bizard, town-major of Montreal, the island at the mouth of the Rivière de la Prairie; it also took the name of its owner and still carries it today. Since it was not on the main route of the Indian fur carriers, there is no record of brigandage on the island. Bizard conducted his dubious fur-trading operations at the small settlement that was the beginning of the city of Montreal.

There was, however, another fortress at the mouth of the Ottawa. A small log building, on a basement of masonry, was built at the extreme western tip of the island – today in the municipality of Senneville – by one of the officers of the Carignan Regiment to whom, when they were disbanded, grants of land were made by Talon. This Captain du Gué sold his land and building in 1679 to the two great merchants of the day, Jacques Le Ber and Charles Le Moyne, father of the famous brothers. Le Moyne died in 1685 and Le Ber bought his partner's share and began to improve the property, one of the structures he erected being a fortified windmill. This small outpost was attacked by the Iroquois in 1687 and again in 1691 but the attacks were successfully repulsed, although the windmill was burned. A stronger stone fort was constructed in 1692, a building that must have been one of the earliest Canadian masonry structures outside Quebec. Called the Château de Senneville, it served as a fortress and saw action even in 1776, when Benedict Arnold established headquarters there during the American invasion of Canada. Its remains may still be seen today.

The idea of forts on the Ottawa seems strange today but when built they indicated clearly the importance that the Ottawa Waterway had already come to occupy in the life of New France. The St Lawrence route had been opened up but for at least a century more the Ottawa remained the main route to the west and to the south since it was so much shorter and removed from the dangers of attacks from New York. The Ottawa was the first part of the water route to the Mississippi and so to New Orleans, the thin line of communication that alone would link together the North American empire of France, a route that was to be carefully surveyed in 1720–23 by Père Charlevoix. As the seventeenth century reached its close, the Ottawa was still the route followed by the Indians to bring their furs down to Quebec, Trois Rivières, and Montreal, even as it was also the way that some used for attacks on the new settlers.

The more aggressive merchants of New France were slowly pushing their outposts up the route used by the Indians, as evidenced by the forts at 'le bout de l'île.' Another of the officers of the Carignan Regiment, Philippe Carrion du Fresnay, obtained upon his discharge what is now Carillon Island and established a trading post at this western end of the Lake of Two Mountains. Carillon is thought to be a corruption of his name. As but one further indication of the early activity in fur trading on the Ottawa, Nicolas d'Ailleboust de Manthet spent the winter of 1694–95 as far upstream as north of Calumet Island, this being the start of Fort Coulonge, one of the oldest of all river settlements. Bois-de-Coulonge (formerly Spencerwood) in Quebec City is another use of the name of the family seigniory of this intrepid early trader. And up and down the waterway, in increasing numbers, went fearless young Frenchmen, soon to be widely known as *coureurs de bois*, braving the dangers of the Indian territories in the search for fur.

This early activity is the more surprising when the small population of New France is remembered. The French have never been noted as colonizers and, despite all the efforts that were made, the total population of the little settlements on the St Lawrence was only 3,215 in 1665. Furs were the economic support of the new colony since the income from their sale had to provide the operating expenses for all local administration. From the start, beaver predominated. It is said that before the coming of the white man to North America, the beaver population was probably ten million. The animals were easily trapped so that as early as 1626 individual traders were taking as many as 22,000 skins annually back to France. It was this trade, as Harold Innis so clearly demonstrated in *The Fur Trade in Canada*, that activated so much of the adventurous travel up and down the Ottawa Waterway. Small wonder that this small fur-bearing animal, of such interest that it was mentioned by Pliny in his *Natural History* and discussed in amusing detail by Sir Francis Bacon, became the national symbol of Canada. The beaver skins were principally used for making men's beaver hats, which became very fashionable; a replica may be seen in Beaver Hall, the London headquarters of the Hudson's Bay Company, where it is noted that Samuel Pepys bought one in 1661 for £4.5.0, a large sum for those days.

Smuggling furs began early, carried out in large measure by the *coureurs de bois*, the name generally applied after about 1700 to those who ventured on their own, or at least without official authority, up the rivers and streams in the search for furs. *Voyageurs* were those who similarly journeyed up and down the Ottawa Waterway and its connecting lakes, rivers and streams, but as members of recognized and authorized trading ventures. In both cases, young Frenchmen worked with Indians who served initially as guides, the *coureurs de bois* often wintering with them in their camps, adapting themselves to the relatively carefree life of the wilds. Repeated efforts were made to limit the number of those going up the Ottawa to trade in furs, such as the edict in 1681 granting amnesty to all *coureurs de bois* who returned to the colony immediately, and the granting of twenty-five official licences a year. Before this royal command was registered with the Sovereign Council, the inevitable happened and two hundred men in sixty canoes left hurriedly for the west.

A regular pattern for the trade along the Ottawa Waterway was for the canoes to leave Montreal in the spring; supplies would be obtained at Michilimackinac and the men would then proceed to Lake Superior or Lake Michigan, winter with the Indians and do their trading, return to Michilimackinac the following spring or early summer, and then proceed down the Ottawa Waterway with their loads of furs to Montreal, their round trip involving an absence from their homes of at least a year. As greater and greater distances had to be travelled in the search for good furs, the absences might last for two or even three years.

Some of the *coureurs de bois* hired Indian maidens to accompany them on their journeys down the waterway to Montreal. This interesting practice did not find favour with the Church. Indeed, it was said that the greatest obstacle to the conversion of the Indians to Christianity was their association with lay Christians. Père Carheil, a Jesuit missionary at Michilimackinac at the turn of the century, went so far as to charge that there was 'a continual flux and reflux of these prostitutes who go from one mission post to another without stop, causing the most enormous and horrible scandal in the world.'

It was not until July 1701 that the continued efforts of successive French administrators finally succeeded in ensuring continuance of trading in the future. In that month, about 1,300 Indians from over thirty nations gathered in Montreal at the invitation of the Governor, Chevalier de Callières, many having come down the familiar Ottawa route. A treaty was finally drawn up which was, in effect, an admission of defeat for the Iroquois; but they were still a powerful enough force to ensure that furs from the Great Lakes would come down the Ottawa to Montreal and so to Paris rather than being deflected through Iroquois territory to Albany and the London market. The treaty signing was marked by a great feast but the governor had taken the precaution of placing a strict ban on the use of liquor so that all passed off peacefully.

The threat of competition from the English was always present after the formation of the Hudson's Bay Company, and was made the more pointed

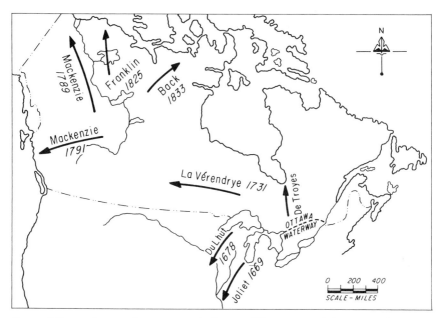

Some of the explorers who came up the Ottawa Waterway and the routes they followed.

after Henry Kelsey first came inland from the bay to trade in the Assiniboine country in 1690. The threat became very real following the signing of the Treaty of Utrecht in 1713, under the terms of which France ceded to Great Britain Rupert's Land, still a rather undefined area but containing the valuable hunting grounds of the west. When, in addition, the British established a fort at Oswego on Lake Ontario in 1720, the French empire on the St Lawrence was even more dependent for its economic well-being on the lifeline provided by the Ottawa Waterway. Its value as the first part of the route to Louisiana was similarly enhanced for the years that yet remained until 1763, when France deeded this part of her North American possessions to Spain.

Pierre Gaultier de Varennes, Sieur de la Vérendrye, was pre-eminent in this exploration of the west. With his three sons, he opened up the prairies for trade with Montreal and the posts he founded were extended, after his death, until one was established in 1751 on the Saskatchewan within sight of the Rocky Mountains. La Vérendrye made his first journey to the far west, naturally up the Ottawa, in 1731. His travels and discoveries in the west, important and interesting though they are, cannot be a part of our story but his numerous journeys between Montreal and the western plains hold a special place in the history of the Ottawa Waterway which he and his sons came to know so well.

It was as a result of such journeys up and down the Ottawa Waterway that, by 1763, there existed a well-recognized route to the western plains, where small posts had been established for fur trading, especially in the Winnipeg area, in direct competition with the Hudson's Bay Company whose men came south from the bay. There had been serious Indian wars to the south, notably the second Fox War that lasted from 1727 to 1738, so the new possibilities that La Vérendrye had opened up, in tapping the rich fur resources of the plains and adjoining lakes, provided welcome relief for the Montreal fur merchants. Portages and trails were improved. Supply depots had been established, notably that at Michilimackinac but also at Kaministiquia on the western route. Such records as exist suggest that the peak in the transfer of furs from the west to Montreal during this period was about 1745; but the trade continued steadily down the years, despite all the turbulent events in the outer world.

When the ice went out of the Ottawa each year the spring flotilla of canoes would set out for the west. In the shorter days of fall, canoes loaded with the bales of furs from the west would come through the lakes, up the French River, across Lake Nipissing, and then down the Mattawa and the Ottawa to deliver their loads to the warehouses of Montreal. Only when the travellers reached Montreal would they hear news of events that reached their climax in 1763 with the Treaty of Paris and the transfer of power in eastern North America from France to Great Britain. Quebec and all of Nova Scotia joined Newfoundland and the colonies to the south to constitute for the next two decades a British North America which included the entire Atlantic seaboard and all contiguous territory.

One of the many surprising features of the Ottawa story is the sudden transition at this critical time from the exclusively French trade in furs up and down the river to aggressive trading by English-speaking merchants, leading to the beginnings of the North West Company in 1779. It must be realized, however, that although some of the Atlantic coast settlements were well developed by 1763, New France was still a relatively small colony clustered along the St Lawrence River, with little in the way of agricultural development or in trade apart from furs, France having really done very little to promote its overseas interests. In 1759, for example, the populations of Quebec, Montreal, and Trois Riviéres were only, respectively, 7,995, 4,432, and 800, with one-quarter of the total population living in urban communities, the drift from country to city having already started.

Official activities during these middle years of the century were almost all directed to resisting the attacks of the British, so that those engaged in the fur trade were very much on their own. As British forces began their final attacks, British merchants were right behind their advance, since the British army still depended on private firms for its supplies and much of its logistic support. Although, following the transfer of power, some of the leading French merchants returned to France, others remained and friendly and close relations between merchants of both tongues quickly developed, the fur trade itself being one of the early examples of true bilingualism in a country which was later to become distinguished internationally for this unique feature of its social and cultural life.

British merchants coming to New France from New York and Albany knew well the fur trade down the Ottawa if only because of the rival trading for furs at Albany. They quickly made good use of their new opportunities. Passes for travel to the 'upper country' were issued as early as 1761. Alexander Henry was one of the earliest of the new traders. He appears to have been connected with the fur trade at Albany; he supplied goods to the English army at Oswego and followed it down to Montreal. Returning to Albany for more supplies, he came back to the St Lawrence and consulted with a Monsieur Leduc at Fort Lévis (where he sold goods to the garrison) and gained much useful information about the fur trade up the Ottawa. He left Lachine in 1761 with a French-speaking companion, Étienne Campion, and a guide, and proceeded to Michilimackinac, which he used as his headquarters. Here he had the agonizing experience of watching the entire British garrison of over seventy men massacred by Indians, although he himself managed to escape.

This was a part of the Pontiac uprising, eventually put down but only after much strife. For two years, 1763 to 1765, no passes up the Ottawa could be issued, but no sooner was the uprising over than the British general, James Murray, was able again to issue permits for travel to the upper country. The Montreal merchants were so well established as to have their own spokesman at Michilimackinac in the person of the redoubtable Major Robert Rogers (leader of Rogers' Rangers). He urged the establishment of a separate fur-trading colony with its capital at Michilimackinac but fortunately this early example of separatism got no further than a suggestion.

In 1767, it was recorded that 'one hundred and twenty canoes with £40,000 in merchandise cleared at the fort of Michilimackinac and went off to winter at traders' outposts on Lake Superior, Lake Huron, Lake Michigan, and "La Baie." Fourteen of these went beyond Lake Superior to the far northwest.' It is almost certain that all would have come up the Ottawa, although the trouble of negotiating its thirty-six portages was becoming increasingly serious for shipments of trading goods. That the St Lawrence route was being considered as an alternative is indicated by the round-trip journey of James Morrison, a merchant of Montreal, made in 1767. He went from Montreal through Niagara and Detroit up to Michilimackinac but returned to Montreal by way of the Ottawa, trading as he went.

Small vessels were soon in use on Lake Ontario and Lake Erie for conveying heavier goods to the upper country, and well before the end of the century the British government had started work on the first small canals, predecessors of the St Lawrence Seaway of today. The Ottawa route, however, continued to be the main channel for the fur trade. The camaraderie that had developed between French- and English-speaking merchants in the sharing of experiences up the river and in the market-places is well indicated by the fact that of the group which protested, in December 1766, against the rule confining traders to the fortified posts, thirty-six were French-speaking and thirty-four English-speaking.

Typical of individual journeys up the Ottawa waterway was that of John Long, an independent trader who left La Chine early in May 1777 with two large birch-bark canoes, having ten Canadians in each (the term Canadian being then used in English to describe French-speaking residents). At La Chine 'the Indian goods are put on board very carefully; the dry merchandise in bales about eighty pounds weight, the rum, powder, and shot in small kegs ... Custom has however made the Canadians very expert, and I must do them the justice to say they encounter these difficulties [in poling etc.] with uncommon cheerfulness, though they sometimes explain, "C'est la misère, mon bourgeois."' This was to be the experience of many hundreds in the years ahead as the waters of the Ottawa carried down their great cargoes of valuable furs on their way to the markets of the Old World.

The trade, and so travel on the Ottawa, increased rapidly despite occasional difficulties with Indians, since their antipathy to the new English-speaking traders, shown in the Pontiac uprising, continued for some time. James Finlay was probably the first English-speaking trader to reach the west; he wintered near the old Fort à la Corne in 1767 or 1768. Benjamin and Joseph Frobisher made their first venture into the upper country in 1769 but were robbed by Indians, an experience that did not deter them from quickly repeating their venture. They became leaders in the trade, as did others whose names appear around this time as obtaining licences for travel to the west – Lawrence Ermatinger, Maurice Blondeau, James

McGill, John Askin, Forrest Oakes, to mention but a few. In 1775 McGill, Benjamin Frobisher, and Blondeau obtained jointly a licence for twelve canoes, three guides, and seventy-five men, with a cargo of 100 gallons of rum and brandy, 24 kegs of wine, 64 kegs of gunpowder, 90 bags of ball and shot, 150 rifles, 150 bales of dry goods, 15 trunks of dry goods, 12 boxes of ironware, 12 nests of brass kettles, 100 packages of carrot and twist tobacco, 50 kegs of hogs' lard and tallow, and 60 kegs of pork. This list is given in detail in order to show how the trade had grown in a mere decade; this was the cargo for one outfit only. The joint French-English character of this partnership will be noted, and it is not without significance that James McGill, Joseph Frobisher, and Simon McTavish all married French-speaking ladies. McTavish, who was to become the commanding figure in the North West Company, had moved from Quebec to Montreal probably in 1775, an indication of the growing importance of Montreal. He made his first trip up the Ottawa in 1776, reaching Michilimackinac in May to tell the surprised residents of that important post about the 'great matters transacted since last Summer in Canada.'

Unsettling as were the immediate results of the passage of the Quebec Act and the aftermath of the American Revolution, finally confirmed in 1783 by the Treaty of Versailles, they did not seriously affect the fur trade up the Ottawa but they did concentrate all attention on the Canadian West, since the hunting grounds south of the Great Lakes and the outlet provided by the Mississippi had been lost. As the distances to be travelled steadily increased, so also did the complexity of equipping annual expeditions from Montreal. Partnerships were the only answer, leading to the successively larger groupings represented by the North West Company.

The significance of the Ottawa Waterway as the first section of the routes followed in the making of these long journeys, is well shown in a report on the fur trade that was made by Benjamin and Joseph Frobisher to Governor Haldimand, dated 4 October 1784:

The Inland Navigation from Montreal, by which the North-West business is carried on, is perhaps the most extensive of any in the known world, but is only practicable for Canoes on account of the great number of Carrying places ... Two sets of men are employed in this business, making together upwards of 500; one half of which are occupied in the transport of Goods from Montreal to the Grand Portage, in canoes of about Four Tons Burthen, Navigated by 8 to 10 men, and the other half are employed to take such goods forward to every Post in the interior Country to the extent of 1,000 to 2,000 miles and upwards, from Lake Superior, in canoes of about one and a-half Ton Burthen, made expressly for the inland service, and navigated by 4 to 5 men only, according to the places of their destination.

The large Canoes from Montreal always set off early in May, and as the Provisions they take with them are consumed by the time they reach Michilimackinac, they are necessitated to call there, merely to take in an additional Supply, not only for themselves but also for the use of the Canoes intended for the Interior Country and the Consumption of their servants at the Grand Portage, but as these Canoes are not capable of carrying the whole of such Provisions it thence becomes necessary to have a Vessel or Boats upon Lake Superior for that Transport only.

Another report of about the same date gave £250 as the total cost for taking a loaded canoe (worth £500 with its full load, including 200 gallons of rum and wine) from Montreal to Grand Portage.

This 'Inland Navigation from Montreal' was indeed one of the most extensive in the world, eventually linking with Montreal posts as much as three thousand miles away. It was unique through a fortunate combination of geographical factors. The remarkable physiography of Canada that makes possible travel by canoe from Atlantic to Pacific and from the Atlantic to the western Arctic coast was naturally basic to the transportation system so well developed by the partners of the North West Company. Availability, throughout most of the regions traversed, of birch bark for the construction and repair of canoes was another vital factor. The bark came from the tree known scientifically as *Betula papyrifera* but colloquially as the white, silver, paper, or canoe birch, a tree found throughout all parts of Canada served by the Ottawa Waterway. Based on the accumulated experience of the preceding century, the *canot de maître* had been developed for the trade between Montreal and the Grand Portage at the western end of Lake Superior. These splendid craft were usually about thirty-six feet long (forty feet being not unknown) with a beam of six feet. Over a framework of white cedar, strips of bark up to thirty feet long, skilfully obtained from mature trees (preferably in warm weather), would be formed into the hull, sewn together with *wattape* (roots of the spruce or juniper), and made watertight with spruce or pine gum. All these materials were available from the forests through which all the waterways passed, so that repairs could be carried out readily on the spot when accidents occurred. It was usual, however, to carry at least a spare roll of birch bark in each canoe. Canadians of today can fortunately see what these magnificent craft looked like, since the National Museum of Man in Ottawa possesses a modern example, built by Matt Bernerd of the Golden Lake Indian reserve in 1957 under the sponsorship of D.A. Gillies of Braeside, one of the recent leaders in the lumber trade of the valley.

Even when looking at this fine example, it is still difficult to imagine that these craft regularly left Lachine with a cargo of four tons of freight, all carefully wrapped into packs for transfer on men's backs over the portages. Crews would vary up to fourteen although between eight and ten men was the more usual complement. Beyond the Grand Portage, the *canot du nord* was used because of the increasing difficulties of portaging; smaller in size (usually about twenty-five feet long), it was handled by a crew of from five to eight and could carry between one and two tons of freight. Between the two major types was the *canot bâtard*, intermediate in size. It was used for express passenger and other services when speed was essential.

Part of the freight loaded at Lachine was the necessary food (and drink) to be consumed on the journey to the lakes. Here, too, geography was helpful since the country around Lake Huron was well known to the Indians as suitable for growing corn, the name 'Indian corn' being a reminder of its ancient use in Canada. Before the maize country was reached, however, much food was necessary, and this was usually provided by dried peas and beans, sea biscuit, and salt pork. Such were the rigours of the journey up the Ottawa that little time was available for utilizing the berries that grew in summer in profusion in the woods, but supplies of them might be obtained from Indians, as also of maple sugar and of dried fish. This does not appear to be a very satisfying diet but with the essential ration of rum it sustained the *voyageurs* in their rigorous and strenuous work. Because of the salt pork in their diet, the men who worked the Ottawa Waterway part of the route to the west were known as *mangeurs de lard*, or 'pork-eaters.'

These men were the real secret of the successful operation of this phenomenal transportation system, the *voyageurs* constituting one of the most remarkable of all groups of workers in Canadian history. Simple men, French-speaking in the main, close friends of the Indians who frequently travelled with them, they were a class apart. David Thompson, one of the greatest of early travellers, said of the typical *voyageur*: 'When he has a moment's respite he smokes his pipe, his constant companion and all goes well; he will go through hardships but requires a belly full at least once a day, good tobacco to smoke, a warm blanket and a kind Master who will take his share of hard times and be first in danger.' So vital was pipe smoking that distances were measured regularly in *pipes*, the distance traversed between the hourly stops on long stretches of paddling during which a quick smoke could be obtained. Much has been written about the

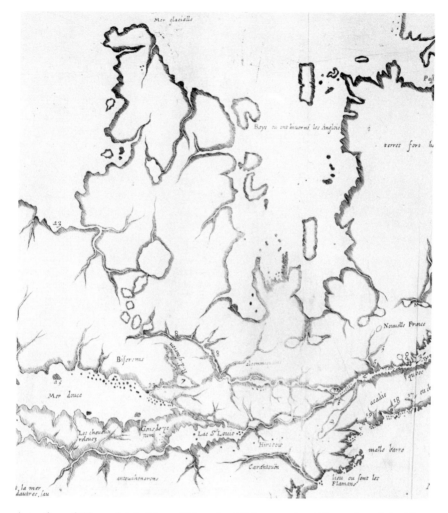

A section of Champlain's Map of Canada, 1616, reproduced from the original in the John Carter Brown Library, Brown University. It shows the Ottawa Waterway clearly and not too inaccurately.

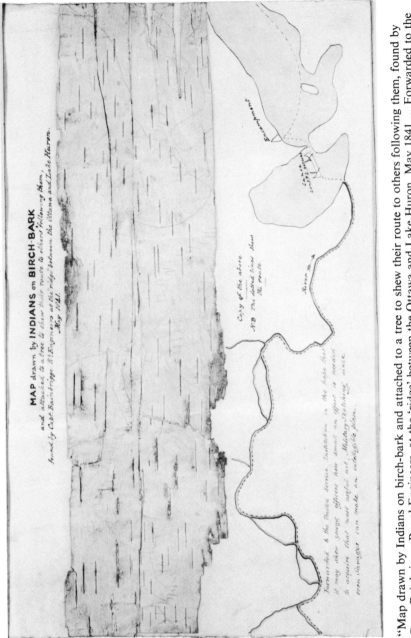

MAP drawn by INDIANS on BIRCH-BARK
and attached to a tree to shew their route to others following them,
found by Capt. Bainbrigge R. Engineers at the ridge between the Ottawa and Lake Huron.
May 1841.

"Map drawn by Indians on birch-bark and attached to a tree to shew their route to others following them, found by Capt. Bainbrigge, Royal Engineers, at the 'ridge' between the Ottawa and Lake Huron, May 1841 ... Forwarded to the United Service institution in the hope that it may shew young officers how small an effort is needed to acquire that most useful art, Military Sketching, since even Savages can make an intelligible plan." The original is in the Map Room of the British Museum.

52

A somewhat romantic view of Chaudière Falls painted just after 1791 by Thomas Davies, who served in Canada in the late 1700s.

53

Philemon Wright's buildings at the north end of Chaudière Falls, as painted by Lieut. Col. Henry Du Vernet about 1830; it is the only known painting by him.

54

'Tracking' canoes on the French River at the Le Duc décharge. A painting by Major J.E. Woolford, R.E., probably early 19th century.

55

W.H. Bartlett print showing the Chaudière Falls and the first Union Bridge as seen from the east with the small settlements of Hull (right) and Bytown (left), about 1840.

March (Horaceville) by W.H. Bartlett about 1840 showing the early settlement, the church (of which the ruins still stand), and a primitive timber raft with living-quarters and 'sweeps.' In Lac Deschenes, looking upstream.

This painting of Horaceville (about 1850) is by Mrs. M. Pinhey, a member of the family of one of the original settlers.

*voyageurs* and their phenomenal physical powers, days of fourteen hours' duration being their regular schedule when en route, but much of it has romanticized this fine group of tough, rough, powerful men. More typical was the statement by one of them that he had saved ten lives, had had twelve wives and six dogs, and spent all his money on pleasure – but added that there was no life as happy as a *voyageur's*.

He also knew fifty songs. The *voyageurs* were musical by nature; singing came naturally to them as they stroked their paddles in rhythm. Their songs remain one of Canada's cultural treasures. Every Canadian who delights in joining in *Alouette*, now recognized around the globe as typically Canadian, is echoing one of the best known of all the *voyageurs'* songs. *À la claire fontaine* was another that is now the happy heritage of all Canada. It is not difficult to imagine that one hears the ripple of the waters of the Ottawa as these songs are sung. And for those who do not sing even *Alouette*, the songs can still be enjoyed through the medium of a fine recording of twelve of the best known, sung by young Canadians of today, the disc being available from the Minnesota Historical Society.

These are the songs of the men who took the trade goods up to the lakes and brought down the furs. They took out the partners from Montreal to the annual meetings with the wintering partners at Grand Portage, until the great post had to be moved to Kaministiquia on the Canadian side of the border after 1803. It was renamed Fort William in 1807 in honour of William McGillivray, the only partner who made the journey up the Ottawa in his own private canoe. John Jacob Astor used the Ottawa at this time; the first canoe load of the overland party which was to establish his fur-trading post on the Columbia River left Lachine in the summer of 1810. The *voyageurs* assisted also with the transfer of British troops up and down the Ottawa for the manning of posts such as that at Michilimackinac and later when it also had to be moved, at St Joseph Island. They carried occasional travellers, and the young men recruited for service with the company at its distant posts, whose introduction to the land of Canada was always provided by their journey up the Ottawa Waterway. This service was provided between Montreal and Fort William, around the turn of the century when it was close to its peak, by 373 men, including eighteen guides and five clerks. These figures are cited in one of the most famous of all contemporary descriptions of the fur trade of Canada, that which prefaces the famous journals of Alexander Mackenzie in the volume in which these were first published in 1801.

This famous book has as its full title: *Voyages from Montreal on the River St. Laurence through the Continent of North America to the Frozen and Pacific Oceans; in the years, 1789 and 1793. With a preliminary account of the Rise, Progress and Present State of The Fur Trade of that country.* The accounts of these two great journeys are written in diary form, clearly based on the travel journals written up by Mackenzie each day. The records start only at Fort Chipewyan, but Mackenzie came to this far outpost, as a young partner in the North West Company, by the usual route, starting with the Ottawa Waterway which he knew so well. The journey to the shores of the Arctic Ocean, down the great river that now bears Mackenzie's name, and back again to Fort Chipewyan, in 102 days only was an amazing feat by any standards. The second journey, in 1793, to the Pacific Ocean, called for the courage and stamina that mark Mackenzie as one of the great travellers of all time. Bernard de Voto, an American writer, has paid this tribute: 'In courage, in the faculty to command, in ability to meet the unforeseen with resources of craft and skill, in the will that cannot be overborne, he has no superior in the history of American exploration.'

Mackenzie returned to Montreal from his second great journey by way of the Great Lakes and called on Governor Simcoe at Niagara, leaving with Mrs Simcoe the skin of a sea otter to prove that he had been to the Pacific Ocean. His earlier journeys had given him a detailed knowledge of the Ottawa Waterway and the rest of the route through the lakes to the west. It is not, therefore, surprising to find that his two journals are prefaced in the book by a *General History of the Fur Trade from Canada to the North-West* which includes what may well be the best of all descriptions of the famous Ottawa route, from Montreal all the way to Fort Chipewyan.

Dr Kaye Lamb, in his splendid 1970 edition of the journals and letters of Mackenzie, suggests that this account of the fur trade may have been written by Roderick Mackenzie, Alexander's cousin, but its inclusion in the original 1801 volume sets the seal of the great traveller upon it. The account states that in the summer of 1798 were delivered 106,000 beaver skins, 32,000 marten skins, 1,800 mink skins, and over 40,000 other skins of a dozen varieties. All but 13,364 beaver skins and about 3,000 other skins went to the London market, the exceptions being sent to China through the United States. The quantities give some idea of the extent of the trade. And here is just the start of the journey, up the Ottawa, that is so graphically described:

Leaving La Chine, they proceed to St Ann's, within two miles of the Western extremity of the island of Montreal, the lake of the two mountains being in sight, which may be termed the commencement of the Utawas

River. At the rapid of St Ann they are obliged to take out part, if not the whole of their lading. It is from this spot that the Canadians consider they take their departure, as it possesses the last church on the island, which is dedicated to the titular saint of the voyageurs.

Surprisingly, Mackenzie does not mention the apparently invariable custom here of the *voyageurs*; but Peter Pond, in his somewhat unusual journal, did so (1770):

... this Church is Dedacateed to St Ann who Protescts all Voigeers   heare is a Small Box with a Hole in the top for ye Reseption of a Lettle Muney for the Hole father to Say a Small Mass for those who Put a small Sum in the Box   Scars a Voigeer but Stops Hear and Puts in his mite and By that Meanes they Suppose they are Protacted

This idyllic scene was captured in verse by Thomas Moore, a young Irishman who in 1804 made a journey from Niagara Falls to Montreal, and later to Halifax, during a visit to North America. His 'Canadian Boat Song' is believed to have been written while he stayed with Simon Fraser at Ste Anne de Bellevue. The song starts:

> Faintly as tolls the evening chime
> Our voices keep tune and our oars keep time.
> Soon as the woods on shore look dim,
> We'll sing at St Ann's our parting hymn,
> Row, brothers, row, the stream runs fast,
> The rapids are near and the daylight's past.

One would like to know to whom Moore spoke during his brief visit, since this was at a time when acrimony among the partners was intense, Alexander Mackenzie (by then knighted) having already broken away in 1799 to form his XY Company, later known by his own name.

The *voyageurs* themselves would not have been involved directly in all the troubles that were beginning to disturb the trade, but many must have been the discussions among the passengers they carried in their canoes. The matter of strong drink was a cause of discord, its sale to the Indians, often diluted with water, being a continuing blight on an otherwise splendid record. In the year 1803, for example, over 20,000 gallons were taken up the Ottawa, all in small kegs, over three-quarters of it by the North West Company, the remainder by the XY Company.

Indicative of the feelings of the traders themselves on this matter is this extract from the minutes of the annual meeting of the North West Company for 16 July 1811, when all parties were again united:

The Consumption of Liquor in all the Trade carried on by the North West Company ... was next examined (at present estimated at 10,000 Gallons, including Spirits) in order to ascertain the least possible quantity that might be made to Answer should the *Saints in Parliament* – in their mistaken notions of Philanthropy – persist in the Intention of abolishing the use of that Article wholly in the Trade – and it is the general opinion that even one Half of the above quantity or 5,000 Gallons if restricted to that small quantity, might still serve the Trade was it found advisable to make any offer of that kind to Parliament, in order to prevent its total prohibition.

There were, however, more serious matters than even the quantity of liquor for the partners to worry about. On the broader national scene, war between Great Britain and the United States was imminent. The actual outbreak of hostilities in 1812 naturally caused alarm amongst the partners. It led to the assembly at the lakehead of a flotilla of 47 *canots de maître* carrying a cargo of furs valued at £200,000 and their dispatch to the mouth of the French River under the care of 135 North West men, all armed. They escaped the American vessels then patrolling Lake Huron and safely reached Montreal (this great brigade was yet another of the sights on the Ottawa that one would like to have seen). Although fighting did take place on the lakes, there was little serious interference with the fur trade, but travel of British military personnel and supplies up and down the Ottawa showed again the strategic importance of the Ottawa route.

No sooner was the War of 1812 concluded than the Earl of Selkirk embarked upon his ill-fated expedition to the Red River country, his projected settlement cutting across the regular North West fur trade route to the west. Trouble was inevitable; a bitter feud developed. When several partners of the North West Company were arrested by Selkirk at Fort William in 1816, following the Seven Oaks Massacre in which Nor'Westers were implicated, they were sent down for trial to Montreal along the Ottawa Waterway, their own river, as they had every right to think of it. What feelings they must have entertained as they travelled the familiar route! Next year, however, McGillivray was on the Ottawa again, going up to the lakehead to take possession of Fort William. The very unusual character of such journeys will be realized when all the portaging is remembered, the nightly sleeping in simple tents; but prisoners were safe only when in the company of canoe travellers, such were still the hazards of the forests around, and escape was therefore impossible.

Change was in the air, however. The North West Company had assisted in the improvement of the portage road at Niagara Falls. As early as 1812 William McGillivray had himself studied on the ground the possibility of a portage road from Lake Ontario to Georgian Bay, as yet another means of improving the Great Lakes route. (This led to the development of Yonge Street.) There was talk of canals to improve river navigation, the North West Company having itself constructed a small stone lock at Sault Ste Marie at the turn of the century, large enough to handle the *canots de maître* which were hauled through by oxen. Politically, the new country was awakening, and the Constitutional Act of 1791 divided the first colony of Quebec into Lower and Upper Canada with the Ottawa River as the boundary. Traffic on the river was not much affected directly by the halting beginnings of government. But behind these developments was the ever present threat to the Montreal fur trade from the north, where the Hudson's Bay Company had steadily been consolidating its position on the shores of the bay.

As early as 1774 the inland post at Cumberland House was established, so that penetration of the western fur-bearing regions by the Honourable Company was almost contemporaneous with the development of the North West Company. Despite the advantage that Hudson Bay provided through the shorter routes from the plains and across the sea to England, the aggressive policies of the North West Company (the 'Pedlars from Quebec,' as they were derisively known by loyal Hudson's Bay men), and their masterly organization of the long transportation route, kept them well ahead of their rivals. In 1795, for example, the North West Company controlled 79 per cent of the total fur trade in Canada, the Hudson's Bay Company only 14 per cent, and independent traders the remaining 7 per cent.

The continuing trade war between these two remarkable companies is a fascinating part of Canadian history. Expert management of transport along the Ottawa route and its connections was partially responsible for the success of the North West partners, but the difficulties of the route must have been of constant concern, especially when the partners gave thought to and discussed the savings to be made if only their western furs could be taken out and their supplies brought in through Hudson Bay. It is not surprising, therefore, to find that approaches were made to the Hudson's Bay Company over two decades by successive North West men for some type of accommodation, permission to sail into the bay being the most obvious. Negotiations got nowhere but the rivalry was steadily intensified, a vessel being actually sailed into the bay by the North West Company at the turn of the century. In the winter of 1814–15, moreover, Colin Robertson was in Quebec organizing for the Hudson's Bay Company, at great expense, a brigade of sixteen canoes with their crews to go up the Ottawa route to the Red River country, in direct competition with the North West Company on their own route.

The first two decades of the nineteenth century saw many such unusual uses of the Ottawa Waterway. When reading of the final stages of the fur-trade war (and that is not too strong a word), the excitement of the rivalry often obscures the critical importance of the Ottawa River in all the comings and goings. Despite the valour of the men who made the Ottawa such a busy and effective transportation route, the trade war could not possibly continue. Amalgamation of the two companies, so long proposed (this being one topic discussed by Mackenzie with Simcoe in 1793), was finally effected on 26 March 1821. Welding together the operations of the two great enterprises was naturally a difficult and long-drawn-out procedure. As a first step, one of the London governors of the Hudson's Bay Company arranged to inspect the establishments and routes of the North West Company in company with one of the North West partners. Nicholas Garry was the governor who had this responsibility; he was accompanied on his journey up the Ottawa by Simon McGillivray of the North West Company, who had the corresponding duty of inspecting the Hudson's Bay Company's establishments that they were able to visit on their long journey to York Factory. One inevitable result of this inspection was the decision to concentrate all travel to and from the western posts through Hudson Bay. Many thought that this meant the end of the Ottawa Waterway as an important line of communication for the fur trade but this conclusion was completely disproved by one of the most colourful of all the men of the Ottawa, Governor George Simpson.

There has rarely been a better example of the right man in the right place at the right time. To the good fortune of the Company, and indeed of Canada, Simpson controlled with a firm hand the development in Canada of the amalgamated Hudson's Bay Company from its inception at that council meeting in September 1821 until his death almost forty years later. Although he did not live to see the end of the two centuries of monopolistic trading, he did represent the Company admirably in London before the parliamentary committee of 1857, the report of which led to the final deed of surrender in 1869. Born at Loch Broom in Scotland in 1787, George Simpson came to Canada as a very young man, being appointed to act as *locum tenens* for the governor at Norway House in June 1820. He led a party into the Athabasca country later that summer and so participated in the final struggle between the two companies. At the 1821 joint council meeting, he was appointed governor of the Northern Department, tribute indeed to his ability. He served also as acting governor of the Southern Department until William Williams retired officially in 1826, when he became acting governor-in-chief of all the Hudson's Bay territories in Canada, the full title being conferred on him in 1839. That he was a lover of the Ottawa from the days of his early travelling on it was well shown when he decided to settle in Lachine, choosing this spot rather than Montreal, which was a 'sink of dissipation and extravagance.' He spent his first few winters as governor mainly in the Red River colony, and his summers travelling throughout the vast area over which he had command. He went as far as the Pacific coast in his effort to meet personally with his staff, and developed in this way an *esprit de corps* that in a remarkably short time replaced the old antagonisms of 1821.

Simpson's residence at Lachine, a large stone building previously used as an inn (but now, alas, demolished), was indeed the Hudson's Bay House for Canada. A companion stone warehouse still stands close to the entrance of the Lachine Canal, the starting point for all the governor's phenomenal journeys to the west. Lachine was convenient for the winter but the council meetings were still held at Norway House and to them the governor went faithfully every year, usually combining attendance at the meetings with travels throughout his domain. In his service to the company he made five transcontinental trips to the Pacific coast, generally by canoe; twelve round trips across the Atlantic for London consultations and personal business, including his marriage in 1830; and one trip around the world, much of the Canadian part of which was made entirely by canoe. When to this record are added his annual inspection trips, all by canoe, often covering more than 4,000 miles, Simpson's journeys constitute a truly remarkable record of travel for one man, especially in mid-nineteenth century. The Ottawa was always the starting point, and on it and its associated waterways Simpson developed the art of long-distance canoe travel to its highest point. He used a *canot du nord*, always well maintained and brightly painted. He had his own specially selected crew of *voyageurs*, who must have been mighty men indeed, from the records we have of their prowess. He always had with him his own piper, Colin Fraser – and perhaps the writer may add that he once held under his arm the pipes that Fraser played.

Chief Trader Archibald McDonald has left us a graphic pen picture of the arrival of the 'Little Emperor' at Norway House in the course of an epic journey from Hudson's Bay to Fort Langley and the Columbia River in 1828: 'As we waft along under easy sail, the men with a clean change and mounting new feathers, the Highland bagpipes in the Governor's canoe, was echoed by the bugle in mine; then these were laid aside on nearer approach to port, to give free scope to the vocal organs of about eighteen Canadians to chant one of their voyageur airs peculiar to them, and always so perfectly rendered.' Always immaculate in dress himself, Simpson was insistent upon his crew putting on a good appearance at every post they visited. Short in stature, being only five feet six inches tall, he kept himself in fine physical condition. Amongst other practices, he always took an early morning plunge into whatever cold water was available ('this pernicious custom,' as one of his young clerks described it many years later, recalling that he was expected to do the same when travelling with his chief). A man of few words, he was once persuaded by his wife to say grace at dinner when no clergyman was present. 'Lord have mercy on what is now before us,' is said to have been his contribution to the pleasures of that evening. Old photographs of his fine residence show that he kept portraits of Napoleon on his walls so that he probably knew his widely used nickname. He lived up to it, being intolerant of any inefficiency and abrupt to the point of rudeness in issuing some of his commands. Behind the stern and severe demeanour of the governor, however, was a man who asked of those who worked with him no more than he was willing to do himself.

Fortunately, he has left for us in his own words an account of what a typical day's travel on the Ottawa with him was like:

Before bidding good bye to our old friend, the Ottawa, let me here offer a description of a day's march, as a general specimen of the whole journey. To begin with the most important part of our proceedings, the business of encamping for our brief night, we selected, about sunset, some dry and tolerably clear spot; and, immediately on landing, the sound of the axe would be ringing through the woods, as the men were felling whole trees for our fires, and preparing, if necessary, a space for our tents. In less than ten minutes our three lodges would be pitched, each with such a blaze in front as virtually imparted a new sense of enjoyment to all the young campaigners, while through the crackling flames were to be seen the requisite number of pots and kettles for our supper. Our beds were next laid, consisting of an oil-cloth spread on the bare earth, with three blankets and a pillow, and, when occasion demanded, with cloaks and great coats at discretion; and, whether the wind howled or the rain poured, our pavilions of canvas formed a safe barrier against the weather. While part of our crews, comprising all the landsmen, were doing duty as stokers, and cooks, and architects, and chambermaids, the more experienced voyageurs, after unloading the canoes, had drawn them on the beach with their bottoms upwards, to inspect, and, if needful, to renovate the stitching and the gumming; and as the little vessels were made to incline on one side to windward, each with a roaring fire to leeward, the crews, every man in his own single blanket, managed to set wind and rain and cold at defiance, almost as effectually as ourselves.

Weather permitting, our slumbers would be broken about one in the morning by the cry of 'Lève, lève, lève!' In five minutes, woe to the inmates that were slow in dressing; the tents were tumbling about our ears; and, within half an hour, the camp would be raised, the canoes laden, and the paddles keeping time to some merry old song. About eight o'clock, a convenient place would be selected for breakfast, about three quarters of an hour being allotted for the multifarious operations of unpacking and repacking the equipage, laying and removing the cloth, boiling and frying, eating and drinking; and, while the preliminaries were arranging, the hardier among us would wash and shave, each person carrying soap and towel in his pocket, and finding a mirror in the same sandy or rocky basin that held the water. About two in the afternoon we usually put ashore for dinner; and, as this meal needed no fire, or at least got none, it was not allowed to occupy more than twenty minutes or half an hour.

Such was the routine of our journey, the day, generally speaking, being divided into six hours of rest and eighteen of labour. This almost incredible toil the voyageurs bore without a murmur, and generally with such a hilarity of spirit as few other men could sustain for a single forenoon. But the quantity of the work, even more decidedly than the quality, requires operatives of iron mould. In smooth water, the paddle is plied with twice the rapidity of the oar, taxing both arms and lungs to the utmost extent; amid shallows, the canoe is literally dragged by the men, wading to their knees or their loins, while each poor fellow, after replacing his drier half in his seat, laughingly shakes the heaviest of the wet from his legs over the gunwale, before he again gives them an inside berth; in rapids, the towing-line has to be hauled along over rocks and stumps, through swamps and thickets, excepting that, when the ground is utterly impracticable, poles are substituted, and occasionally also the bushes on the shore. Again, on the portages, where the tracks are of all imaginable kinds and degrees of badness, the canoes and their cargoes are never carried across in fewer than two or three trips – the little vessels alone monopolizing, on the first turn, the more expert half of their respective crews. Of the baggage, each man has to carry at least two pieces, estimated at a hundred and eighty pounds avoirdupois, which he suspends in slings of leather placed across the forehead, so that he has his hands free to clear the way among the branches of the standing trees and over the prostrate trunks.

But, in addition to the separate labours of the land and the water, the poor fellows have to endure a combination of both sorts of hardship at least three or four times every day. The canoes can seldom approach near enough to the bank to enable the passengers to step ashore from the gunwale and, no sooner is a halt made, than the men are in the water to ferry us on their backs to dry ground. In this unique department of their duties they seem to take a pride; and a little fellow often ambitiously tries to get possession of the heaviest customer in the party, considerably exceeding, as has often been the case in my experience, the standard aforesaid, of two pieces of baggage.

These words appear in the first of the two volumes in which his journey around the world was described. Published over his name in London in 1847, and dedicated to the directors of the Hudson's Bay Company, the volume may have been ghost-written in part but it carries the authentic ring of the Little Emperor. He had been knighted in London by Queen Victoria in January 1841, probably for the assistance he gave in providing facilities to Arctic explorers, and to the forces at the time of the 1837 troubles. He set off in early spring across the Atlantic to Boston, thence up to Montreal and Lachine. This part of the journey is briefly described, but once the departure from Lachine is made, the record is clear and full. We must give at least one description of the entire journey along the Ottawa Waterway from Lachine, up the Ottawa and Mattawa, across Lake Nipissing and down the French River. Whose better than the greatest canoe traveller of them all? Sir George Simpson's own account of the journey with which this volume is concerned is, therefore, included as an appendix.

The Ottawa River in these changing years was used by many others in addition to the governor of the Honourable Company. Explorers were still using it as their gateway to the unknown. Captain John Franklin, probably the greatest of all Arctic explorers, who 'put the roof' on the map of Canada, made his second journey to the Arctic in 1825 by way of the Ottawa route, returning the same way in 1827. Captain George Back similarly used the Ottawa route in 1833 on his first expedition to the Arctic coast. On Franklin's return journey he stopped at the mouth of the Rideau River as the guest of Lieutenant Colonel John By, who invited him to lay the foundation stone for the first of the great entrance flight of locks at the start of the Rideau Canal. Colonel By, all his men, and all his supplies for the building of the canal, similarly came up the Ottawa between 1826 and 1832, while farther down the river, Lieutenant Colonel Henry Du Vernet in his little camp at Grenville used the river for bringing men and supplies for the building of the Ottawa River canals. Governors and other notable visitors came up the Ottawa to view these military works, as the two Canadas slowly developed into the beginnings of the Canada of today.

What may be more surprising, in view of this, was the continued trade in furs on the Ottawa. The Hudson's Bay Company maintained eight active posts in the Ottawa Valley and another at North Bay, all forming part of the Montreal Department, and all but one supplied from Lachine. Canoes with their cargoes of furs were still to be seen throughout Sir George Simpson's residence at Lachine, indeed throughout the century. A photograph (page 110) shows Indians bringing a canoe load of furs into the Ottawa River in 1902. By 1840, however, beaver hats were going out of fashion in Europe, the silk hat taking over; but as this market faded the more elegant use of beaver furs for ladies' wear began, a change for which the company was ready. In the year 1860, a focal point in the story of the Ottawa, more than 9,000 beaver skins and 15,000 muskrats were taken at Lac des Sables and Fort Coulonge alone, so the Governor was never far from the detailed operation of the trade which he administered so well.

Simpson's interests, however, went far beyond furs in canoes. He appreciated what the coming of steamships would mean for his beloved river; and so in 1849 he became a partner in the Ottawa Steamer Company and loaned money for the construction of some of the new steamboats. Next came the start of railways in the transportation revolution of the century; Sir George had his eye on this development also. Most significant for him was the extension of United States rail connections in the direction of the Red River and, later, the construction of the first steamboat on that north-flowing stream. When St Paul was the western rail terminus, goods were taken thence by rail and then on carts across the plains as far as the Red River Settlement. At Sir George's instigation, the Hudson's Bay Company in 1858 had sent a shipment of goods for the west by way of New York, then by rail to St Paul, and by cart to the Red River Settlement, at a spectacular saving in cost. Until Canadian rail transport could be used, at first from the lakehead to Winnipeg and then in 1885 all the way by rail, the Red River route was increasingly used, apart from late in the year 1862 when Sioux Indians successfully interfered with its operation. Sir George Simpson himself travelled by rail to St Paul in 1858, and thence overland to the Red River, finally by canoe to Norway House for the annual meeting of the council. He repeated this in 1859 but had to abandon his journey at St Paul in 1860 when he suffered his first serious attack of illness.

Prior to this, with that foresight with which he was gifted, he had associated himself with railway development in eastern Canada, being elected to the board of the Quebec, Montreal, Ottawa and Occidental Railroad, more commonly known in later years as the North Shore Line. He must have been unique in thus combining interest in canoe travel, steamships, and railroads. Although the governor had given up, finally, his arduous journeys up the Ottawa, the Ottawa route continued to be used for official Company business. Simpson's successor as governor, Alexander Grant Dallas, came from Fort William in 1863 by 'the old canoe route' as far as Ottawa, just renamed from Bytown. He was accompanied by Edward Hopkins, who served as secretary to Sir George and later advanced in the Company's service to be chief factor, retiring to England only in 1870. He was a man of wide interests, godfather of Gerard Manley Hopkins, the poet. After tragically losing his first wife from cholera, he married Frances Anne Beechey, known for her paintings of river scenes in Canada, in some of which she herself appears as the 'lady in the canoe.' A reproduction of one of her vivid paintings, so intimately connected with the Hudson's Bay Company, is on page 109. She travelled widely with her husband. They came down the lakes by canoe, up the French River, across Lake Nipissing and down the Ottawa certainly as far as Pembroke in August 1869, this being the last official Company travel by canoe that it has been possible to trace. Canoes still came down the Ottawa but the steamships, then the railways, and finally the highways eventually displaced them for all but journeys of adventurous pleasure.

All this Sir George Simpson may have foreseen, but canoe travel was probably uppermost in his mind in the happy summer of 1860. With the faithful Hopkins, the old gentleman (for he was now seventy-three) got back safely by rail to Montreal and then supervised arrangements at the summer home that he had built for himself on Dorval Island for the reception of Edward, Prince of Wales. The Prince, the first heir to the throne to visit Canada, laid the foundation stone for the new Parliament Buildings in Ottawa – so soon to be the Parliament Buildings of the new country of Canada – and officially opened the Victoria railway bridge across the St Lawrence at Montreal. One can readily imagine the satisfaction of the Little Emperor in thus having the opportunity of entertaining the son of his Queen in his own home. After a great meal had been enjoyed, and the Prince had listened to the band that played on the lawn, the entire party embarked in part of the great flotilla of canoes that Sir George had assembled for this splendid occasion. They set off across Lake St Louis for Lachine, the Prince in the leading canoe, with the royal standard fluttering at its bow, the governor directing the procession from a following canoe.

Three days later, Sir George suffered an apoplectic stroke while driving in his carriage from Montreal to Lachine. He was taken to his home by the side of the river he loved and there he died, six days later, on 12 August 1860. When his body was placed on a special train at Lachine for the journey to Montreal, a group of Indians, 'his Indians,' sang a 'wild and doleful dirge.' An era had ended.

# FOUR

# Travellers' Tales

*Le samedy I. de Iuin nous passasmes encor deux autres Sauts: le premier contenant demie lieuë de long, & le second vne lieuë, où nous eusmes bien de la peine; car la rapidité du courant est si grāde, qu' elle faict vn bruict effroyable, & descendant de degré en degré, faict vne escume si blanche par tout, que l' eau ne parost aucunement ...*

Let Champlain's own words begin this selection of extracts from the records left by travellers on the Ottawa Waterway. This was his first encounter with really swift water, at Carillon, Chute à Blondeau, and the Long Sault.

It was here we had such difficulty, for being unable to portage our canoes on account of the thickness of the woods, we had to track them, and in pulling mine I almost lost my life, because the canoe turned broadside into a whirlpool, and had I not luckily fallen between two rocks, the canoe would have dragged me in, since I could not quickly enough loosen the rope which was twisted around my hand, which hurt me very much and nearly cut it off. In this danger I cried aloud to God and began to pull my canoe toward me, which was sent back to me by an eddy such as occurs in these rapids. Having escaped, I gave praise to God, beseeching Him to preserve us.

This, the first account of a journey on the Ottawa, is still one of the most vivid. Here Champlain tells of an experience on his return downriver, accompanied by a flotilla of canoes:

Continuing our journey, we arrived at the Chaudière falls, where the natives celebrated their usual ceremony, which is as follows. Having carried their canoes to the foot of the fall, they assemble in one place, where one of them takes up a collection with a wooden plate into which each puts a piece of tobacco. After the collection, the plate is set down in the middle of the group and all dance about it, singing after their fashion. Then one of the chiefs makes a speech, pointing out that for years they have been accustomed to make such an offering, and that thereby they receive protection from their enemies; that otherwise misfortune would happen to them, as the devil persuades them ... When he has finished, the orator takes the plate and throws the tobacco into the middle of the boiling water, and all together utter a loud whoop. These poor people are so superstitious, that they would not think they could have a safe journey, unless they had performed this ceremony here...

I often find myself thinking of this scene when crossing the bridges that today span the Chaudière, hidden though the great river is by the surrounding industrial complex for much of the crossing.

Some of the pioneer journeys up the river of the Récollet and Jesuit missionaries have already been described. Here are instructions issued in Paris in 1638 by the Jesuit Superior, directed to *Nostre Compagnie qui seront enuoiez aux Hurons*, as summarized by Francis Parkman:

You should love the Indians like brothers, with whom you are to spend the rest of your life. – Never make them wait for you in embarking. – Take a flint or steel to light their pipes and kindle their fire at night, for these little services win their hearts. – Try to eat their sagamite as they cook it, bad and dirty as it is. Fasten up the skirts of your cassock, that you may not carry water or sand into the canoe. – Wear no shoes or stockings in the canoes; but you may put them on in crossing the portages. – Do not make yourself troublesome, even to a single Indian. – Do not ask them too many questions. – Bear their faults in silence, and appear always cheerful. – Buy fish for them from the tribes you will pass; and for this purpose take with you some awls, beads, knives and fish-hooks. – Be not ceremonious with the Indians; take at once what they offer you; ceremony offends them. – Be very careful, when in the canoe, that the brim of your hat does not annoy them. Perhaps it would be better to wear your night-cap. There is no such thing as impropriety among Indians. – Remember that it is Christ and his cross that you are seeking; and if you aim at anything else, you will get nothing but affliction for body and mind.

We have already seen how graphically the Chevalier de Troyes described the start of his journey up the Ottawa in the early spring of 1686. He was so interesting a writer, and his journal is so human a document, that one wishes it were known to all Canadians, at least through the excellent translation of Kenyon and Turnbull. The extracts that follow are from his story of his first journey into the wilds of Canada, with a company fully equipped for their daring attack on the English forts on Hudson Bay. Here they have just left what is now Grenville:

We left at daybreak, and camped at Petite Nation some eight leagues away. On the nineteenth, we broke camp very early to go to a place called la Chaudière about nine leagues upstream. We did not get there because it was necessary to stop to repair our canoes. We also went up the Du Lièvre River to pick up a canoe which was cached there ... Throughout the trip, we had several times encountered bands of Christian Iroquois, who urged us to remain for a time with them so that they could entertain us. As we were pressed for time, we could not accept their kind invitation. Some gave us presents of meat, while others offered to go hunting for us. Some of their best men even offered to accompany me. I thanked them but declined their offer. That night, the weather was extremely bad.

I had a Canadian tied to a tree to punish him for an insulting remark that he had made. Several unruly characters almost started a mutiny because of this, but I shortly led them back to their duty. Father Silvie was of great assistance in this task ... Then on the 21st I left for Chaudière Portage. The voyageurs had given it this name because part of the river there falls among a frightful confusion of rocks, and at the bottom, spurts out as if from a kettle ... The twenty-fourth, we came to Cat Portage. This place got its name because it is filled with sharp rocks which, in a manner of speaking, scratch the canoes of the voyageurs ...

After mass on May 5th, we left for the portage at the end of a narrow stretch of the river. This stretch of river is some seven leagues long, bordered on the north by a high mountain which drops straight and sheer into the water. The middle of this rock wall appears black, caused perhaps by the natives' offerings of tobacco which they shoot at the rock by attaching them to the ends of their arrows. The natives call this rock 'The Bird.' According to the custom of our people, a man must be baptized here the first time he passes this rock. Several of our men, not wishing to abandon this time-honoured custom, dived into the water so we camped at the foot of the portage.

As noted in Chapter Three, one of the first English-speaking adventurers to obtain permission from General Gage (Commander-in-chief of the British forces), and to secure the necessary passport from the town-major at Montreal, for a journey to Michilimackinac was a fur trader from the east. This was Alexander Henry, senior of the two men of this famous name who early penetrated the west. (His younger namesake was his nephew, whose journey was made almost forty years after that of his uncle.) He had been told that the route up the Ottawa River was 'the shortest and that which is normally pursued by the canoes, employed in the Indian trade.' And so he set off from Lachine on 3 August 1761 on a journey that was to keep him in the west until his return to Montreal on 15 October 1776. In his later years, he wrote down the experiences of his 'premature attempt to share in the fur-trade of Canada, directly on the conquest of the country, [which] led the author of the following pages into situations of some danger and singularity.' This is the supreme understatement in the literature of early Canadian travel, since, as previously noted, Henry witnessed the massacre by Indians of over seventy British soldiers on the King's birthday in 1763. He escaped at that time, but was later captured, though he ultimately escaped again. His vivid record makes fictional wild-west stories appear tame.

On his way to these adventures, Alexander Henry travelled up the Ottawa River. Some indication of what lay ahead for him was given by Indians whom he met on the river, such as those encountered on the Lake of Two Mountains from whom he

purchased some of their maple-sugar, and beaver-skins, in exchange for provisions. They wished for rum, which I declined to sell them; but they behaved civilly, and we parted, as we had met, in a friendly manner. Before they left us, they inquired, of my men, whether or not I was an Englishman, and, being told that I was, observed, that the English were mad, in their pursuit of beaver, since they could thus expose their lives for it; 'for,' added they, 'the Upper Indians will certainly kill him,' meaning myself. These Indians had left their village before the surrender of Montreal, and I was the first Englishman they had seen ... [Then comes a brief account of the journey up past the Chaudière and the Chats.]

On July 10, we had reached the Portage du Grand Calumet, which is at the head of the channel of the same name, and which name is derived from pièrre à calumet, or pipe-stone, which here interrupts the river, occasioning a fall of water. The carrying-place is long and arduous, consisting of a high steep hill, over which the canoe cannot be carried by fewer than twelve men ... The ascent of this carrying-place is not more fatiguing, than the descent is dangerous; and, in performing it, accidents too often occur, producing strains, ruptures, and injuries for life. [In a footnote Henry explained: 'a charitable fund is now established in Montreal, for the relief of disabled and decayed *voyageurs*.']

[Above Des Allumettes is] the *rivière Creuse* (called, by the English, *Deep-River*), twenty-six miles in length, where the water flows, with a gentle current, at the foot of a high mountainous, barren and rocky country, on the north, and has a low sandy soil on the south. On this southern side, is a remarkable point of sand, stretching far into the stream, and on which it is customary to baptize novices. Above the river Creuse, are the two carrying-places, of the length of half a mile each, called the Portages des Deux Joachins; and, at fifteen miles further, at the mouth of the river Du Moine, is another fort, or trading house, where I found a small encampment of Indians, called Maskegons, and with whom I bartered several articles, for furs. They anxiously inquired, whether or not the English were in possession of the country below, and whether or not, if they were, they would allow traders to come to that trading-house; declaring, that their families must starve, unless they should be able to procure ammunition and other necessaries. I answered both these questions in the affirmative, at which they expressed much satisfaction.

Naturally, there have been disappointments in assembling these personal writings about travel on the Ottawa – records that one had hoped to find but which cannot now be traced, and eminent travellers whom one had expected to find as visitors to the Ottawa Valley who never did see it, confining themselves to the St Lawrence route to the Great Lakes and the west. John Graves Simcoe, the first lieutenant governor of Upper Canada, did not get to the Ottawa in his four busy years in office. Lady Simcoe also used the St Lawrence route to York and Niagara but she did mention in her diary for 22 June 1792, after recording her journey from Montreal to La Chine in Mr Frobisher's carriage and spending the night in 'an indifferent House called an Inn': 'We embarked at 6. Soon afterwards left Pt Claire and Isle Perrot to the north, and saw the junction of the Ottawa or Grand River with the St Lawrence, the former pouring its dirty coloured water into the transparent stream of the St Lawrence.' It was a refrain that other travellers up the St Lawrence would often repeat.

Patrick Campbell, an army officer who spent the years 1791 and 1792 in

North America, generally in New Brunswick but with one long journey to
Niagara and back through New York State, observed:

Towards evening [of November 6, 1791] we crossed the mouth of the north
river which flows into the St Lawrence, the opening of which is so broad as
to appear more like a Lake than a stream of running water, and not inferior
in width to the St Lawrence itself. I have been informed that this river rises
out of Lake Superior; others say that it passes to the northward ... the
greatest part of the Fur Trade is carried on by it ... it passes the head of
another river which falls into Hudson's Bay; that these two streams pass
within half a mile of each other, and pursue their courses in different
directions ... that the clerks and servants of the Hudson's Bay Company,
and those of Montreal, often meet about the heads of these rivers, and
encroach on each other's territories so much that it creates great disputes
among them; what is more, they encourage the Indians to commit outrages
on each other, and strive who buys best.

Canada's most eminent early explorer and surveyor, David Thompson,
came down the Ottawa River only once, and this at the end of twenty-eight
years of exploration in the west. The final words of his great *Narrative*
provide this conclusion to all his fifty thousand miles of journeying in wild
and unknown country in the service of the Hudson's Bay and North West
companies:

On the fifteenth a vessel arrived [at Fort William] with the news that War
had been declared by the United States, against Great Britain and we were
warned to be on our guard; this made us all look very serious, for the whole
returns of the Company were yet here, getting ready to be sent to Montreal;
everything was expedited every exertion made to get the Furrs off, in which
we were seconded by the Men, who alarmed at the chance of being made
prisoners, and thus deprived of their families and enjoying their wages were
most anxious to arrive at Montreal; we had only a short distance to dread
being captured, being the Falls of St Maries and the straits to Lake Huron,
once in the Lake we held ourselves to be safe by passing to, and down, the
Ottawa River; in which thank good Providence we succeeded, and by the
middle of August with Men and Furrs we were safe in Montreal.

That is just about the shortest known account of the complete passage of
the Ottawa River route from Lake Huron all the way to Montreal. David

Thompson was so splendid an observer and note-taker that the disappointment of this staccato account is the greater. He did see the Ottawa
again, but he never went back to the west, spending his later years at
Terrebonne, Williamstown, and then Longeuil, near Montreal, where he
died (in abject poverty) on 10 February 1857. He was buried, with his wife,
in Mount Royal Cemetery, Montreal, but without any sign to show where
the bodies lie.

One of the most interesting of the records left for us by officers of the
British army who travelled on the Ottawa River in the latter half of the
eighteenth century on their journeys to and from St Joseph Island, was that
written late in life by Colonel George Thomas Landmann of the Royal
Engineers and published in 1852. Landmann was born at the Royal Arsenal
in 1779, his father being an instructor at the Royal Military Academy.
Commissioned in the Royal Engineers ('without passing through the
Royal Artillery') in 1795, he was ordered to Canada in 1797. He had an
adventurous crossing, which included the capture of a Danish vessel that
Landmann boarded.

In Canada, in April 1799, he was directed to build on St Joseph Island a
blockhouse, several other buildings, and a wharf, all without benefit of
drawings or specifications. He found that the whole summer would be used
up if he went by 'the ordinary military route, that is by Kingston, Niagara
and Amherstburgh'; and so he attempted to get passage with a North West
Company brigade. Alexander Mackenzie arranged for him to go up the
Ottawa with William McGillivray. He was entertained before leaving
Lachine at the usual lavish luncheon: 'By six or seven o'clock, I had, in
common with many of the others fallen from my seat and curled up in the
fireplace.' Meanwhile, the clerks had sent two canoes with all the baggage
up to the head of the island. Landmann and his companions went up later in
a calèche (a two-wheeled, one-seated horse-drawn vehicle), over a road so
bad that he was bumped out of his seat, losing his hat, his watch, and his
money. Twice the calèche slid down the bank into the river, but after a
ten-hour journey through the night, they arrived at Ste Anne's, where the
canoes were waiting.

The canoe I was in had twelve men, as had also the other one in company,
and no merchandise, nothing but provisions and our baggage, which gave
us a wonderful advantage in passing the carrying-places, as two trips was
always found to be sufficient to carry the whole. The carriers of the canoe
had the severest work, and as it weighed about fifteen hundred pounds, it is

clear that each man of the six was expected to bear, on level ground, about two hundred and fifty pounds.

At the first camping place ... my shoes were still so damp that I placed them with the upper leathers towards the fire, but at such a distance as I thought beyond the range of mischief, yet on the following morning I found the toes and heels drawn together, and the leather so brittle that on attempting to straighten the soles, they broke to pieces like earthenware. I had no second pair; I was reduced to the necessity of going bare-footed until I arrived at St Joseph's.

He describes vividly the difficulties of the portages on the Mattawa River, one of his worries being that he might be bitten on his bare feet by the snakes he saw; but all was well and they got to Lake Nipissing safely. Like most travellers, he mentions Pointe-aux-Croix, near which they camped for the night:

Here we found a family of Indians, from whom we purchased two fine sturgeons, weighing about sixty or seventy pounds each, and for which we paid a bottle of rum, (half water) ... Whilst the tent was erecting, I observed one of our men cut off the tail and piece of fish weighing about seven pounds, and toast it in the fire; in the course of an hour he had eaten it all; and seeing me standing at a short distance looking at him, he held up the bone with a grin of exultation. In like manner the others played their parts, and finished every morsel of one hundred and forty pounds of sturgeon, long before the hour of departure in the morning. From this place we soon entered the French river near its source, and commenced to run down its rapid stream. The Parisien rapid is one of the worst of those inclined shoots, it is very narrow, and requires an extraordinary degree of skill, to descend it with safety through its turbulent waters, and avoid two large rocks under water, one at each end, but on contrary sides, rendering it necessary to cross through the middle of a high ridge of water formed by the velocity of the current.

After some more details of the difficult descent of the French River, he pays tribute to the *voyageurs* and their hardihood and skill:

No men in the world are more severely worked than are these Canadian voyageurs. I have known them to work in a canoe twenty hours out of twenty four ... the quantity of food they consume is incredible ... They are short lived and rarely are fit to voyage after they have attained their fortieth year, and sixty years seems to be the average of their existence ... These [are] men of a high courage, who have proved that they hold the effeminacies of civilised life in contempt.

In the summer of 1800 Landmann set a record for the journey from St Joseph Island to Montreal. He relates how he bought a light canoe, 25 feet long, and hired a former guide named Le Duc and nine *voyageurs*, all specially picked. He knew that McTavish had once made the journey in 7³/4 days; he was determined to beat this record. The party arranged their equipment so that all could be transported in one trip over each portage, with Landmann himself carrying a full load. They were favoured with good weather across the lake and so reached the mouth of the French River in thirty hours. Then started the hard work of portaging up the French River and into Lake Nipissing, down the Mattawa, and then down the Ottawa. They were held up at Lachine, impatiently waiting for a guide to lead them down the Lachine Rapids; but even so they reached Montreal in 7¹/4 days. All the men were exhausted and had sore eyes because of the forest fires between which they had paddled for a long stretch of the Ottawa, the contents of the canoe catching fire at one point as well as men's clothes. They were bruised and hurt by the heavy hailstones which fell in the storm that quenched the fire.

This was the heyday of the North West Company, when through canoe traffic on the waterway was probably at its peak. Competition with the Hudson's Bay Company, however, was casting its shadow ahead, conflict between the two great companies being accelerated by the strange episode of Lord Selkirk and his settlement at Fort Garry. The Earl of Selkirk had landed in New York in 1815, at the start of his fateful residence in North America. He spent the winter in Montreal, where he was almost ignored by the North West partners even though he had come out authorized by the Hudson's Bay Company, of which he was a large shareholder, to discuss terms of amalgamation with them. Behind his back, he was known as 'Lord Moonshine' or 'The Bible Peer.' One could put this down simply to the strong antipathy of the partners to anything connected with the Company, were it not confirmed from a more surprising quarter.

Lord Selkirk had met a Lieutenant von Graffenreid, a Swiss mercenary soldier who had come to Canada to fight in the War of 1812 with the Swiss Regiment de Meuron, taking part in the ill-fated battle of Plattsburg. The regiment was disbanded after the conclusion of the war, but von Graffenreid was engaged by Lord Selkirk to command the bodyguard at the Red

River Settlement. With a picked group from his regiment, he travelled from Lachine to Toronto in June 1816. Here they met Lord Selkirk and his party and the combined group proceeded up the portage to Lake Simcoe and over to Penetanguishene on Lake Huron, then an active naval base. Here Lord Selkirk was greeted with huzzahs and salvoes – which, tactlessly, he did nothing to acknowledge. The commander of his bodyguard comments as follows in his diary, a translation of which has been kindly made available to me by Mr Rudy Josephson: 'but as he refrained from doing so … I began to believe that he lacked common sense, which proved to be borne out later on.'

On his way up from Lachine Lieutenant von Graffenreid had stopped in the Lake of Two Mountains. (This was apparently used as a route from Lake St Louis to the St Lawrence in order to avoid the Coteau Rapids, to such an extent that surveys were made by the Royal Engineers for a connecting canal at this point between the Ottawa and the St Lawrence.) He had twenty-seven men with him; they were to go up the St Lawrence in two batteaux, but he wanted his men to have experience with canoe travel and so obtained a canoe for this purpose before proceeding. He comments:

On a nearby mountain, Mont Calvaire, on which were three chapels built by missionaries one could enjoy an excellent view of the St. Lawrence River and its many very beautiful islands covered with trees and pretty villages … a group of Indians who were passing by carried beaver pelts as well as marten and other pelts; besides this they had a number of beaver glands containing valuable castor oil. Two tame young beavers were also carried along which they fed bread, milk and bark. Several Indians had with them bundles which were worth from two to three hundred Louis d'Or.

Von Graffenreid stayed at Fort Garry for one year after the departure of the Earl of Selkirk but got very bored, having little to do in his military capacity. He was eventually relieved by a Captain Matthey on 26 August 1818 and although pressed to stay on, decided to leave for Montreal and Europe. A party was made up of three canoes, each manned by nine Iroquois, and they set off for the east, this time following the Ottawa route. Here is von Graffenreid's record of the latter part of his long journey:

We passed by the River 'Serpent' under favourable winds which is the half way mark of Lake Huron, and on October 10 we go up the Rivière des François and we found the right way, not without difficulty. On the 12th, we passed through Lake Nipissing and reached the Rivière des Vases where we had to overcome many portages. The banks of all these rivers are richly covered with crosses which have been put there for those who had accidents. If we didn't have to wait so frequently for the other canoes and at the same time had to make repairs on ours as well as the others, we would have made the journey much more quickly. Finally on October 14th, we entered the Great River the Ottawa, where I had to submit to the ceremony of baptism, because I had never travelled on this river before. At the same time all the canoes were newly repaired with pitch. This river too has numerous, partly very dangerous rapids and one of them nearly cost us our lives. The last one, le Grande Sault, is five hours long [?] and is navigated with pilots who are especially stationed here. I welcomed with hearty rejoicing the view of pretty American [sic] farmhouses and gardens ... On the 21st, we camped during a heavy rain on the shore of the Lake of Three [sic] Mountains where I had already been earlier. After a long and dangerous trip lasting fifty days I finally reached the much looked-forward to City of Montreal where, immediately upon my arrival, I paid Lord Selkirk a visit.

The merging of the Hudson's Bay Company with the North West Company is reflected in the following passage:

The Hudson's Bay Company having made an Arrangement with the North-West Company, it became necessary that one of the Directors of the former Company should accompany Mr Simon McGillivray, a Partner of the latter, to Montreal and from thence to proceed thro' the Indian Country to Fort William and from thence visiting the different Posts belonging as well to the H.B. as to the N.W. and the Red River Settlement to proceed to York Fort, and from thence to embark for England. Myself being the only single man in the Direction it became imperative on Me that I should not hesitate to undertake this long and tedious Journey.

These are the opening words of one of the most revealing and human accounts of the journey by canoe up the Ottawa Waterway and on to the west – the diary of Nicholas Garry, then the deputy governor of the Hudson's Bay Company, after whom Fort Garry was named. The diary was handwritten on both sides of sheets of Whatman paper, bound in book form so arranged that it could be locked. Written in canoes and in camps, it was difficult to decipher. But Garry's grandson transcribed it and made it available for publication by the Royal Society of Canada, to which it was presented in 1900 by Sir John Bourinot.

Garry had sailed from Liverpool on 6 April 1821 and arrived in New York on 10 May. Leaving New York in the steamboat *Chancellor Livingstone*, he reached Albany after a voyage of twenty hours and then took a carriage to Montreal. There he attended communion service at St Paul's Church, the Reverend Mr Bethune officiating. 'A singular incident occurred to me. Mr Henry, an old Gentleman of 85, the first Englishman who went in to the interior of the Hudson's Bay Territory was next to me on my Right.' Nicholas Garry had done his homework; he knew about Alexander Henry's remarkable stay in the west and, as later entries in his diary make clear, he had read Alexander Mackenzie's journal.

Garry went to Lachine on 7 June and later drove to Ste Anne's where his company was assembled, the canoes having been paddled up from Lachine.

Our Party consists in Mr William McGillivray, Mr Simon McGillivray and myself, Mornis[?] an old Canadian Voyageur as McG's servant, an English Boy servant to his brother and my man Raven, one Guide Langue, 12 Canadian Voyageurs, an Illisquois, Thoma, making in all 19 [20?] Persons. Our canoe is 36 feet in Length and about 6 Feet extreme Breadth.

They made a late start on their first day, leaving Ste Anne's only at eight o'clock that morning.

At 1 o'clock we approached the Long Sault and landed at a small village [Pointe Fortune] where Mr Miles Macdonald is living in a deranged state of mind. Here our Canoe was towed up by Ropes about one mile. During a Distance of 15 miles there are several Décharges and Portages which are called the Rapids of the Long Sault. At last we landed on the Upper Canada side and walked about 5 miles and on Travelling through Woods were dreadfully attacked by Mosquitoes. Here Government is making a Canal to avoid the Rapids of the Sault, in the same manner as the Canal intended to be made at Montreal is to avoid the Rapids of St Louis at LaChine ... At the Top of the Canal we found an encampment of the Staff Corps commanded by Captain Duvernet and Le Merrick [?] who received us most hospitably. Mrs Duvernet, an Italian Lady, appeared to be a very agreeable amiable Woman. At seven o'clock we embarked and at about eight encamped and drank Tea with a Mr Grant formerly in the service of the North West [Company]. At two o'clock in the morning we embarked ... The Weather was at Intervals raining when we were dreadfully annoyed by the Mosquitoes. The sturdy little Canadians little minding their stings were covered with Blood and our sufferings on many occasions were dreadful. For the Protection of our Faces we had Veils but when we were exposed to their Attacks it was a misery in the most Frightful Shape ... The Night is passed under the Sufferings of Bites and Stings, and if at last, worn out, Sleep should close the Eyes the call to embark now awakens you to the renewed Attacks of a Host of bloodthirsty and insatiable Enemies; a Digression occasioned by the Bite of Mosquitoes, Sand Flies, Spiders, etc.

But he stuck it out, despite all discomforts. Later in his journey, when the flies were rather less troublesome, he was able to enjoy the feelings experienced by all travellers on Canada's waterways:

In nature's Wilds all is Independence, all your Luxuries and Comforts are within yourself and all that is pleasurable within your own Minds: and after all this is Happiness, if there is such a thing in the world, which no mortal can say ... Our Dinner Table was a Hard Rock, no Table Cloth could be cleaner and the surrounding Plants and Beautiful Flowers sweetening the Board.

This was on the Winnipeg River; back on the Ottawa, Garry told of his delight at the Chaudière Falls:

We had scarcely Time to admire the beautiful Scene when the Chaudière in all his Wildness and Majesty appeared before us. The Imagination cannot picture anything so wild and romantic. The Ottawa dividing itself into two streams forms an extensive Island covered with the finest Trees (principally Oak), in a bed of Long Grass and beautiful Verdure ... The Beauty of the Scene is perhaps a little destroyed by the Appearance of Cultivation. A Mr Wright an American has built a little Town near the Falls, and Deal Mills.

After mounting the second Portage at Des Joachims, Nicholas Garry had his first encounter with sand flies:

Here we were dreadfully annoyed by the Mouchestik or Sand Fly, a little black treacherous Rascal more venemous than the Mosquitoes and so insidious that you cannot keep them off. Our People were streaming with Blood, indeed their Sufferings were this Day very great; the Heat was excessive, the Thermometer 90 in the Shade, the carrying Places over rugged Mountains without shelter from the Sun and the Attacks of Mosquitoes and Mustiks. But they were still all Animation, no Man shrinking from his Duty, all anxious to get on. At 9 we encamped but had to cut away Trees to enable us to fix our Tent. An immense Fire and Smoke relieved us from our Enemies.

Near Roche Capitaine they

passed the Encampment of an Indian; the Poles of the Tent remained and his Bath or Sweating House and Frame to stretch the Beaver. The Bath is a sort of little Tent of Wood over which shrubs are placed to keep out the Air. In the middle are red hot Stones on which they pour water and every Aperture being closed the Heat occasioned by the Steam becomes excessive. This they consider a Remedy for all Complaints particularly for Rheumatism. It is exactly on the Principle of the Russian Bath, the Indian indulging himself in the same Luxury as the Russian in jumping from the Bath into the River or rolling himself in the Snow, after parboiling.

Along the way, the party experienced some of the pleasantries that redeemed the hardships of canoe travel – finding on one portage a 'Letter written on an Egg from Mr. McCloud, who had preceded us by two Days'; on another 'a Piece of Bark on which was written a "Present for Mr. Garry" and on looking about we found a Pile of Stones ... [covering] a small Land Tortoise which are very common in this Country.' He delighted in 'an immense quantity of Butterflies. A blue Butterfly with blue wings the most beautiful I have ever seen.' But nothing, probably, so interested this visitor as an encounter on Turtle Lake, close to the final portage over into Lake Nipissing:

On entering the Lake we met 4 Canoes with Indians with a Deputation of 80 Warriors going to Lord Dalhousie. One of the Indians had killed another and they were going to intercede for the Culprit. The Chief was a fine old Man apparently about 70, designated by the Feather in his Hat, a common Goose Quill. The young Men were very well looking. I only observed one Female who was probably the Wife of the Son of the Chief, as she was sitting behind him. She had a most beautiful intelligent Countenance the finest black Eyes and a Complexion which would have been considered as a Brunette and not darker in any Country. We made the Chief a Present of Tobacco and Biscuits ... Our Journey has been this Day a most fatiguing one for our Men and the most miserable to us Bourgeois ... comprehending almost everything, except meeting the beautiful Indian.

There were other lovely ladies who sailed on the Ottawa. One of them kept a diary of her journey; her name was Frances Simpson. Sir George Simpson, in his active days in the west, is known to have followed the general practice of marriage *à la façon du pays*, a practice that was even acknowledged by his Company; some of the children born of these liaisons carried his name. In September 1829, however, he went to England and there met and was attracted by his eighteen-year-old cousin, Frances Simpson; they were married on 24 February 1830, in Middlesex. Simpson was accompanied on this trip to England by Chief Factor McTavish, who also married a young lady, also on 24 February, but in Edinburgh. The couples travelled together to Canada by way of New York, the two ladies having an enjoyable time in Montreal before leaving for the west. Simpson appears to have been able to keep his new wife clear of any entanglements with his Canadian offspring, but McTavish was not so fortunate and encountered some domestic difficulties even in Montreal.

After less than a month there, they set off to the west on one of Simpson's speedy journeys. Mrs Simpson kept a diary, which has fortunately been preserved. Her journal shows that despite the long hours of travel each day, dangers, and weather that included much rain and some near-freezing periods, she never lost her cheerful outlook nor ceased to enjoy her experiences.

They set out on 2 May 1830, from Lachine, and even on this day they started at 4:00 a.m. The combined party travelled in two of the large canoes, 'Mr. and Mrs. McTavish & Maid Servant in one, & Mr. Simpson, Myself and Servant in the other, accompanied by Messrs. Keith and Gale who kindly volunteered to favour us with their company for a day or two. The two canoes [were] manned by 15 hands each, all strong, active, fine looking Canadians.' Typical of Sir George's travel habits was their first stop:

At 9 o'clock we put ashore for breakfast, above the Rapids of St. Ann – the water being too shallow for the Canoes to touch the bank, Mrs McTavish & myself were carried in the arms, and the Gentlemen on the backs of our sturdy Canadians, which (as may be supposed) caused a hearty laugh both at, and to, such of the company as were novices ... the cloth was laid on the grass, & spread with Cold Meat, Fowls, Ham, Eggs, Bread & Butter everyone sat down in the position found most convenient, and each made the most of the time afforded. Mr Simpson (after looking at his watch) gave the call of 'Take Away' – the breakfast party were on their feet in a moment, the things washed, packed and the Canoe off again, within the 45 Minutes usually allowed for this meal.

They stopped at what is now Oka and again at St Andrews, where they had a two o'clock dinner, accompanied by port, madeira, and champagne (in honour of the ladies), but went on to spend the night at Chute à Blondeau. 'Arose at 2 a.m. with aching bones – the people were aroused by Mr. Simpson's call of Levé, Levé, Levé.' This was to become a familiar diary entry. They were on their way again by three o'clock.

They spent the next night near the mouth of the Lièvre River after a pleasant day:

The Sun intensely hot today and the water of the Grand, or Uttowas river as smooth as glass; the Country on either side a thick Forest; the trees near the edge of the Water low, & branching, chiefly Aspen; while those behind were Pine, straight as Arrows, and growing to an enormous height: everything was calm & quiet, not a sound to be heard excepting the stroke of the paddle and the clear mellow voice of our principal vocalist, Tomma Felix, singing 'La Belle Rosier' and other sweet Voyageurs airs.

On the third day they visited Mrs John By and her daughters whose home was near the construction camp for the Rideau Canal, in the clearing in the woods that was to become Bytown and later Ottawa. Snow fell on the night of the sixth, so that canoes, paddles, and equipment were ice-coated in the morning. It was, therefore, not surprising that two young recruits in the crews deserted into the bush, one man having already been lost in this way. This was near Des Joachims. They stopped to search for them 'with the assistance of an old Indian Woman & her children (whom we found on the Portage) ...' and the men were found.

A Court Martial was held upon them, composed of the old voyageurs (who are all upon their honor, & never desert), the sentence of which was a dozen lashes with their leather carrying straps: and in spite of their tears, and entreaties, would (I believe) have been carried into effect, had not Mrs McTavish and Myself, called to their aid our most persuasive arguments, and obtained their pardon.

At one particularly difficult portage, an old Indian named Nicholas tried to carry Mrs McTavish in his arms, but found he was not up to it. He offered to take her on his back instead.

Mr Simpson who was coming on after us, persuaded Mrs McTavish (with some difficulty) as a last resource to do as Nicholas recommended, which she at length agreed to, and on the back of Nicholas accordingly mounted:

the scene however was so ludicrous that the by-standers could not resist a laugh, in which Mrs McTavish joined so heartily, that poor Nicholas was thrown off his equilibrium, stumbled forward, fell on his face, and gave his unfortunate rider a summerset over his head, into the mud: throwing her into a situation the most awkward, and ridiculous that ever poor Lady, was placed in. After extricating her with much difficulty, she was at length dragged to the end of the Portage, where we all washed and dried ourselves, and had Breakfast, after which we descended a small river, passed thro' Lake Nipisang, about 40 miles in length, then made a Portage into the French River.

Just one month after leaving Montreal they had got as far as the post on Rainy River, subsequently named Fort Frances after Mrs Simpson, and on 6 June they arrived at Fort Garry. Later they went on to York Factory, which they reached on 26 June.

At the end of her journal, Mrs Simpson looked back over her long trip and said:

Fond as I am of travelling, I own, I felt pleased at the idea of remaining quiet for two months: having traversed in various ways (since the 8th March) a distance of 8,000 miles which, for a novice, is no small undertaking. I must here observe, that a Canoe voyage is not one which an English Lady would take for pleasure ... putting up some evenings drenched to the skin, and finding the Encampment so wet, as to render it impossible to dry any of our wet clothes, when it became necessary to wear them the following day in the same state. Many of these difficulties may be in some measure overcome, by persons accustomed to travel thro' the Country in this manner, so that I possessed the greatest advantage as Mr Simpson from frequent experience, knew how to appreciate every comfort that could be obtained, and kindly provided me with many things he had never before thought of – viz. Indian Rubber Shoes, Umbrellas, and a thin Oil Cloth as a covering from the rain.

With this foretaste of the plastic raincapes of today, we must leave Mrs Simpson. Unfortunately, she was in ill-health throughout her short stays in Canada. She was under almost constant medical care, such as could be provided initially at York Factory, but eventually return to England was clearly essential and she went back, with her husband, in the summer of 1833, never returning to the 'Indian country.' She died in Lachine in 1853 at the early age of forty and one has to wonder whether that gruelling first journey had not, perhaps, impaired her health permanently. Mrs McTavish did stay in Canada, her husband retiring with her to a farm on the Lake of Two Mountains.

There were other unusual incidents on the portages up the Mattawa, records of which have come down to us through the writings of other early travellers. One of the most pleasant of these is related by a traveller to the west who

had a great surprise at the Portage Talon. Picking my steps carefully as I passed over the rugged ground, laden with things personal and culinary, I suddenly stumbled upon a pleasing young lady, sitting alone under a bush, in a green riding habit, and white beaver bonnet. Transfixed with a sight so out of place in the land of the eagle and the cataract, I seriously thought I had a vision of –
    'One of those fairy shepherds and shepherdesses
    Who hereabouts live on simplicity and watercresses.'
But having paid my respects, with some confusion (very much amused she seemed), I learnt from her that she was the daughter of an esteemed Indian trader, Mr Ermatinger, on her way to the falls of St Mary with her father, and who was then, with his people, at the other end of the portage: and so it turned out. A fortnight afterwards I partook of the cordialities of her Indian home, and bear willing witness to the excellence of her tea and the pleasantness of the evening.

The man who enjoyed this experience was an endearing character, John Jeremiah Bigsby, M.D. Born in 1792, he started his career with the Army Medical Corps in South Africa but came to Canada in 1821 as medical officer with a large detachment of a German rifle regiment in the English service. A keen amateur geologist, he was able to make extensive observations when he was appointed in 1822 as secretary to the International Boundary Commission established under the terms of the Treaty of Ghent. This necessitated a journey up the full length of the Ottawa Waterway to join the other members of the commission.

Returning to England after six years, he wrote the story of his Canadian experiences. It was published in 1850 as a two-volume work with the unusual title *The Shoe and Canoe*. *The Shoe* is readily explained by the prodigious walks that he made – from Hawkesbury to Montreal, for example, covering twenty-five of the sixty miles on the first day. Here he tells of a journey up the Ottawa with a brigade of the North West Company:

The North-west Company provided *munitions de bouche* on the most liberal scale – port, madeira, shrub, brandy, rum, sausages, eggs, a huge pie of veal and pheasants, cold roast beef, salt beef, hams, tongues, loaves, tea, sugar, and, to crown all, some exquisite beaver tail. The men were provided well in a plainer way, and had their glass of rum in cold and rainy weather. I was disappointed and not a little surprised at the appearance of the *voyageurs*. On Sundays, as they stand round the door of the village churches, they are proud dressy fellows in their parti-coloured sashes and ostrich feathers; but here they were a motley set to the eye: but the truth was that all of them were picked men, with extra wages as serving in a light canoe.

Describing his journey up the Lake of Two Mountains, Bigsby says:

Of such use is singing, in enabling the men to work eighteen and nineteen hours a day (at a pinch), through forests and across great bays, that a good singer has additional pay. The songs are sung with might and main, at the top of the voice, timed to the paddle, which makes about fifty strokes a minute. While nearing habitations, crossing sheets of water, and during rain, the song is loud and long.

On the shore of Lac Deschenes, 'it being Sunday, Mr [Father] Tabeau had the tent set up; and he dressed an altar within it with crucifix and candles, little pictures, and clean linen cloth. With his singing-boy and bell he performed a religious service, all the *voyageurs* kneeling round the tent door with great seriousness. I was glad to see this.'

In his travel book Bigsby says little about geology, but from other sources we know that he was collecting specimens and fossils whenever possible. He found an unusual fossil on the flat Table Rock then so prominent a feature of the Chaudière. He took this specimen back to England where it was figured and described, although not named, by G.B. Sowerby in 1825. As the science of palaeontology developed, the importance of this Ottawa River fossil became apparent since it proved to be the first specimen of its kind known to science.

A few years before his death in 1881, Bigsby decided to donate a gold medal to the Geological Society of London (where he had done a lot of voluntary cataloguing work, endearing himself to the staff). This medal is still awarded biennially by the Society to an eminent geologist not over the age of 45, preferably one who has done work in North America. On one side of the medal is a profile of Dr Bigsby; on the other a reproduction of the famous fossil he found at the Chaudière, described, on the medal, as 'Found – 1822 – Canada.' It is a moving experience to handle one of the prestigious Bigsby medals and to see this evidence of its close link with canoe travel on the Ottawa Waterway.

One of the many interesting men to have left us some record of travels on the Ottawa was a Canadian still but little known, even though he was the first white man to see the Churchill Falls in Labrador, discovering them on a journey across Labrador from Fort Chimo, a rigorous journey which he was the first white man to make. His name was John McLean. He was born at the hamlet of Dervaig on the island of Mull in the Highlands of Scotland in September 1799. Coming to Canada as a young man, he joined the service of the Honourable Company and spent his first twelve years in the Ottawa Valley, for nine of them in charge of the post at Lac des Sables on the Lièvre River. In his later years, he wrote a splendid book on his early experiences in the course of which he says:

On the 25 April 1833, I embarked on board of a steamboat at Lachine, and reached Hull on the 27th. Here the regular conveyance by land carriages and steamboat ended, and the traveller in those days was obliged to wait his passage by the canoes of the shanty men, or hire a boat or canoe for himself. I had recourse to the latter expedient, and reached the post of the Chats, then in charge of my esteemed friend Mr McD — l, on the 30th. Captain Back arrived on the 1st of May, put ashore for a few supplies and my wards, and immediately re-embarked.

This must have been one of the first steamboat journeys for one of the Company's intrepid canoe men. The reference to Captain Back will ring a bell in some minds. This was Captain George Back of the Royal Navy, on his way to the Arctic. McLean had 'found, on arriving in Lachine, that I had been appointed to conduct some of Captain Back's party, who proved rather troublesome to him at Montreal, to the Chats, and there to await my passage to the north by the Brigade.' Steamboat travel was probably safer, even in those days, with these miscreants than confined journeying in a canoe. 'The brigade consisted of three Montreal canoes, laden with provisions for the trip, and some tobacco for the southern department; and manned by sixty Iroquois and Canadians, the latter engaged to winter, the former for the trip.' Then follows an account of the familiar daily routine of fast canoe travel which McLean was to follow until he reached the valley of the Mackenzie River.

Captain George Back was setting out on the first of his two expeditions to the Arctic. He had crossed the Atlantic in the *Hibernia* to New York, coming up to Montreal where he was, like so many travellers, given every assistance by George Simpson. Arriving at Lachine on 23 April 1833, he 'found them far too assiduous in their libations to Bacchus to be subject to any less potent influence'; so he left as soon as he could in two canoes with picked crews. They started in the Lachine Canal and

were followed by the dense crowd on the banks. A few minutes brought us to the St Lawrence and, as we turned the stems of our little vessels up that noble stream, one loud huzza bade us farewell! Both our *maitre-canot*, and the other which was of smaller dimensions, were rather lumbered than loaded ... the crew was an unavoidable mixture of old hands and '*mangeurs de lard*' or green-horns; and there was scarcely one who had failed to take advantage of the last opportunity of getting drunk. At the head of them was Paul, an old Iroquois guide, who was, however, otherwise invaluable, as, I really believe, he knew the situation, of every dangerous rock in the whole line of rapids between Montreal and Hudson's Bay.

Captain Back had read Sir Alexander Mackenzie's famous work, and other books already published at that time about canoe travel in Canada, and so he treated the details of his own journey quite lightly, but he did note:

By the kindness of Colonel Duvernet, the canoes were permitted to go through the government canal, which cuts off the dangerous rapid of the *long Sault* [at Grenville]. They were afterwards towed by the steam-boat which plies between that place and Bytown, a village beautifully situated on the heights between the Rideau and the Chaudière Falls; in which latter, only the evening before several raftsmen had been unfortunately engulfed. Lieutenant Kains, who commanded the steam-boat, could not be prevailed upon to accept any remuneration for the important service thus rendered to us.

After picking up his three troublesome men from John McLean at the Chats, following his first experience with a portage, he went on to Fort Coulonge. 'The houses above this were far apart and the population comparatively thin; but, on my return in 1835, I was agreeably surprised to see many comfortable dwellings erected in the interval, surrounded by smiling cornfields, and animated groups of both sexes, who looked from the windows or stood on the banks to see us pass.' This is clear indication of the rapid settlement that was then taking place in the upper Ottawa Valley. In this interval, Captain Back had reached the Arctic coast in his search for

Captain John Ross. The maps he then made, as far east as Montreal Island, were so accurate that they were in use until 1948.

John McLean was back again on the Ottawa in 1843 en route to Fort William, this time in charge of the brigade. He left Lachine on 29 April, 'but the crews were so intoxicated that we were compelled to lay to on an island near by, to allow them to recover from the effects of their carousels.' At Lachine, he had been 'joined by Captain Stalk of the 71st., and Lieutenant Lefroy of the Artillery; the former accompanied us on a jaunt of pleasure, the latter on a scientific expedition.'

The idea of a scientific expedition in 1843, as distinct from one for exploration, may seem strange to some readers but this was not the first such venture to have been initiated by the Royal Society of London. Lieutenant (later General) Lefroy had already been on a similar expedition to St Helena (where he had seen Napoleon's body exhumed), when he was ordered to Canada to continue his observations of terrestrial magnetism, a programme that had been suggested to the Royal Society by Baron Von Humboldt. In Canada he first visited the military observatory that was established in Toronto in 1840 but then returned to Montreal to prepare for his long journey to the Mackenzie Valley, which he penetrated as far north as Fort Good Hope, spending the winter at Fort Chipewyan on Lake Athabasca taking regular observations. In Montreal he 'called on Sir George Simpson; he is the toughest looking old fellow I ever saw, built upon the Egyptian model, height two diameters, or like one of those short square massy pillars one sees in an old country church. He gave me much definite information … He is a fellow whom nothing will kill.'

Lefroy reached Fort Garry on 28 June and there found Sir George Simpson who had passed them on 5 May, when they were near the Chats, on one of his own journeys to the west. Lefroy reported upon his journey in a series of letters home, one written from Lac des Chats on 6 May to his cousin Julia Lefroy who lived at Church Oakley in Hampshire, containing this vignette of his camp:

Imagine a table rock shewing its grey face between patches of moss and grass with young fir and juniper growing about out of the crevices; three large birch bark canoes, the prettiest vessels that float, lie bottom upwards with keel to the wind, the open side to the fires; and under them and before them are standing or lying some fifty voyageurs and Indians, talking French Patois, with more oath than you would like to hear, and the light plays on the white tents behind and their red shirts and caps in true Rembrandt effects.

This is enough to give a good impression of Lefroy's delightful personality. He became good friends with McLean. This must have helped McLean in his later life since he quit the Company in 1845 in a huff and lived in Guelph and Elora, Ontario. His long life ended on 8 September 1890 while he was living with his daughter in Victoria, where he is buried in the Ross Bay Cemetery. Lefroy died just six months before this at the end of a distinguished career which included the governorships of both Bermuda and Tasmania. He served also, late in life, as chairman of a committee of the Royal Geographical Society studying permafrost in Canada.

In 1833 Sir George Simpson took up permanent residence in Lachine, in the large stone house purchased by the Company which soon came to be known as Hudson's Bay House. In directing the far-flung affairs of the Company Simpson was ever ready to assist worthy travellers. As early as 1827 he had provided Lieutenant Colonel John By with a canoe and a picked crew of *voyageurs* for By's first trip along the route of the Rideau Canal which he had come out from England to build. Simpson seems to have been glad to render special assistance to members of the churches who wished to serve in the west. In 1843 he assisted Bishop Provencher of the St Boniface Mission on the Red River to make a visit to Montreal, in the course of which this pioneer priest called, in September 1843, at the mother house of the Sisters of Charity, better known as the Grey Nuns of Montreal, in order to appeal for volunteers to staff a school at St Boniface. Of the thirty-eight sisters in the house, eighteen offered their services; four were selected. Equipped with specially designed clothing (including long green veils – 'Thus disguised,' said Sister Lagrave, 'we belonged neither to this world nor the next'), and after being courteously received by Sir George at Lachine, they set out on 24 April 1844 in one of two canoes, the other occupied by Chief Trader McPherson and his family.

Sir George, accompanied by Bishop Provencher on his return to St Boniface, passed them on Lake Nipissing, and found the four sisters 'weatherbeaten but enduring with fortitude the hardships of their strange journey.' Sister Valade, who was to be Mother Superior of the new mission, helped with the cooking. Sister Lagrave, her first assistant, seems to have been always cheerful, singing with the *voyageurs* as they paddled. Captain Doré had solemnly warned his crews that they must be careful of their language in view of their special guests.

It was Sister Lagrave who, writing to the Mother Superior in Montreal, told her:

Yesterday we ran several quite dangerous rapids. The canoemen uttered cries of delight in clearing these rapids. I too enjoyed it, but our sisters were pale with fright ... You know that I am not as light as a feather [her nickname was 'La Bonne Grosse'] and when it comes to climbing rocks, pushing through thickets, crossing ravines on dry and rotten trees, I think twice about it – but there is no turning back. We have suffered no serious accident.

She spoke too soon since, just before reaching the post at Sault Ste Marie, she slipped and sprained her left ankle very badly. Despite the pain, she remained cheerful, even joking with her *voyageurs*. First aid from her fellow travellers availed but little. She was urged to stay at Fort William but the sisters all agreed that she should go on, even in the smaller canoes, and so she was carried (in a specially built frame) by her *voyageurs* over the worst portages but remained in the canoe, alone, for all the rapids through which the canoe could be steered down or hauled by ropes. They reached the Red River in mid-June, and on the last day of their journey refused to stop until they reached St Boniface at one o'clock in the morning.

Another clerical traveller to the Red River, also assisted by Sir George Simpson during this same season of 1844, was the Bishop of Montreal (and Quebec), the Right Reverend George Jehoshaphat Mountain:

On the morning of May 16th, I embarked in my canoe at *La Chine*, nine miles above Montreal, where the Company have an important *Depot*. Arrangements were all made for me in the most excellent manner, and with the most careful attention, by direction of Sir George Simpson, the Governor of the Company's Territory. A new birch-bark canoe was provided, of the largest class ... The crew were picked men, and most of them were, more or less experienced voyageurs. One had accompanied Captain Franklin to the Arctic regions in 1825 ... We were seventeen persons in canoe. Our baggage, bedding, and provisions, with the equipments of the canoe and the tent, were estimated, I think, at the weight of a ton and a half. We travelled for some days up the Ottawa, with Settlements or detached habitations within our reach; and, in fact, we were far up river before we bid adieu to the region where Steamers have penetrated; and inns have been established at intervals connected with their trips; but we fell at once, to avoid all delay and make sure of keeping our people together, into the habits and rules of the voyageur, and our only recourse to the houses was to procure milk, for which payment was always refused, for our tea.

Some older readers may recall the pleasure they had as boys in reading the adventure stories of R.M. Ballantyne. The very first book that I myself remember reading was *Martin Rattler* in a blue-bound Everyman edition. Born in Edinburgh, Scotland, on 24 April 1825 and christened Robert Michael Ballantyne, although always known by his initials, Ballantyne was apprenticed at the age of sixteen by his father to the Hudson's Bay Company 'if he was agreeable.' R.M.B. was agreeable and so arrived at York Factory on Hudson Bay in August of 1841 but left almost immediately for Norway House, where he stayed as a clerk until June 1845. He then went on to the Red River post but was unsettled there and so pestered the chief factor that he left for the east on 20 August 1845 with the hope of a position at one of the King's Posts on the Quebec coast. He travelled with another Mr McLean, a light-hearted Highlander, and the latter's wife in a canoe manned by a crew of eight. 'The young and pretty Mrs McLean helped with the cooking and kept the men's clothes in repair … One can admire the pluck and endurance of this early Victorian lady of twenty three, hampered with the long skirts and flounces of the period … She was expected … never for a moment to show that she felt the slightest fear of being hundreds of miles from any form of civilization.'

They were on the Lake of the Woods on 7 September and here they met Dr John Rae on his way to York Factory. 'After a few minutes conversation (on a flat rock) we parted and pursued our respective journeys.' Instead of changing into one of the larger *canots de maître* at Fort William, they crossed Lake Superior safely in their lighter craft, reaching Sault Ste Marie on 12 October. Here Mr and Mrs McLean left Ballantyne to proceed by way of the Great Lakes, but he continued up the French River, noticing fourteen rough wooden crosses on the shore of Lake Nipissing marking the graves of a canoe's entire complement lost in a gale. Then on Sunday 19 October

we commenced descending the magnificent river Ottawa [actually the Mattawa], and began to feel that we were at last approaching the civilized nations of the earth … The scenery on the Ottawa is beautiful, and as we descended the stream it was rendered more picturesque and interesting by the appearance occasionally, of that, to us, unusual sight, a farmhouse … On the fourth day [after camping in the woods despite the proffered hospitality of settlers] we came in sight of the village of Aylmer, which lay calmly on the sloping banks of the river, its church spire glittering in the sun, and its white houses reflected in the stream. It is difficult to express the feelings of delight with which I gazed upon this little village, after my long banishment from the civilized world … I wandered about the streets, gazing in joy and admiration upon everything … but especially upon the ladies, who appeared quite a strange race of beings to me – and all of them looked so beautiful in my eyes (long accustomed to Indian dames), that I fell in love with every one.

They reached Lachine on the afternoon of 25 October 'having been journeying in the wilderness for sixty-six days' and averaging thirty-five miles a day throughout.

Ballantyne was first ashore, to be greeted by Chief Factor Duncan Finlayson. The next morning he drove with the factor to meet Lady Simpson and Mrs Finlayson, her constant companion. He was extremely shy but Lady Simpson kindly wrote later to his mother that 'he is, without exception, the handsomest young man I have seen in Canada.' *Hudson's Bay or Everyday Life in the Wilds of North America*, from which most of the foregoing quotations have been taken, was the beginning of Ballantyne's long career as a writer. He died in Rome on 8 February 1894 and is buried there in the English cemetery, his grave marked by a white marble monument erected 'by Four Generations of Grateful Friends in Scotland and England.'

Other famous British writers of the eighteenth century travelled in Canada. Few readers of *Barchester Towers* might imagine that Anthony Trollope, who led a busy dual career in the British Post Office and as a writer, would have found time to have sailed the Ottawa. He paid a long visit to North America over the winter of 1861–62, starting and finishing in Boston but including a Canadian visit that permitted brief stays at Quebec City, Montreal (where he met Sir William Logan, by whom he was fascinated), Ottawa, Prescott ('one of the most wretched little places to be found in any country' – but that was in 1861), and Toronto (where the 'University is the glory' of the city). And he relates that from Montreal

we went up to the new town [Ottawa] by boat, taking the course of the river Ottawa. We passed St Anne's, but no one at St Anne's seemed to know anything of the brothers who were to rest there on their weary oars ... This boat conveyance from Montreal to Ottawa is not all that could be wished in convenience, for it is allied too closely with railway travelling ... But the river is seen, and a better idea of the country is obtained than can be had solely from railway cars ... As one ascends the river, which by its breadth forms itself into lakes, one is shown Indian villages clustering down upon the bank. Some years ago these Indians were rich, for the price of furs, in which they dealt, was high; but furs have become cheaper, and the beavers with which they used to trade are almost valueless. That a change in the fashion of hats should have assisted to polish these poor fellows off the face of creation must, one supposes, be unintelligible to them ... The children of the Indians are now fed upon baked bread, and on cooked meat, and are brought up in houses.

We are thus reminded of canoe days, even though Anthony Trollope was travelling in a steamboat, before proceeding from Ottawa to Prescott on one of Canada's first railways, for the time of transition had come. The tales that travellers had to tell of their journeys up and down the Ottawa waterway changed likewise. Some of these we shall have occasion to look at briefly in later chapters. Explorers, fur-traders, and missionaries followed by soldiers and merchants, a few travellers for pleasure, then the seekers after good timber, some ladies of high courage, pioneering bishops and priests – all travelled the waters of the Ottawa by canoe on their way to the Great Lakes, to the west, to the Arctic. No record was made of some of the greatest and most poignant journeys, but we know what rigours every traveller had to endure from the vivid accounts of which this chapter presents merely a sampling.

We will take leave of the great days of canoe travel on the Ottawa with another typical river scene, described for us by one of Canada's greatest early surveyors, Joseph Bouchette, the surveyor general of Lower Canada. In his famous book, *The British Dominions in North America*, published in 1832, he describes his journey up the Ottawa. On the way back he stopped at Kinnell Lodge, the residence of an extraordinary character among the early settlers, Chief McNab; it was located just to the west of the mouth of the Madawaska River.

The characteristic hospitality that distinguished our reception by the gallant chief, when in 1828 we were returning down the Ottawa, after having explored its rapids and lakes, as far as the Grand Calumet, we cannot pass over in silence. To voyageurs in the remote wilds of Canada, necessarily strangers for the time to the sweets of civilization, the unexpected comforts of a well-furnished board, and the cordiality of a Highland welcome, are blessings that fall upon the soul like dew upon the flowers. 'The sun was just resigning to the moon the empire of the skies' when we took leave of the noble chieftain to descend the formidable rapids of the Chats. As we glided from the foot of the bold bank, the gay plaid and cap of the noble Gael were seen waving on the proud eminence, and the shrill notes of the pipes filled the air with their wild cadences. They died away as we approached the head of the rapids. Our caps were flourished and the flags (for our canoe was gaily decorated with them) waved in adieu, and we entered the vortex of the swift and whirling streams.

# FIVE

# Lumbering on the Ottawa

Jacques Cartier, on his first voyage of discovery in 1534, landed at four places on Prince Edward Island 'to see the trees, which are marvellously beautiful and sweet smelling: and we found them to be cedar, yew, pine, white elm, ash, willow, and several others unknown to us.' And a little later, when in the Baie des Chaleurs, he noted and recorded the great spruce trees 'tall enough to mast a ship of three hundred tuns.' Other early visitors to North American shores similarly observed the grandeur and extent of the untouched forests. Champlain has repeated references in his journals, for example, to the trees that lined the shores of the water routes that he traversed. And when he returned to France in September 1611 he took with him a quantity of split oak for use in wainscoting and window frames, in all probability the first export of timber from Canada to Europe.

This was not, however, the first North American shipment, since there is some record of pine being taken from Maine to England as early as 1605. But not until towards the end of the eighteenth century were more than token shipments of wood carried eastwards across the Atlantic. Then started one of the major chapters in early international trade, trade that continues to this day even though in greatly modified form, trade that reached one of its peaks in the middle of the nineteenth century when the Ottawa River was the scene of some of the greatest rafting of square timbers down to the sea that this continent was ever to witness.

Developments in ship-building and other construction during the Industrial Revolution led to a great increase in the demand for timber, and especially for large squared timber and long solid spars for use as masts on the wooden ships then universal. Even when the change to iron and then to steel ships eventually eliminated ship-building as a market for Canadian timber, other uses for wood developed. The wide use of frames of heavy timbers, securely connected together in what was called 'mill construction,' examples of which can still be seen in old industrial buildings, once provided a corresponding market in the building field. As iron, then steel, and eventually reinforced concrete came into use in building and engineering construction, so did this market also disappear, but not before the start of a demand (still increasing) for lumber for the frame buildings that are so widespread today, especially for residential construction. And as the days of big timber started to fade, a small beginning was also made in the use of smaller logs for chipping as the first stage in the making of paper, a use of timber in which Canada today leads the world.

A political development caused the first great change in the nature of the Canadian timber trade, and a military manoeuvre created the tremendous demands for timber that Canada had to meet at the opening of the nineteenth century. Prior to the American Revolution, Great Britain had encouraged imports of timber from New England, and especially long spars for use as masts, even establishing a system of bounties for some types of colonial timber. This source of wood was naturally cut off abruptly after 1783, greatly to Canada's benefit. Britain's major source of timber, however, continued to be the Baltic countries, transportation from which cost only a third as much as transatlantic shipment.

A modest start in the purchase of timber at Quebec by British merchants was made in 1803, but the Berlin Decree of Napoleon, issued in November 1806, proved to be the real turning point. This eventually closed all ports of France and her satellites to British ships. It was not long before the ports of Denmark, Prussia, and Russia were also closed to them, and thus all normal Baltic timber supplies were cut off. The British Admiralty was especially alarmed, for this was still the time of wooden ships and war was in the air. A rapid and very great increase in exports of Canadian timber to England followed. By one of those coincidences that enliven the pages of history, the first raft of square timbers from the Ottawa was sold at Quebec in the very month in which the Berlin Decree was issued.

In the absence of roads and railways, moving timber by water was the only possibility. Large timbers could be trimmed from logs in the woods, skidded or hauled to the nearest watercourse, and then floated downstream. This was done in the great days of Ottawa Valley lumbering on most of the tributaries to the main river and even on many of the tributaries of the tributaries. The great logs were floated down until they reached the main river, where they were assembled and lashed together in rafts. As already indicated, such a raft of square timbers came floating down the St Lawrence River into the harbour of Quebec in August 1806. It was owned by, and in command of, the pioneer settler of the Ottawa district, Philemon Wright.

Wright was a native New Englander who left his home in Woburn, Massachusetts, in 1796 to see if he could find a suitable location for the resettlement of his large family. He came again in 1797 and on this trip was attracted by the land around the Chaudière on the Ottawa River. He repeated his visits in the two following years, becoming so convinced that this was where he wished to settle that he obtained a grant of a large area on the north bank of the river, the location of the city of Hull today.

He started his great trek from Woburn on 2 February 1800, with five families, seven sleighs, eight oxen, and fourteen horses. The little caval-cade reached Montreal on the tenth day of the month but did not stop, proceeding up the Ottawa along the poor trails that linked the small settle-ments around the Lake of Two Mountains. After three more days of travel, they reached the foot of the Long Sault, then the limit of settlement. Here they had to rearrange the teams so that they could proceed in single file, the men going ahead to make a road through the snow and, once the rapids were past and travel on the ice of the river was possible, to test its thickness to ensure the safety of the party.

On their first day on the river itself, they met an Indian with his squaw and child. After recovering from his astonishment, especially at the oxen, the Indian directed his wife to pull the small sleigh with her child to the river bank, where she was to make herself comfortable while he acted as the party's guide. He went ahead, testing every step of the way with his small axe. They camped each night on the adjacent river bank. Naturally they made slow progress; it took them six days to cover the 64 miles from the head of the Long Sault to the site of their new home. The Indian accom-panied them all the way, staying with them on the final night before leaving them to return to his squaw and child. He was given a great send-off, with such presents as were possible, and sped on his way with three huzzahs from the full company.

This was at the beginning of March 1800, with snow still on the ground. But the first tree was immediately felled with the special axes that the party had brought with them and the clearing in the forest that was to become Hull was started. Philemon Wright was visited very soon after his arrival by the chiefs of the two Indian tribes, Algonquin and Iroquois, which had villages on the Lake of Two Mountains. They laid claim to the land and wanted to know by what right Wright was cutting trees on it. There was much good-humoured argument, settlement being finally referred to the authorities at Quebec, who decided against the Indians. Their goodwill over the outcome is shown by the fact that they decided to make Wright a brother chief so that if any further discussion developed, settlement would be made among fellow chiefs. By the Chaudière, therefore, was held for the new white man one of the famous Indian ceremonies that have been continued down to this day.

The welfare of the struggling little settlement depended on the sale of timber. The first raft contained seven hundred logs, over nine thousand boards, and several thousand staves, all of which must have been hand sawn. It was formed by the lashing together of twenty cribs, the techniques of raft construction having been developed already on the St Lawrence River. It started on its long journey on 11 June but did not reach Quebec until 12 August. It was not until November, as previously noted, that the timber was sold, since Wright had reached Quebec with his shipment of staves past the contract date. He had managed to make the tortuous journey with a crew of only four men, including one of his sons, Tiberius. The very last timber raft went down the Ottawa just over a century later, in 1908; it was specially organized by J.R. Booth, one of the great lumbermen of the valley, to recognize the tercentenary of Quebec. It was assembled on the Coulonge River and contained 150,000 feet of square and waney timber, worth almost $100,000. Its captain was Noe Valiquette, who had a crew of eighty men. Thereafter such large timber as was taken out of the Ottawa Valley went by rail.

For just over one hundred years, therefore, the Ottawa River carried on its waters these most unusual, ungainly craft – for so they must be described since they contained living and sleeping accommodation for their crews, frequently carrying deck loads as well. An average Ottawa River raft might contain up to one hundred separate cribs and thus from 2,000 to 2,400 timbers, a total volume of 80,000 to 120,000 cubic feet of first-class white pine, usually with some red pine included. In mid-century such a raft might be worth $12,000; as timber grew scarcer, the value went up to $25,000 by the 1880s, and to over $100,000 by the turn of the century.

It would now be almost impossible to assemble such a raft on the Ottawa, so thoroughly was the valley logged in those early days. White pine is still obtained there, but of smaller size than the great logs that used to form the rafts, sticks sixty feet long and trimmed square to twenty-four inches on each side being then commonplace. It is impossible to estimate with any degree of accuracy the total volume of this splendid wood that was taken down the river. Such figures as 85 million pieces of pine taken out between 1826 and 1894 are merely an indication of the magnitude of the Ottawa timber trade. They serve as a good reminder of the remarkable effect that Napoleon's action in 1806 had upon the whole economy of the Ottawa Valley.

It was the river and its tributaries that made this trade possible. In the winters, selected trees would be cut down (with axes in the early years, later with saws), squared with broad-axes by skilled woodsmen, stamped with the owner's mark and skidded with horses to the bank of the nearest watercourse. There are records of squared timbers being floated down even so small a stream as the Brennan River at Killaloe Station between 1840 and 1875, the greatest days of big timber. To assist with the driving of the timbers in the spring, the trimming was always finished off by pointing the ends. Guided on their way by expert river-men, the logs would be floated down successively larger streams until they reached the Ottawa. There they would be assembled and sorted into groups of similar lengths, prior to building individual cribs.

Two timbers about 25 feet long were first picked out, flattened near their ends, and bored to take the oak pins used for connecting the transverse timbers to them. On this simple framework the whole crib would be built up, between one and two hundred cribs being coupled together by red pine cap-pieces longitudinally and with chains transversely to form the raft. The term 'dram' is also encountered in some of the older accounts of rafting. It sometimes means the crib, but is more accurately used to describe a few cribs fastened together, several drams then forming the completed raft. One crib, usually near the centre of the raft, would be fitted out as the cookery crib (the 'cambuse') with a central open fireplace and raised sand ovens in which bread could be baked. Small bunk-houses or cabins in which the raftsmen slept, rolled up in their blankets, completed the equipment of the normal raft. Details of raft construction are given by Dr Charlotte Whitton in *A Hundred Years A-Fellin'*, a fine book issued in 1942 to mark the centenary of one of the well-known valley firms, Gillies Brothers and Company Limited.

Rowlocks were always fitted to the outer cribs since the rafts were steered with the aid of large oars or sweeps when the river current was sufficient to move them. When the weather was appropriate, sails were used to aid progress in earlier days, but after the advent of steamboats on the river, tugs were invariably used for hauling on long stretches, as they continue to be today for the modern equivalent, the booms of pulpwood and saw-logs. In the absence of tugs, rafts could be 'kedged' – hauled slowly forward on cables secured to an anchor placed well ahead, by means of a windlass on the raft operated by teams of men. Down the rapids, the rafts would almost invariably be split up into individual cribs, each guided skilfully by a small team of four or five men under a leader called the pilot. Even when timber slides were in use, this was still a dangerous task requiring unusual skill. When cribs were taken right through rapids, such as the Long Sault, it was one of the most hazardous of all river operations. The rapids safely run, the cribs had to be reassembled, pinned, and lashed together again to form the complete raft, which would then set off on its slow journey to the head of the next rapids. Small wonder that it took sometimes two years to get a raft from the Upper Ottawa to Quebec, although the more usual journeys from that part of the river adjacent to Ottawa involved an absence of one or two months.

Life on the rafts was a world in miniature. Some of the cooks were legendary, some of the tales akin to folklore. It is on record, for example, that in 1854 a large crib was caught against a rock at the Chaudière, the eight men upon it being marooned until rescued, after a six-hour vigil, by means of a line thrown to them over the raging water of the falls. Even more remarkable was the experience of the lone river-man who in 1864 managed to reach this same flat rock after a nasty accident, and had to wait there for three days with his feet in water until rescued with the aid of Indians who used bows and arrows to get a line out to him. With hazards like this – and the Chaudière was but one of many places along the river where such accidents could easily happen – it is not surprising to find that some of the very earliest public works constructed in Canada consisted of improvements to the Ottawa River and its tributaries in order to facilitate the passage down the river of floating logs. Some of these works are still maintained on the main river, although most of those on tributaries have long since disappeared. Their construction and successful operation constitute yet another of the untold stories of the Ottawa.

Before the union of the provinces in 1841, no river works had been carried out with public funds, although a number of private owners, led by Philemon Wright, had taken the initiative themselve to create such improvements at the major rapids. The first slide on the river was that constructed in 1829 on the north side of the Chaudière by Wright; it was purchased by the government for $40,000 in October 1849. A second Chaudière slide was built in 1835 by G. Buchanan, who also constructed the first slide at Chats Falls in the same year, both these works being taken over by the government in 1845 and thereafter publicly maintained. Hugh Bolton built one at Portage du Fort in 1839 but it was carried away by the spring flood of 1840, being rebuilt in 1841 by John Poupore.

David Moore constructed a long slide at the Calumet Rapids in 1843 and was allowed to charge five cents for each crib that used it. His heirs were compensated when it was rendered useless by later government works, the arbitration being settled only in 1861. This incident is mentioned to indicate the difficult legal problems that surrounded the construction of any works on the river or its tributaries, mainly because what would benefit one group of users might cause harm or at least difficulties to others. The first legislation to deal with such problems goes back to the year 1828. Thereafter, legal problems about the use of the Ottawa persisted almost until the end of the century. Quite the most famous, although coming at a later date than we have been so far considering, was the passage by the Ontario legislature of the Rivers and Streams Act. This was disallowed three times by the government of Canada as infringing on federal jurisdiction; but Ontario persisted, carrying its appeal to the Privy Council, which decided in favour of the province. Thereafter, private dams were allowed on tributary streams and the way was paved for further increases in provincial powers.

By the 1870s there were in use on the main river alone, quite apart from many more works on the tributary streams: 2,000 feet of excavated canals, 3,834 lineal feet of timber slides, 29,855 feet (more than five miles) of booms, almost 2,000 feet of small bridges giving access to the river works, 52 piers in mid-river, three slide-keepers' houses, and three storehouses. Many more works were yet to be built, but I give this outline of the situation in the seventies since it was in 1870 that the Upper Ottawa Improvement Company came into being officially and took over all works for log control. The Department of Public Works continued to be responsible for major works up and down the river, however, its major improvement being a rock-filled crib dam of timber right across the river at Carillon, and, later, control dams at the foot of Lake Temiskaming and at the Chaudière Falls in Ottawa. Both the original and the second (1870) dam at Carillon included a timber slide. In more recent years, when almost all rapids on the Ottawa have been flooded out by major hydro-electric dams, passage for logs past the dams has had to be provided for by modern log chutes. Thus the civil engineering works on the Ottawa River necessary for assisting the passage of timber have an unbroken history of well over 150 years.

Timber slides are well described by their name. Built of heavy timbers, almost always on or near one of the river banks at the site of the more precipitous rapids, they consisted of inclined sluiceways with well-formed timber bottoms and sides high enough to guide the cribs as they floated swiftly down on the thin stream of water admitted to the slide by a control sluice. The floor of the slide was extended well out into the river to ensure that cribs and logs would be able to float clear as soon as they had descended the slide, thus obviating the danger of jams at the lower end. Remains of slides are still to be seen up and down the river, while the many photographs that were taken in the latter part of the nineteenth century of these characteristic features of eastern Canadian rivers, and especially of the Ottawa, have made them generally familiar to Canadians, even though the last use of the big slides was more than fifty years ago.

One of the best known of all the Ottawa slides was that on the Hull side of the Chaudière. Even more famous was the Bronson slide on Victoria Island. Its location close to the centre of the nation's capital naturally enabled many visitors to Canada to see it and to watch with fascination the large timbers, either in cribs or singly, rushing down to plunge into the river waters at the foot of the descent. Even more exciting was to watch the expert river-men who would often 'ride the crib' down the slide, being thus able to assist more speedily with the reassembly of the raft at the foot.

Only rarely were visitors allowed to experience the thrill of a ride down a log slide, but it became a feature of the visits of very eminent people to Ottawa following one of the most carefully planned events of this kind, in 1860, for Edward, Prince of Wales. He reached Ottawa on a memorable evening at the end of August. After the luncheon which followed the laying of the foundation stone of the new Parliament Buildings on the day following, the Prince was driven over the suspension bridge at the Chaudière, under a 'Lumbermen's Arch' built of 200,000 lineal feet of plank assembled into a magnificent arch merely by piling, with no fastenings. At the entrance to the timber slide, he was escorted with his aides onto a specially prepared timber crib which then descended the slide under the guidance of expert river-men, floating safely at the foot into the middle of the small bay, there to be greeted by a huge company of gaily dressed lumbermen in a hundred birch-bark canoes. Two thousand people, in six river steamers that had been assembled at Ottawa for the great day, watched the performance, and an estimated twenty thousand more spectators lined the banks to cheer.

Two days later, the Prince left Ottawa and sailed up Lac Deschenes, ascending the portage at Chats Falls, at the head of which there took place one of the most memorable ceremonies in the whole history of the Ottawa

Waterway. Stepping on to a vast raft of timber, the Prince was presented with a formal address by a Mr Mason on behalf of the men of the river. Inscribed on birch bark, it read thus:

We, the Raftsmen of the Upper Ottawa, constitute a body of 13,000, the bone and sinew of Canada. We take advantage of meeting Your Royal Highness upon a raft, respectfully to offer you our hearty welcome and to express our loyalty, our devotion, and our affection for the Queen. God Bless you. May Your Royal Highness long remain Prince of Wales.

In some ways this simple but gracious act symbolized the peak of rafting on the Ottawa, one that must surely have been long remembered by the royal visitor. The governor of the Hudson's Bay Company presented to the Prince a beautifully made birch-bark canoe, the later history of which is unknown. His Royal Highness's private reaction must have been akin to the possibly apocryphal reply of John Buchan when, as Lord Tweedsmuir and governor general of Canada, he was presented with a very large moose head, beautifully mounted. After expressing thanks he said that he thought it would look well in St Paul's Cathedral.

The Prince of Wales's example at the Chaudière was followed by some of the governors general and their ladies in succeeding years. The Earl of Dufferin and the Marquis of Lorne were two representatives of the Queen who enjoyed this experience, as did a few other important visitors. Detailed mention can, however, be made of only one other descent of the Chaudière slide, which occurred in 1901 during the visit to Canada of the Duke of York and his lovely wife, the 'Princess May,' (later King George V and Queen Mary), at the end of their world tour which took place just after the death of Queen Victoria. Leading lumbermen of the Ottawa Valley combined to arrange this event, which was witnessed by far larger crowds than its precursor of 1860. A special car, beautifully equipped, had been built by the Ottawa Electric Railway Company, and this was used to convey the royal visitors from Rideau Hall through the streets of Ottawa and over the bridge to Hull and the head of the slide.

Five cribs had been prepared for the use of the royal party and their entourage, which included prominent Canadians. In the manner of such events, the first crib to descend the slide was filled with newsmen covering the royal tour. The Duke and Princess were on the second, members of their party on the third, and Sir Wilfrid and Lady Laurier on the fourth. Fortunately all went well and safely. Canoe races on the river followed, and then came a picnic in the Rockcliffe woods. Lumbermen had built here a

A typical river scene in the 1860s, painted by Frances Anne Hopkins. It is believed the lady in the canoe (one of the north type) is the artist herself, as she is known to have accompanied her husband, a Chief Factor with the Hudson's Bay Company, on several journeys.

Indians bringing a load of furs from Lake Kipawa into the Ottawa in 1902. The canoe, on its way to a Hudson's Bay Company post, also carries rolls of birchbark.

The south end of the Union Suspension Bridge at Ottawa, photographed by
W. Notman about 1870, lumber piles and barges, with the rocks of Chaudière,
showing clearly at the bridge.

Lumbermen 'riding the crib' down a timber slide on the Chaudière. Note the original centre block of the Parliament Buildings, burned in 1916, with the Library, which still stands, and the original West Block.

A sketch from the *Illustrated London News*, 1860, showing the lumbermen's regatta that greeted Edward, Prince of Wales, on his visit to Ottawa. The entrance locks of the Rideau Canal can be seen in the centre background.

The Duke and Duchess of York on the crib on which they descended a timber slide at the Chaudière in 1901. The floating booms indicate that the party is approaching the head of the slide.

A flotilla of river boats – pointers in the foreground – greeting the Duke and Duchess of York after the royal couple had descended the timber slide in 1901.

One of the last of the great timber rafts on the Ottawa, 1899, passing the old Parliament Buildings.

typical shanty for the royal visitors to see. They put on a demonstration of tree-felling, followed by dancing and a luncheon of pork and beans. The idea of the future Queen Mary descending the Chaudière timber slide and finishing her outing with pork and beans fills one with delight; but all who have read her biography will experience no surprise even if this is their first introduction to this adventure of Princess May, since it was so entirely in keeping with her venturesome and lively character.

Philemon Wright's lumbering activity was soon surpassed by others who followed him up the valley. Hamilton Brothers had bought a small sawmill at the head of the Long Sault in 1810 and they built this into one of the major timber enterprises on the lower part of the river. Similar activity gradually developed up the river but it was not until mid-century that lumbering on the Ottawa really became big business. Bearers of some of the great names in the industry were already in the valley. James Gillies had come from Scotland in the early 1820s; John Egan began his operations at Quyon shortly after; Allan Gilmour became active in timber purchases, as the start of the famous firm of Gilmour and Hughson, in the early thirties. It was not until 1848 that Thomas McKay built his first mill at Rideau Falls. Ezra Butler Eddy came up to the valley from Vermont only in 1851 and was soon making matches in his home. A carpenter named John R. Booth, coming from Waterloo, Quebec, started his spectacular career at about the same time. These were great names, as were many others, too numerous to mention here, but all were aided in their success by the transport of their products on the Ottawa Waterway.

From the start there was some degree of co-operation despite the intensity of competition. As early as 1832, the Crown Timber Office granted what came to be known as the Gatineau Privilege, restricting rights for logging on the Gatineau to Philemon Wright's three sons and four other timber men, including George Hamilton from Hawkesbury. Renegotiated in 1835, the Privilege lasted until 1843. An Ottawa Lumber Association was formed in 1836 by most of the small firms for mutual benefit, although the Wrights were not among the members. Quite the most important of these co-operative ventures was the Upper Ottawa Improvement Company, known throughout the valley as 'I.C.O.' It is in some ways a unique organization, not the least of its claims to distinction being that it is now well past its centenary.

It was in 1868 that the concept developed of all the companies bringing logs down the Ottawa River getting together and doing this co-operatively, thus avoiding all the problems and difficulties that separate and competitive log drives were creating. Following the initial meetings of various company representatives, the I.C.O. was formed and received its charter under the authority of an Act of the Dominion Parliament, since an interprovincial river was involved. This granted the company power to take over from the Department of Public Works all existing river works for log control, and to make the necessary arrangements for their future maintenance and for moving timber from the foot of the Des Joachims Rapids as far as Pine Tree Island at the foot of the Chaudière Rapids. The company also took over, on lease, the famed Bronson timber slide down the Chaudière. Amendments to the original Act were approved in 1875 and 1888 respectively, which had the effect of giving the company control of all log movements from the head of Lake Temiskaming at the foot of the rapids on the Quinze River as far as the foot of the Chaudière. Individual companies continued to do their own cutting and hauling to the main river, either on land or down tributaries of the Ottawa, but once the logs reached the Ottawa the Improvement Company took over their movement to the respective mills. The sound sense of this arrangement is obvious and it has worked well for over one hundred years.

Until relatively recent years, the I.C.O. had its head office, most appropriately, on Victoria Island, amid the waters of the Ottawa River at the Chaudière. I once stood in a replica of the original board room just after examining the first minute book of the board of directors, an experience that made singularly real the earlier days on the great river. But the ancient building in which the office was housed, on Middle Street, has now been destroyed, so slight is Ottawa's concern for its own history. The company continues its widespread operations, still co-operatively, from a more modern office in the complex of Eddy Company buildings but still at the Chaudière. In its earliest years, the I.C.O. had its towing done by existing river navigation companies, notably the Union Forwarding Company, but the Improvement Company took over this steamship enterprise around the turn of the century and thereafter did all its own towing, as it continues to do today.

In the early years of the century I.C.O. had a fleet of varied steamboats, one of which still sails Lac Deschenes. With the development of the modern diesel engine, it was inevitable that the more interesting steamboats should gradually disappear, to be replaced by relatively impersonal large diesel tugs, of which the company now operates a fleet of twelve, together with a much larger number of smaller service vessels. These boats operate from twelve stations along the river, known as 'booms' since all are related to the major holding booms operated on the river. Through the changing pattern of lumbering on the Ottawa, the I.C.O. has continued its good service; but we must look at the changes that have taken place before considering what the company does today.

On the rafts, in addition to cambuses and sleeping huts, were often large barrels, carrying down the river yet another product of the forest in the form of potash or lye, a typical barrel holding 600 to 700 pounds of this earliest of manufactured chemicals. To the early settlers, trees were a nuisance to be cut down as they made a start at clearing land. This was no selective cutting, as for timber or sawn lumber; everything had to be felled if possible. It was soon found that by burning large quantities of wood and leaching the ashes potash was obtained which could be sold for cash, usually the only cash that many early settlers were to see for years. Sixty full-grown maple trees were destroyed in order to fill one of the large barrels. Some idea of the forest cover that was thus removed is given by the export from Montreal in 1821 of 35,765 barrels of potash, not all from the Ottawa Valley although it was for long a major source. After the leaching of the ashes in wooden troughs, the resulting liquid had to be boiled down, the salt crystals being ladled out into coolers when the proper degree of concentration had been reached. One may still see, occasionally, one of the cast-iron potash kettles which constituted a major product of the pioneer iron foundry of Les Forges Saint-Maurice near Trois Rivières. (Any kettle that bears the initials *F St M* cast in it is an antique of real value.) But after all this work, the settler might expect to receive $8 for a complete barrelful, or possibly as much as $10 depending on transportation costs, even though the barrel might be sold in Montreal for $30.

A glimpse of what the valley was like in the days of the timber trade is given in one of the few books on the valley published in the last century, a fascinating volume by James Gourley, in which the author relates that

these lands were so thickly covered with forest, trees standing near each other and of so large a growth as almost wholly to exclude the sunshine from the soil in the leafy season 'when summer was green' ... Hardwood trees of fifty and sixty feet high were plentiful, some white pines there were whose height was found to be a hundred feet from tops to the ground. We helped square one 73 feet long 24 by 25 inches four straight lines over three hundred cubic feet and we have seen larger than this one ... The density of these forests, the interlacing of the bows and their thick green foliage or frondage account for the abundance of water then flowing in rills and for the disappearance of these waters when the country was denuded of this thick, close covering. Then little river beds have disappeared before the plow and the present generation could hardly point out their place. Yet some of them with water not over three inches deep and twelve inches wide ran the whole summer.

Transport of large logs down the river was the start of the lumber business on the Ottawa but it was a natural development that, as the market began to increase, sawmills should be established so that lumber in smaller sizes could be made available for sale. The first sawmill in the Bytown area was built in 1831 by Jean-Baptiste Saint Louis (one of the contractors on the building of the Rideau Canal), although the Hamiltons were well established at Hawkesbury by that time. Thereafter sawn lumber steadily increased in importance even though the great rafts of timber continued to make their stately progress down the river throughout the century.

The first sawmills naturally were water-driven. With the hydraulic machinery then available, capacity was severely limited, but good small businesses were built up by those fortunate enough to be able to use some of the easily controlled waterfalls on the main river or its tributaries. As in so many other branches of industry, it was the advent of steam power that revolutionized the sawing of lumber.

The first steam mill in the Bytown district was that of J.C. Blasdell. This was located on the south bank of the Ottawa near the outlet from MacKay Lake, in what is now Rockliffe. Fuel was immediately available in the form of waste wood from the sawing operations, known generally as slabs. The new mill could produce over one million board feet in a working season. Remarkable as this was at the time, in contrast with the production of the older water-operated mills, it was but the beginning of steady development that was to see a total production from mills in the Ottawa area alone of 343 million board feet in 1896, of which J.R. Booth produced 115 million. This was probably the peak year; but the business was on a vast scale.

Storage of the products of the mills, while drying and prior to shipment, was in itself an immense problem as may be judged from many of the photographs of Ottawa taken just before the turn of the century, showing the storage grounds, piled high with lumber, all round the Chaudière. Some sawn lumber was carried initially downriver on the decks of the larger rafts but this was slow and inconvenient. Barges were developed and barge building started on the Hull side of the river, an industry that assumed some importance, especially when the building of steam tugs was also undertaken. It has been estimated that there were as many as 250 barges and 50 tugs in use at the peak of the sawn-lumber industry towards the end of the century; many of these were built in the Hull shipyard. There were 'Blue Barges' and 'White Barges.' The former were as large as they could be and still navigate through the locks of the Ottawa River canals and the Rideau Canal; each one carried about 300,000 board feet of lumber. The white barges, with strange-looking square ends painted white, carried only up to about 175,000 board feet, their smaller size being necessitated by the dimensions of the locks then in use on the Erie Canal system in New York. These locks were only 18 feet wide and 110 feet long, with an available depth of 7 feet.

Mention of the Erie Canal shows how far the lumber of the Ottawa was transported on the barges and explains also why it was that almost all the barges had quarters for the accommodation of the bargee (to use the old English term) and possibly also his family. Some went down the Ottawa River, through the Ottawa River canals at Grenville and the lock at Ste Anne's to the Lachine Canal, where loads destined for Montreal were unloaded. Many barges, however, continued down the St Lawrence River past Montreal to Sorel, there turning into the Richelieu River, through the lock at St Ours and the Chambly Canal and finally into Lake Champlain, to unload usually at Burlington, Vermont. This pleasantly situated town developed into an important lumber centre, its good rail connections facilitating economical transport to the New England states. Other barges, loaded at Ottawa or at the small wharf at Ironsides which served the mills on the Gatineau River, would take a different route, through the Rideau Canal to Kingston. From Kingston, some would proceed to Clayton, New York, where rail connections were again available; but others would cross the end of Lake Ontario as far as Oswego, there to enter the spur canal which led to the main Erie Canal, a spur still in use as part of the modern New York Barge Canal. Ottawa barges thus had access to the Mohawk Valley and, at Albany, to the Hudson River and New York.

It was not uncommon in the great days to see as many as fifty barges either loading or waiting to be loaded from the vast lumber yards around the Chaudière and at the mouth of the Gatineau. As with the lumber business, so also did the shipping business have its noted figures. One of the early leaders was Moss Kent Dickinson, the 'King of the Rideau,' who at the peak of his activity owned as many as sixteen steam tugs and eighty-four barges. At a later date, Dennis Murphy was a large-scale operator on the river, even buying out the small private fleet that J.R. Booth had developed for his own use. Under Murphy's direction, almost all the organizations concerned with lumber shipments from Ottawa were amalgamated in 1892, forming the Ottawa Transportation Company. Initially the company had eight steam tugs and sixty-seven barges, the numbers indicating that the peak had been passed for river transport. There were still to be several decades, however, before the shipping of lumber down the river and the Rideau Canal would cease. Twenty new barges were constructed even in the first decade of this century. The timber trade down the Ottawa remained steady throughout the early 1900s, but the number of tugs and barges slowly declined, five tugs and less than forty barges remaining at the outbreak of the First World War. It will have been noted that all this transport of lumber by water was from Ottawa to points downstream or down the Rideau Canal. The great barrier of the Chaudière was the compelling reason for this; no navigation locks have been built to surmount it, although often proposed. Gradually, as settlement extended up the river, it was the Upper Ottawa Valley, above the Chaudière, that produced most of the lumber shipped to the markets of the world. Some of this came down-river as logs in the annual drives, to be sawn in the Ottawa mills. But there were large mills up the river too, and it was to serve them that some of the most interesting railway construction of the region took place. The availability of rail transport from the late seventies was yet another factor that led to the decline and eventual disappearance of transport of sawn lumber down the Ottawa Waterway.

What the lumbering industry used to be is shown by a singularly interesting outdoor Logging Museum, developed by the Ontario Department of Lands and Forests, located close to the eastern entrance of Algonquin Park. In one of the attractively arranged showcases are details of the great activity of the Canada Atlantic Railway at its peak. Also to be seen in the museum are a typical logging locomotive; a small log cabin that once served J.R. Booth as an office; examples of equipment and tools that were used, including a complete 'alligator' (to be described shortly); and a large squared log from a tree estimated to have been 170 years old when cut down. To stand by this great log of beautifully clear timber is one of the best of all reminders of the magnificent wood that the Ottawa Valley provided. Small wonder that the timber trade attracted men from near and far. Even the Hudson's Bay Company once made a short foray into the timber business, on Lake Temiskaming, in 1840–41; but the fur business was their preserve and to it they confined all their later attention. At the London Exhibition of 1862 there was exhibited a 'deal' (the largest type of plank sawn from a complete log), fifty inches wide and six inches thick; and this was probably by no means the largest that was produced.

There were, however, problems for the lumber business – problems that seriously affected the Ottawa River. The first of these was the disposal of waste material from the sawmills, generally sawdust and the slabs already mentioned as the residue from squaring round logs. Some, but by no means all, of the slabs were used as fuel for the boilers of the steam-power plants serving the sawmills. Much of the waste material, however, after being broken into fragments in a 'hogging machine,' got into the river, where it remained in view for a long time. Inevitably there were complaints from almost all residents along the river, and from the citizenry generally as settlement in the valley progressed.

One of many inquiries into the problem was made in the summer of 1888 by Sandford (later Sir Sandford) Fleming, one of Canada's greatest early civil engineers, on behalf of a committee of Ottawa lumber manufacturers. Their concern shows that even in those early days industry was not unmindful of its responsibilities for pollution control.

Assuming 10 per cent wastage, Fleming calculated the annual volume of waste material from 300 million board feet of lumber would amount to 92,592 cubic yards. After taking borings and making soundings, he recommended the dredging of about 10,000 cubic yards of sawdust from below the entrance to the Rideau Canal. With this and careful control of waste disposal, he foresaw no danger that navigation would be interfered with 'for centuries to come.' (Even today, despite the years that have passed since sawmilling stopped, test borings regularly encounter sawdust, and it remains a problem when engineering works such as bridge piers have to be constructed in the river bed.) Fleming found that mill waste was not unwelcome to everyone:

... there are a large number of families settled along the river banks between Ottawa and Grenville who appear to have selected the site of their habitations on account of the supply of fuel which is annually floated to their doors. During the summer months numbers of women and children may be seen regularly at work on boats and canoes gathering in from the stream their winter's supply of fuel. There is in reality a considerable population dependent upon the mills for their winter firewood which thus costs them only the trouble of gathering it.

One cannot escape the feeling that here Sandford Fleming was making the best of a bad job, but his careful observations leave no doubt that this supply of free firewood was a factor in settlement.

This mill waste was closely related to the other great problem – that of fire. Down through the years, as one studies the records of the time, one reads again and again of the destruction of mills by fire. Mill waste cannot be always blamed with certainty but it was undoubtedly a contributory factor to many of the fires which led to such repeated economic losses. The Gilmour Company was especially unlucky, having a major mill burned to the ground in 1874 and another in 1893, in each case just as an economic depression was starting. The Edwards mill at Rideau Falls burned in 1907, and was replaced by a group of singularly unattractive buildings that remained there until the clearing up of Green Island and surroundings in the fifties, followed by the building of the new Ottawa City Hall.

The fires were not restricted to the mills even though the mills and their lumber yards presented a special hazard when any fire did occur. Hull was burned down in part in 1875, in 1880, and again in 1888; but it was the fire that started in the north of Hull on 26 April 1900 that is still talked about as the 'great Ottawa fire,' even though it started on the other side of the river. So fiercely did the flames rage through the crowded wooden buildings that soon the mills and stockpiles at the Chaudière were alight. The fire jumped the river and soon destroyed a good part of Ottawa, devastation extending as far as Dow's Lake. All of the Eddy establishment was destroyed, although some of the older stone buildings were eventually rebuilt. J.R. Booth alone lost 55 million board feet of lumber stored in his yards. This was the last of the great fires since improvements in water supply, in fire-fighting, and, above all, in fire-prevention measures combined to limit such fires as did still occur.

Little would be gained by any broad review of the damage done by forest fires in the Ottawa Valley; but, as a reminder of the devastation they can bring, here is an eyewitness account of one that was long remembered. It is taken from a collection of letters by an English visitor to Canada, George T. Borrett. Writing to his father from Ottawa on 22 August 1864, he said:

I am now in the future capital of the two provinces of Upper and Lower Canada. My journey here was made by rail to Lachine, a few miles west of Montreal, and thence by steamer up the Ottawa river. We had anticipated a fine day's excursion, but unfortunately the bush had taken fire, and the country for miles and miles around was enveloped in clouds of smoke. At times the fog was so thick that we had to stop and drop our anchor; at others we were delayed by frequent soundings; once we made a complete circuit, and only discovered that we were returning to Montreal when the sun broke through the fog upon the wrong side of us ... It is difficult to give you any idea of what one of these fires is like. It is by no means easy to convey an impression of what is signified by 'the bush.' You must picture to yourself a tangled forest of closely-packed moderate-sized trees, with a dense undergrowth of shrubs; pines will be the most prevalent trees, but beech, maple, oak, sumac, walnut, and poplar, may all be included under the general term 'pine forest.' Imagine this mass of leaf to extend over a flat swampy area of hundreds of square miles, broken only here and there by the log hut of some lonely settler, or the freshly cleared corn-field of a newly arrived farmer. You must then suppose the underwood to have taken fire from some seemingly insignificant accident – a spark from a settler's pipe, perhaps, or a lighted ember from his log fire; and the heat of the sun's rays has so scorched the trees that they burn like torchwood down to the very roots, and so the fire is communicated to the parched turf or soil of the swamp, which smoulders away like peat for days and weeks and months, till rain falls and extinguishes the fire, after it has eaten its way into the earth perhaps three feet deep.

Vital as was the control of pollution and of fire, essential as was the development of technology, the basic factor in the success of the lumbering industry was the skill of the Ottawa river-men. As a young man I watched them and learned much from them. To see them building a structurally excellent crib from a design in their own heads, launch it smoothly into swift water, and site it with precision, to see them handling the pointers that were their special craft, was to see artists at work.

To show how widely these river-men were known and how highly their service was valued, we may turn back to a page in history known to too few Canadians. On 26 May 1884, General Charles Gordon was isolated at Khartoum after the Mahdi, self-proclaimed divine guide of Islam, had captured Berber on the Nile. The British House of Commons voted £300,000 for a relief expedition under the command of Lord Wolseley, then Adjutant General. This was General (later Field Marshal) Wolseley, who had commanded the Red River expedition of 1870. He remembered his fine experience with Canadian river-men and *voyageurs* during that difficult journey. Having won support for a rescue attempt by way of the Nile, he turned to Canada for the experts to man the small craft needed to navigate the rapids of the river's upper stretches.

On 21 August, the governor general received a request for the services of '300 good *voyageurs.*' Since the British government was to pay all expenses, the prime minister of Canada did not object to such a force being raised, even though it was to represent the first participation (although on a very limited scale) by Canadians in an overseas war. Lord Lansdowne was the governor general. His military secretary was Lord Melgund, later to be the fourth Earl of Minto and himself a governor general of Canada. Lord Melgund took complete charge of recruiting the *voyageurs* that had been requested. In little more than three weeks, he had assembled almost four hundred suitable men from half a dozen scattered points, brought them to Quebec, had them medically examined, documented, and issued with personal equipment and uniform clothing, with officers selected and the vessel which was to transport them to Egypt duly inspected, all with the aid of just two office assistants and a small advisory committee.

Three hundred and sixty-seven men were recruited, of whom 159 came from the Ottawa and 92 from Manitoba (some of whom were not entirely suitable, through unwise selection); 56 were Indians, and the remainder came from Trois Rivières, Sherbrooke, and Peterborough. They were commanded by Major (later Colonel) F.C. Denison of Toronto. The Ottawa men assembled in the city before leaving. The governor general with his lady went down to Quebec to see the expedition off on its journey, making an appropriate and felicitous speech. The men crossed the Atlantic on the *Ocean King*, with a coaling stop at Sydney where one man deserted (replaced by a MacDonald, who then represented the Maritimes to make the company truly Canadian), and the thirst of many of the river-men was suitably, if only partially, assuaged, as occurred also when a stop was made at Gibraltar.

In Egypt, the British-built whalers were towed by river steamers upriver to the first cataract. The Canadian river-men soon got to work at their accustomed tasks and, using Kroomen (as local inhabitants were called) as their crews, they worked the boats up the second, third, and fourth cataracts. (Later, they brought them back by shooting the rapids in true Canadian style.) The river-men were instrumental in getting the relief expedition and its supplies up and over the cataracts, although just too late to rescue General Gordon, through no fault of theirs. The men had been engaged for a six-month period, but when this expired there was still work to be done and they were offered extensions. Six foremen and 83 river-men accepted, generally English-speaking Canadians; most of the Indians and French-speaking Canadians preferred to return to their homes. This was a group of men who worked together in perfect harmony. Only sixteen of them were lost, and those not during the actual operations of the River Column, as the expedition was called. In a formal report to the governor general, Lord Wolseley said that 'the services of these voyageurs have been of the greatest possible value, and further, ... their conduct throughout has been excellent. They had earned for themselves a high reputation among the troops up the Nile.'

Wherever Ottawa river-men work, they like to have, if at all possible, Ottawa River pointers. These now traditional craft were first developed in 1850 by John Cockburn, a boat-builder who was persuaded by J.R. Booth to develop a strong, stable boat suitable for river driving. Their wide, shallow shape will be familiar to all who know the river, since they are still in use all along the Ottawa – and not only there. More than fifty were used on the St Lawrence during the construction of the St Lawrence Power and Seaway project. They are to be found all over Canada wherever there is river work to be done in shallow and swift waters. And they are still being built by John Cockburn and Son, the principal of this century-old firm being the grandson of the founder. The firm's pointer-building plant is now in Pembroke, having been moved there by the founder ten years after developing his fine original design in Dey's Arena, Ottawa.

So successful has this design proved to be that the only significant change down the years has been the production of square-ended pointers to which an outboard motor can be attached. Fifty per cent of today's pointers, however, are still the standard double-ended, pointed, shallow craft with wide flat bottoms and flared sides, this unusual design resulting in an unloaded draft of only $1^{1}/_{2}$ inches for a fifty-foot pointer which will weigh about half a ton. Controlled and propelled by oars, they can be swung around with a strong stroke of one oar; in the hands of skilled river-men, they are most graceful craft and ideally suited to their unusual tasks. They are built of white pine planking, with cedar for the ribs and red pine or white spruce for the oars. Their distinctive brick-red colour has never changed down the years.

The pointers were not, however, the only river craft specially developed for lumbering. Even more unusual were the queer-looking 'Alligators,' now out of use on the Ottawa. Conceived and designed by another Canadian, John Ceburn West, they were made in Simcoe, Ontario, the firm of West and Peachey having both Canadian and u.s. patent rights. They shipped Alligators, therefore, to many points in North America but one of the chief areas of service was the Ottawa Valley. Essentially, the Alligators were amphibious vessels, fitted with a powerful winch in the bow. This immediately took the place of the old horse-capstans, mounted on small rafts; but the mode of operation was the same, a steel cable being attached to a forward anchor and hauled in – as the tow was slowly inched forward – until the anchor was reached. It was then reset as far forward as possible, and the hauling begun again. The unusual feature of the Alligators, however, was the provision of flat bottoms of sturdy construction such that, under the hauling power of the winch, the vessels could pull themselves out of the water, as at a portage between lakes, and proceed overland on timber skids placed on the ground, possibly greased to reduce friction. It was said that they could even haul themselves up a one-in-three gradient.

The maker's advertisement stated that they were 'the lumberman of the day, a multum in parvo, economizing time and labour and entirely doing away with the almost endless annoyances to which lumbermen of late years have been subject.' The men who had to operate these weird-looking craft might have expressed their virtues rather differently, since the large winch and centrally located steam boiler and engine, together with the arrangement of the clutch so as to have the same engine drive both paddle wheels (or screw) and the winch, made accommodation always crowded. The Alligator at the Algonquin Park Logging Museum, the *William M*, was used until 1943 by Gillies Brothers in Cedar Lake. The illustration on page 153 shows a typical Alligator afloat in a boom at Arnprior in 1908. The original patents expired in 1932, and since that time vessels of the same type, although now known as 'Winch Boats,' have been produced at Owen Sound by Russel Brothers Ltd, naturally with diesel power instead of the wood-fired steam engines, and steel hulls in place of the old wooden ones. Simple and rather crude as they were, the old Alligators made a significant contribution to the great days of lumber movement down the Ottawa Waterway.

To cut and trim the trees woodsmen need the best of steel axes, even though the modern portable power saws now perform much of the more laborious work. Here, too, the Ottawa Valley had its special service, and still does as these words are written, the Walters Axe Company being yet another firm serving the lumber industry that has passed its centenary; it is still located in Hull as it has been throughout its history. Founded in 1868 by Henry Walters, a cutlery maker from Sheffield, England, the company was operated for more than fifty years by his son, Morley P. Walters, until his death in 1969. Walters was the oldest living graduate of McGill when he died in 1969, and was indeed one of the grand old men of the Ottawa Valley. Always distinctive with his tweeds and deerstalker hat, he went regularly to his works until almost his hundredth year.

The skilled use of axes can be witnessed at the log-cutting competitions that are still a feature of fairs up and down the valley. So also is the art of log-rolling – the term being used in its literal sense – an art that displays the unique sense of balance of the experienced river-men. To watch river-men of today working on the booms, especially if they have to walk the logs to release a jam, is a memorable experience.

To assist them with this dangerous work, river-men have from the earliest times used special boots. With heavy caulked soles, lumbermen's boots are specially distinguished by the pattern of half-inch steel spikes set into the soles, giving the wearers a firm grip on the wood. The making of such boots is yet another of the arts associated with the lumber business. It is still being exercised by the skilled workmen of a century-old firm in the valley, Farmer Brothers Limited of Arnprior. Founded in 1869 by William Farmer, who came from Wales to Perth in 1855, and first operated by William and his two brothers, the company still maintains its works in Arnprior, now under second-generation management. Samuel Farmer, father of the three founders, also engaged in boot manufacture up the Madawaska at Combermere. This venture faded with the decline in lumbering activity but the Arnprior business continued, its peak probably in the first decade of this century.

Surely there is something significant and appealing in the fact that in the Ottawa Valley there are today four companies, each well over one hundred years old, still serving in a special and intimate way the movement of lumber down the waters of the great river. Despite the disappearance of logs from so many other of the rivers of eastern Canada, they still move down the Ottawa. Apart only from the building and navigating of the great rafts of squared lumber and the operation of the famed Alligator boats, all the traditional operations of lumbering are still to be seen in the Ottawa Valley and on its river, continuing much as they have been carried on for more than a century and a half, although now with the help of modern tools and other technical aids, especially in communication.

Cutting and trimming of trees is still carried out every year, although now by well-organized operations working out of camps that would have been regarded as palaces by woodsmen of a century ago. The logs, both pulpwood and saw-logs, are hauled out of the bush over the snow and ice of specially constructed winter roads to designated unloading depots. These may be at the mills, truck hauls having been steadily increasing in distance, or they may be at railway yards where logs can be conveniently loaded on flat cars. On the larger tributaries, however, and in many places on the main river itself, the logs are carefully piled on the winter ice of the rivers or lakes.

Modern technology is now assisting in even such an apparently simple operation as piling logs on ice, for the piling grounds are specially prepared, when once the ice begins to form, by regular flooding to increase the thickness of the ice cover, and by embedding logs in the ice to serve as reinforcement, similar to steel rods in reinforced concrete. Ice sheets thus strengthened can bear heavy loads, large areas being regularly covered with piles of pulpwood up to about six feet high. With the coming of spring, the ice will melt and at failure will dump the accumulated log piles into the rising waters of lakes or streams.

Then starts the spring drive, an operation still to be seen on the Ottawa itself, on the Coulonge and the Gatineau in the main valley, and on some of the tributaries feeding into Lake Temiskaming. In the woods, each log will have been cut exactly to length, four or eight feet long for use as pulpwood (the longer length for modern mills) or twelve to sixteen feet long in the case of saw logs, sawing still being carried out on a major scale at the mills of Gillies Brothers at Braeside and those of J.E. Boyle Ltd. at the mouth of the Coulonge River. And each log will have its owner's brand mark stamped on its ends.

Once the logs are in the Ottawa, either the river itself or where it broadens into Lake Temiskaming, the men of the Upper Ottawa Improvement Company take charge. It is they who conduct the main river drive, who man the floating booms towards which the logs are steadily driven. At the booms, the logs will be sorted according to ownership. Key locations for the holding booms, as they are called, are just above the large concrete dams of the water-power plants that have now drowned out almost all the rapids on the main river. Carefully designed modern log chutes are incorporated in the dams and down these the logs are fed, the speed and volume of their passage being remarkable to witness. At close hand, the skill of the river-men is a joy to watch. Their easy use of their long pike-poles, their peaveys and their cant-hooks (tools still in regular use, all designed long ago as a result of long experience in log-handling) is a display of skilled artistry.

In still-water parts of the river, as below some of the dams or in the wider lake-like sections, loose booms consisting of big timbers chained together are used to surround large collections of logs. The two ends of the floating boom are fastened to one of the I.C.O. powerful tugs and this modern version of the timber raft is hauled downstream, either to the next dam or to the mill to which the logs are assigned. At each mill an ingenious contraption called a jackladder, with its lower section below water level, picks up the logs in a steady stream as they are fed to it by the river-men and carries them up to the conveying system which will deposit them in the vast piles of logs so familiar at every major pulp and paper mill.

The Improvement Company regularly handles 33 million logs down the

Ottawa from the head of Lake Temiskaming each year, in its co-operative work for the E.B. Eddy Company, the Canadian International Paper Company, and (now) the Consolidated Bathurst Company with its own paper mill and the Gillies Mill which Bathurst now controls. Below the Chaudière, the Canadian International Paper Company handles its own wood from the Gatineau and other sources and this includes the movement of about 30 million logs down the Ottawa annually.

Work on the river does not cease with the main drive since inevitably there will be loose logs that break away from the booms and float off on their own to the shores, as well as 'deadheads,' the logs that have lost some buoyancy and can just be seen on the surface. All these strays can be a menace and a nuisance alike to pleasure craft and to residents along the river banks. Especially in recent years, both the Improvement Company and C.I.P. have devoted special efforts to removing these stray logs as a service to the public which uses the river for recreational purposes to an increasing extent. Surveys have shown that this service is widely appreciated; it provides further evidence of the growing concern for all aspects of the amenity of the great river, even though much still remains to be done before the Ottawa can again truthfully be called the Grand River.

It is not given to all to be able to witness the felling of trees in the bush, their storage on the winter's ice, or the exciting drive of the logs down the swift-flowing waters in the spring and early summer. This is an interesting feature of the river's continuing use in the service of man, exciting indeed when witnessed on some of the smaller streams feeding the Ottawa. I can vividly recall seeing 'one million logs,' as I was told by the men in charge of the drive, come down the Montreal River many years ago, on their way to Lake Temiskaming and eventually to the Temiskaming mill. We had to facilitate their passage through the construction works that spanned the river at what was to be the Upper Notch water-power plant, and this at the peak of the spring flood which brought its own problems to the construction operations. But with skill that is vivid in memory even to this day and in what seemed an incredibly short time despite some trouble with jams upstream, the loosening of which was thrilling to watch, the logs were passed through, the river-men called their goodbyes and another drive was on its way downstream.

This fascinating use of the river can still be seen at many points above Hawkesbury. A particularly convenient viewing point is the Rockliffe Lookout in Ottawa where the sorting work on the booms at the mouth of the Gatineau can be clearly seen and, if the time is right, one may watch a large boom full of pulpwood being towed slowly down-river to the great

Gatineau mill. It requires but little imagination to replace the diesel tug with a steam tug in the mind's eye, and but little more to think of the small pulpwood logs as the great squared timbers of yesterday. It was timber such as this that first brought affluence to the valley and livelihood to many of its early settlers.

# SIX

# Canals and Steamboats

If one crosses the Ottawa River today by the Sir George Perley Bridge from Hawkesbury into Quebec, and takes the road that veers sharply to the left at the northern end of the bridge, one will quickly come to the small village of Grenville. Near a curve in the road one will see what is almost the equivalent of a village green, a quiet and pleasant spot on a summer day. There is water to be seen in the background. A short walk will bring into view the surprise of a well-built masonry ship lock, unusual in that there are no lock gates at either end; the carefully carved stone quoins are well worn but now empty. The water in the lock is at the same level as the river, clearly visible off to the right (or west). This is the level to which the water in the river has been backed up by the great Carillon hydro-electric dam twelve miles downstream. The dam has greatly changed the appearance of the valley in this area, one of its main effects having been to submerge almost completely the Ottawa River canals. The lock that still remains at Grenville was the upstream guard lock of the Grenville Canal. Its predecessor was built here in the 1820s as a vital part of the defence of British North America.

The idea of this serene rural setting having anything to do with defence may seem to some readers to border on the absurd. Even more remarkable, however, is the fact that the original lock here was built slightly narrower than any of the others on the three original small canals. It was, therefore, the bottleneck of the entire Ottawa-Rideau military waterway and caused even the Duke of Wellington profound concern. The thought of the Iron Duke having anything to do with this small canal is difficult to appreciate today, especially since he never visited North America. But he knew it well. As late as 1845, when he had finally retired at the age of seventy-seven, he appealed once again to the Secretary of State for War and Colonies in the British government to eliminate the bottleneck at Grenville by authorizing the rebuilding of the locks. His deep concern for the defence of British North America went back to the time of the War of 1812, which was responsible for the building of the Ottawa River canals and the Rideau Canal. Canoes were still the main means of transport up and down the waterway when these military works were started. By the time they were complete and ready for use, steamboats were sailing the Ottawa. The story of the building of the three small canals between Carillon and Grenville is therefore an appropriate introduction to a review of the century-long use of the Ottawa River by steamboats, yet another phase of the story of the waterway.

'Mr Madison's War' has long been a popular name in the United States for what is more formally known as the War of 1812, surely one of the most unfortunate conflicts in modern history. There had been minor irritations in the early 1800s between Great Britain and the United States but cool heads could probably have solved the problems they presented. Heads, however, were not cool. The British prime minister was assassinated in the House of Commons on 11 May 1812, just after he had made up his mind to repeal some of the orders-in-council which together made up one of the irritants. There was a delay in replacing him and by the time that his successor (Castlereagh) was ready to withdraw the orders it was too late. At the urging of President Madison, the u.s. Congress declared war on Great Britain. The formal declaration was made by the president on 19 June 1812, just three days after the new British prime minister had announced immediate suspension of the orders. With no transatlantic cable, this news reached Washington when it was far too late to stop hostilities.

This is the war of which the historian Charles Stacey has so delightfully said that it 'is one of those episodes in history that make everybody happy, because everybody interprets it in his own way. The Americans think of it as primarily a naval war in which the pride of the Mistress of the Seas was humbled by what an imprudent Englishman had called "a few fir-built frigates, manned by a handful of bastards and outlaws." Canadians think of it equally pridefully as a war of defence in which their brave fathers, side by side, turned back the massed might of the United States and saved the country from conquest. And the English are happiest of all because they don't even know it happened.'

The war was far from popular in the United States but it was fought with bitter losses on both sides, the final result being as close to a stalemate as can be imagined. It was fought on land in both Lower and Upper Canada, but by the end of 1813, American troops had been almost cleared out. Naval battles were fought on the Great Lakes and on Lake Champlain. Eventually, a treaty of peace was signed in the Belgian city of Ghent on 24 December 1814. Not the least of the unusual features of the war was that the final battle, that of New Orleans, was fought after the treaty had been signed – the result again of the slow communication of those days. President Madison officially pronounced the declaration of peace on 17 February 1815. Three days before the news of this action reached London, word was received of Napoleon's escape from Elba and British attention was diverted to the battlegrounds of Europe.

Canadians, however, could not forget the invasion of their country and the dangers that still persisted despite the Treaty of Ghent. This concern is but little appreciated by Canadians today although there is still an active Society of the War of 1812 in the United States, founded only in 1854, but holding regularly an annual commemorative service in Philadelphia (which, by chance, I have attended on three occasions).

A matter of special concern in the years immediately following the end of hostilities was the critical situation of Kingston. It was a vital fortress with an associated naval dockyard serving Lake Ontario and therefore important for the defence of Upper Canada. All supplies for Kingston had, however, to be brought from Montreal up the St Lawrence, by boats in summer or over the snow and ice in winter. British defence authorities had been surprised that the Americans had not ambushed this critical supply line during the course of the war. They may not have realized its strategic importance or, if they did, they were unable to execute an attack, since they too had no roads leading to the banks of the international section of the St Lawrence.

By the end of the war, however, a complete plan for such an attack had been prepared. This was actually disclosed to the general officer commanding in Upper Canada by the American General Brown, 'thinking secrecy no longer necessary.' Action had therefore to be taken without delay to find an alternative route between Montreal and Kingston, since there was widespread fear that hostilities would break out again, so high did feelings still run on both sides of the border. Preliminary explorations had been carried out long before this and it was known that, by using the Ottawa and Rideau rivers, access could be gained to the Rideau Lakes, whence the Cataraqui River could be followed down to Kingston. This was a natural route, long known to the Indians who had served as guides to early military surveyors.

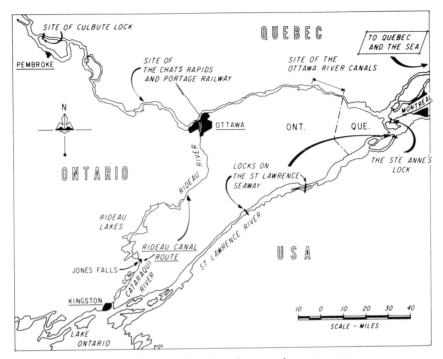

The Montreal-Ottawa-Kingston triangle and connecting waterways.

The sketch map above shows the two routes between Montreal and Kingston. From this it can be seen that even though the Rideau Canal would constitute the major part of the alternative military route between the two locations, it could not be fully effective without the completion of the Ottawa River canals and the lock at Ste Anne de Bellevue. The latter was necessary to bypass the small drop at the Ste Anne rapids. A small wooden lock was built at Vaudreuil for this purpose in 1816, being replaced in 1843 by a masonry lock at Ste Anne de Bellevue.

It will be recalled that upstream of the head of the Lake of Two Mountains there was a stretch of twelve miles broken by rapids – first at Carillon, then at Chute à Blondeau, and finally the Long Sault itself extending from Greece's Point to Grenville and Hawkesbury. As early as October 1815 the British prime minister had expressed the interest of his government in having small canals constructed to circumvent these rapids. This initiated a series of studies of possible locations and estimated costs, the first designs being for very small canals indeed, capable of conveying only the batteaux then coming into use – more substantial craft than canoes for the transport of freight, but still manually propelled. These investigations were made first by officers of the Corps of Royal Engineers but later by officers of the Royal Staff Corps, notably in 1819 by Captain F.W. Mann of this little-known regiment of the British Army.

The Ottawa River canals were in fact constructed entirely by the Royal Staff Corps, despite the general impression that they were the work of the Royal Engineers, as were the Rideau Canal and so many other works that contributed to the early development of Canada. Even the bronze plaques that are mounted near the two ends of the old canals, erected by the Historic Sites and Monuments Board of Canada, repeat this error. It is well, therefore, to know something of this unsung British regiment. It was formed in 1799 when the Duke of York, then commander-in-chief of the British army, wanted additional engineer soldiers for one of his campaigns and was unable to obtain them from the Corps of Royal Engineers. The new regiment served with distinction in Egypt and in the Peninsular War under the Duke of Wellington, carrying out some notable bridge building. Later the regiment constructed the Royal Military Canal, an interesting defence work still to be seen between Shorncliffe Battery and Rye on the south coast of England. Two companies sailed for Halifax in October 1814 and were moved up to work on the early St Lawrence canals in 1815. From this task they were moved again in 1819 in order to start building the Ottawa River canals, upon which they were to be engaged for the next fifteen years. Before the Ottawa River canals had been completed, the Royal Staff Corps was abolished in the great economy move of 1829. The few officers remaining at the completion of the canals were listed in the annual Army Lists, eventually as attached to the Ordnance Department.

The delay in starting the construction of this military waterway is surprising in view of the strong recommendations made for it in 1815. The reasons are complex but one of them was the reluctance of the provincial governments of the time to contribute in any way to its financing, defence being still an entirely British responsibility. It was not until a new commander-in-chief in Canada, the Duke of Richmond, had sent a very strong report on the matter soon after his arrival in 1818, that action was initiated. The Duke of Wellington added his support. The actual start of construction was made on 30 May 1819, when Captain Mann was instructed by the Duke of Richmond to commence work on the Grenville Canal. It seems clear that this humane governor had been influenced by the difficulties encountered by the first settlers coming to reside in Richmond, a military settlement some miles to the west of the present location of

Ottawa. There were about three hundred of them including women and children; their hardships in mounting the Long Sault in 1818 must have been trying in the extreme. Official confirmation reached Canada shortly after Captain Mann had been ordered to start work, but this was qualified by the requirement that payment should be made out of the 'Army Extraordinaries,' a fact that explains the strict limitation of funds during the first seven years of this isolated construction project.

The Duke of Richmond planned to inspect personally the full route of the Kingston-to-Montreal waterway, in the course of the travels he made in the summer of 1819, even though this meant rigorous journeying through virgin forest and along untamed rivers. He did inspect most of the route of the Rideau Canal on foot or in canoe, but he died tragically (from the effects of a bite from a tame fox that must have had rabies), just after leaving the new little bush settlement of Richmond on his way down the small Jock River to the Ottawa. His body, in a plain deal box, was taken in a batteau down the Ottawa River, which he had hoped to inspect, in late August 1819, to be buried in the Anglican Cathedral at Quebec City.

The lack of the detailed written instructions which might have been expected from him caused some difficulty in getting work on the Ottawa River canals started. All the Duke had authorized was work on the Grenville Canal, and so nothing was done on the other two, nor on the Rideau Canal, until 1826, even though all were necessary to the alternative military waterway between Montreal and Kingston. Work on all the canals resulted from the recommendations in a report submitted by a special commission of three distinguished military men, headed by Colonel Sir James Carmichael Smyth, who visited each canal site in the summer of 1825. Thereafter work proceeded with all possible despatch, the Rideau Canal being opened for use in the spring of 1832, and the Ottawa River canals two years later.

The story of the building of the Rideau Canal, under the direction of Lieutenant Colonel John By of the Corps of Royal Engineers, has been told in the author's book, *Rideau Waterway*. The completion in only five working seasons of this great work, with its forty-seven locks and more than fifty dams, large and small, is one of the epic stories of civil engineering in North America. The fifteen years taken for the much smaller Ottawa River canals is in strange contrast. There were, however, extenuating circumstances. Since the building of the canals between Grenville and Carillon has not yet been described, a summary here is desirable because the finished canals were so integral a part of the Ottawa Waterway for a century after their completion. The diagrammatic sketch map on p. 140

shows the locations of the three canals, all on the north bank of the Ottawa River, as were the original portage trails. The dominating position of the Grenville Canal will clearly be seen but the much shorter Carillon Canal and the single lock and very short canal at Chute à Blondeau were equally essential for providing through navigation around the swift water that here made the Ottawa so beautiful and so dangerous.

Captain Henry Du Vernet of the Royal Staff Corps was selected to direct the building of the Grenville Canal, once official approval had been given. Little is known about his background but the record of his work on the Ottawa shows clearly that he was a capable officer and a thorough gentleman. He landed at Quebec on 29 July 1819 with two new companies of the Royal Staff Corps and proceeded upriver to Montreal, and eventually up the Ottawa to Grenville, where he took over from Captain Mann, who then returned to England.

The task of building a canal around the surging waters of the Long Sault with no plans or specifications as a guide, and in country that was still thick virgin forest down to the water's edge, would have daunted any ordinary man. But Du Vernet was no ordinary man, as his letters and reports show clearly. In his first report of November 1819, written after he had returned to Montreal at the beginning of that month, he noted that 'the ground through which the Canal has to pass is still un-cleared and the wood very thick.' At Grenville the soil cover over the bedrock was so thin that 'it was with great difficulty a place could be found to fix a Tent upon it.'

After looking the site over, he stated that his idea was 'to keep on the same level as long as can be conveniently done and to bring the Locks as close together at the lower end as possible; it appears that this can be done in nearly a straight line and that two Locks can be brought together which will save a pair of gates: in all eight Locks will be required.' Little was possible of accomplishment during the few weeks available in the fall of 1819 and much of the summer of 1820 was spent in clearing the bush from along the line of the canal. Excavation work really started in 1821. Du Vernet's detachment did not exceed one hundred men, some of whom had to be used for guard duty, others in the small mess and stores. The unit had to be largely self-contained during the months of summer and fall that were spent at Grenville, as all supplies had to be brought up laboriously from Montreal.

Du Vernet experienced difficulties with the authorities in Montreal (notably the commissary general) in obtaining even the necessary minimum equipment for his camp in the forest. All his complaints, and they were many, were invariably couched in courteous and dignified language,

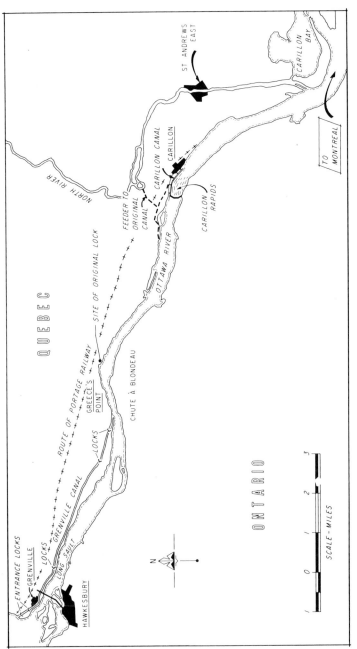

The Ottawa River canals, begun in 1819 and completed in 1834.

written out in longhand by himself or by his one clerk-assistant, the excess of paper work demanded from him being yet one more of the crosses he had to bear. He even had to address the governor in an attempt to obtain more oats for the horses that he used, in addition to oxen, as the work progressed. Several pages could be filled with extracts from Du Vernet's reports demonstrating the continuing incidental difficulties he encountered, quite apart from the main problem of getting the work done.

After clearing along the line of the canal, he faced the task of excavation. Moving the thin layer of soil was easy but excavation was mainly in solid rock. It involved drilling holes, all by hand, in which black powder was inserted for blasting, following the primitive practice of these early days. Blacksmiths had a steady job in preparing the drills. The drudgery of the slow and tedious hand-drilling may be left to the imagination, but the occasional accidents due to faulty blasting techniques were the subject of all too frequent references in Du Vernet's reports.

In addition to the main job, there was careful accounting to be done, for annual expenditure was strictly limited to £8,000. Only once in the years up to 1827 was this amount exceeded (in 1824, when £8,770/2/8³/₄ was spent) so it is not surprising that when Du Vernet returned to England in 1824 for a long leave, not a great deal was to be seen on the ground even though the incomplete excavations for the locks and canal channel represented so much human travail. Captain W.J. King was in command during Du Vernet's absence; he soon found himself facing the same problems, and complained on one occasion to the military secretary to the governor that he had not come out from England to be a public accountant. Du Vernet, now promoted to major, returned in July 1827 and remained until the works were completed towards the end of 1833.

The need for construction of all three Ottawa River canals had by this time been recognized, as well as for the much larger task of building the Rideau Canal. Lieutenant Colonel John By had, as noted earlier, arrived in Canada in the summer of 1826 to direct the latter work. Construction of the smaller canals on the Ottawa continued to remain wholly the responsibility of the Royal Staff Corps. More money was now available and Major Du Vernet was permitted to add to the unskilled civilian labour that he had started to employ supplementing his own men, as early as 1822. Once plans for the two smaller canals had been developed, some work was done under contract by civilian contractors. This may have speeded up some parts of the work but it also led to a new crop of difficulties since the Royal Staff Corps was not experienced in contract work and the commissary general apparently insisted upon controlling the contractual arrangements.

These were among the factors that caused such slow progress, another being an outbreak of cholera leading to the loss of almost all of one working season.

The greatest burden that the commanding officer had to carry, however, was dealing with irate landowners. Although still unsettled, land along the route of the canal had been legally subdivided and, as always happens under such circumstances, it became the most valuable land in the whole Ottawa Valley as soon as it was needed by the Crown. It seems clear from the records that Major Du Vernet had to spend more time in dealing with landowners than in directing the actual work, so vociferous and abusive were these early property-holders.

Quite the worst offender was G.P. Grece – after whom Greece's Point is named (with a spelling mistake). Even as late as 1841, his son was still urging his claims for compensation to Captain Ben Stehelin, R.E., then in charge of the canals, coming to argue rudely with him 'while the Northwest Canoes were passing the detached lock of the Carillon Canal.' In one of his many letters about this matter, Du Vernet said that 'if any inference is to be drawn from the extravagant demands in the late arbitration, Mr Grece's property as well as that of other proprietors similarly situated must be greatly improved instead of injured by said canal.' In an earlier appeal, asking for the assistance of an expert in land values, he said that 'I am not a competent judge of property and some of the Tenants speak no other language than Gaelic,' a sidelight that will interest all Scots-Canadians. The acquisitive landowners thought nothing of addressing their appeals and petitions directly to the governor, now Lord Dalhousie. When he visited the works in September 1823, he saw some of the petitioners, later reporting that 'Mr McMillan and Mr Grece have both conducted themselves with so much violence, and the latter particularly with such outrageous insolence, that I should feel myself justified in refusing them the smallest compensation' – but he added that he would not follow their example.

We must get back, however, to the canal building. The size of locks was a critical matter, as has already been indicated. When work started in 1819, Du Vernet was guided by the size of lock then being contemplated for the new Lachine Canal, with water only four feet deep and width sufficient for two Durham boats to pass one another. There was some reference to 'small steamboats,' but these were late in coming to the Ottawa and nobody before John By had the vision to appreciate what a difference steamboats would make.

The first locks to be built on the Grenville Canal were at the upstream, or western, end; three were finished to the dimensions initially planned of roughly 107 feet long and 19 feet 4 inches wide. I say 'roughly,' since the surveying of the Royal Staff Corps was not accurate, with the result that all three locks differed slightly, the upper or guard lock (at Grenville) being slightly narrower than the other two. The remaining locks on the Grenville Canal, and those on the Carillon and Chute à Blondeau canals, were constructed 128 feet long and 32 feet 6 inches wide, only slightly below the size of the Rideau Canal locks as built after Colonel By had won his battle to have their size increased. Locks on the Ottawa River canals controlled the size of vessels using the Ottawa-Rideau route from Montreal to Kingston, the upper three locks limiting the beam of all such vessels by more than ten feet. It is small wonder that, for as long as the canals were regarded as vital for defence, this bottleneck was of great concern to military authorities, notably to the Duke of Wellington.

To circumvent the rapids known as Chute à Blondeau was a relatively easy matter since they had a fall of only about four feet. A channel about eight hundred feet long had to be excavated, almost all through solid rock, with a single lock installed at about mid-point. This was the first part of the combined project to be constructed by contract. A canal around the Carillon Rapids provided more challenge in design to Major Du Vernet in view of the high land beside the rapids. He had seen how difficult and slow was excavation in solid rock; he knew the urgency with which completion of the canals was awaited. The elegant but unusual solution that he devised can best be appreciated by reference to the sketch map on page 140. Coming downstream, a single entrance lock was to be built with a lift (rather than a drop) of thirteen feet. This would raise vessels into a channel that could be excavated with ease along the lie of the land, well above the river, until a gully was reached just below the rapids, in which two locks could be built descending to river level with a total drop of twenty-three feet.

The idea of using three locks for a fall of only ten feet may seem strange but Du Vernet's plan was endorsed by a special committee of inquiry (of which Colonel By was a member) that was set up in response to the quite violent protests from the Seignior of Argenteuil and the more than five hundred residents of St Andrews and the area round when it was found that a channel was to be excavated from the North River in order to act as a feeder to the Carillon Canal which, in Du Vernet's plan, would lose water in both directions as vessels locked through. This inquiry caused still further delay in the start of work on the Carillon Canal, with the result that it was the last to be finished, including the little feeder channel that caused such local distress. This small ditch (for that is all that it is) may still be seen today; as one stands by its side, it is astonishing to reflect upon the burning emotions that its excavation aroused. Durham boats had been able to use the Grenville Canal from August 1832, once they had been hauled up the Carillon Rapids and Chute à Blondeau, but it was not until the winter of 1833–34 that work on the Carillon Canal was finished. The first vessel passed through the three Ottawa River canals on 30 April 1834.

The relief that this opening must have given to users of the river is clearly indicated by the contents of a politely worded petition signed by merchants in Kingston on 7 May 1832, addressed to the governor (now Lord Aylmer), protesting the delay in the completion of the Ottawa River canals and pointing out their value for the development of trade to the west. This was an entirely new concept for the use of the canals since they were still essentially military works, which remained under military control until 1857. The petition indicated, however, the real beginnings of settlement along the Ottawa and the introduction of the newfangled steamboats which began to use the canals from the start of their service. The canals, as finished in 1834, continued in use until rebuilt in the 1870s, most downward bound vessels continuing to shoot the Chute à Blondeau rather than waste time going through the single canal lock.

Throughout the years of canal building (1819 to 1834) canoe traffic up and down the river continued. Philemon Wright still sent primitive rafts of large timbers down the river. But as settlement developed along the banks of the Ottawa, the settlers needed to have supplies brought in, in addition to the equipment they took with them for the establishment of their new homes in the forest. To begin with, such goods were carted by road from Montreal to Lachine and there loaded into batteaux or Durham boats for shipment upriver. In this way they reached Pointe Fortune or St Andrews, where they were transferred to carts again for the rough trip over the portage trails to Hawkesbury or Grenville. Transhipment into large freight canoes was then necessary for the final part of all journeys to points on the river up to the Chaudière.

Many of those using the north bank at the Long Sault would stop for a visit at the camp of the Royal Staff Corps: there are some happy references in travellers' records to the welcome they received from Henry Du Vernet and his Italian-born wife at their home in the woods at Grenville. Du Vernet was by then a lieutenant colonel; he became a full colonel in 1841 while on the half-pay list. No record of his life at Grenville has yet been found. Somewhere, one likes to think, is the diary that he surely must have kept; one day it may come to light, as may also some of the paintings that he executed, only one of which is known at present (page 54).

Philemon Wright must have met Du Vernet in his journeys downriver as the pioneer lumberman developed his many interests. Not surprisingly, one of these was the improvement of traffic on the Ottawa. Wright had operated a 'packet' (probably a Durham boat) named *Britannia*, for transport of his own freight for some years preceding 1819, in which year he started a public service with a vessel appropriately called *Packet*, between Hull and Grenville. It was fitted with sails but was usually propelled by oars. A few years later (probably in 1824) a similar service was started by 'Judge' MacDonnell between St Andrews and Montreal. As business slowly grew in volume, the need for some improvement became evident. On the St Lawrence steam had already made its appearance, John Molson of Montreal having built Canada's first steamboat, the *Accommodation*, in 1809. She was so successful in her service between Montreal and Quebec that in 1812 Molson built four more steamships.

Despite this relatively early start of steam navigation in Canada, it was not until 1822 that the Ottawa River saw its first steam-propelled vessel. The *Union of the Ottawa* was built in that year by Thomas Mears at Hawkesbury. Philemon Wright was one of the financial backers of this pioneering venture. The vessel seems to have been little more than an elaborate barge with an English-built steam engine mounted on its deck, transferred from an earlier vessel that Mears had built. She served well up and down the Ottawa between Grenville and Hull until 1830 when her name was changed to the *Union* and she was sold to another owner. This, however, was the beginning of a new era on the Ottawa.

By the year 1830, with the prospect of the opening of the Ottawa River canals in view, a further step was seen to be necessary and a syndicate was formed (naturally with Wright as a member) in order to provide a steamboat service between Lachine, Carillon, and St Andrews. The *St Andrews* was built for this service and at about the same time the *William King* was constructed as a replacement for the little *Union*. Both the new vessels were purchased in 1832 by the Ottawa and Rideau Forwarding Company, which had been formed by forward-looking Montreal business men, anticipating the trade that would develop. John Molson, now 'the Honourable,' was president of the company, which began immediately to bargain with the Seignior of Vaudreuil for a tract of his land on which to build a small lock with approach channels to facilitate navigation up the rapids between Lake St Louis and the Lake of Two Mountains. The small lock structure was quickly built and so the company was ready with its small fleet well before the completion of the Ottawa River canals. The company experimented with a stern-wheeler (one of the few such vessels ever to sail on the Ottawa), but the *Shannon*, with accommodation for passengers, was the pride of the fleet, and the precursor of many fine vessels that provided good service between Grenville and Hull-Ottawa for the next eighty years. The monopolistic position of the new company was objected to, especially when it restricted the use of the lock at Vaudreuil to its own vessels. The monopoly was neatly broken in 1841 by Robert Ward Shepherd, the first of a family long associated with steamboats on the Ottawa River. In September of that year, the level of water at the rapids became so low that barges could not be hauled up in the usual way at Ste Anne's. The lock at Vaudreuil not being available to him, Captain Shepherd explored the adjacent rapids in a small boat, found a channel whose existence he had suspected, laid out a heavy anchor at the head of the rapids, and proceeded to 'snag' his two loaded barges up into the Lake of Two Mountains.

After this coup, the company soon agreed to allow rival firms to use its lock, at a charge of eight dollars per barge. This was a short-lived concession since plans for a masonry lock at Ste Anne's had been prepared in 1839, and construction started in 1840. The work was taken over from Lower Canada in 1841 by the Board of Commissioners of the United Province of Canada and finished in 1843. The first vessels passed through in June of that year. Now the complete route between Montreal and Kingston was canalized and through sailings of sizeable vessels started immediately. Until 1851, this route was the 'Seaway,' permitting the passage of even seagoing boats all the way up to Lake Superior, since the Welland Canal had been opened in 1829, linking Lakes Ontario and Erie.

These were years of active development in both Lower and Upper Canada. Indicative of this was the public outcry when the gates on the Carillon Canal failed in July 1842, leading to a three-week closure of the canal system. It was stated that the equivalent of 145,000 barrels of flour was held up at Kingston, sure sign that the new waterway was already being put to good use. It had already become clear, however, that although the canals would well serve the passage of loaded barges, the necessarily slow transit from Carillon to Grenville would not suit the needs of passengers. In the late spring of 1842, therefore, the first through passenger service was initiated between Montreal and Hull and Bytown, as the small town at the entrance to the Rideau Canal was then called, to become later the city of Ottawa after its change of name in 1855. A stage-coach was used from Montreal to Lachine where the steamer *Oldfield* was boarded for the sail to Carillon. A company had been organized to provide stage-coach service parallel with the canal between Carillon and Grenville, where the upper river steamer, the *Albion*, was boarded for the final smooth sail of sixty miles to the Chaudière. Of special note is the fact that Sir George Simpson had an interest in the Carillon-to-Grenville staging company, yet another indication of his astuteness.

Change was in the air and this, too, Sir George recognized since he agreed to serve as president of the Ottawa Steamer Company when this was formed by Captain Shepherd and some partners by purchase of the Jones Company, one of the pioneer operators. It is perhaps ironical that the partners in this steamship company should have held their regular meetings in the old Hudson's Bay House at Lachine. There was change also on the St Lawrence, for two canals were finally being built there to circumvent the rapids. By the year 1842, it was possible for the small steamer *Highlander* to reach Kingston from Montreal under her own power, even though much work was still to be done before the St Lawrence canals were finally complete. This turning-point in travel to the west was reached in 1851, after which all freight for Lake Ontario was taken up the St Lawrence instead of along the longer and slower Ottawa-Rideau route.

With settlement increasing along the Ottawa, its river traffic continued to grow even without the through traffic for the Rideau Canal. Mail was first carried up the river by the Ottawa Steamer Company in 1850. New vessels were built, the *Atlas*, for example, having a length of 150 feet and a beam of 25 feet. Pride of the river fleet was the *Lady Simpson*, acquired in 1850 and first commanded by the veteran Captain Shepherd, who retired in 1853. He was succeeded by his brother Henry William Shepherd who served for the remarkable span of fifty years as a captain on Ottawa River steamers, with never any loss of life on his vessels. In this period, the first sawn lumber was prepared, by water power, at the Chaudière and taken down the river for export to the United States. All this Sir George Simpson witnessed before his death in 1860.

Sir George had kept up his own epic canoe journeys along the Ottawa Waterway until the mid-fifties. His successors in the administration of the Hudson's Bay Company continued using the Ottawa route for canoe journeys until late in the sixties but the coming of the railways finally eliminated this romantic use of the river. Rafts of great timbers continued their slow journeys downstream and their thrilling passage through the rapids after being broken up into cribs. In these mid-century years, therefore, the Ottawa River was a busy thoroughfare, as busy, perhaps, as at any time in its history. This was true not only in the section of the river between Ste Anne's and Ottawa but above the Chaudière also. The barrier formed by this great fall was never canalized, although several proposals for a canal around it were advanced and some even surveyed. Steamships above the

Chaudière, therefore, were always operated quite separately from those below. Because of the Chats and other rapids, there could not be any through sailing, except in each of the great lakes between the major rapids, but an efficient service was gradually built up with stage and portage connections for passengers and freight between each steamer route.

The *Lady Colborne* was the first vessel built on Lac Deschenes. Captain Grant (the first captain of the little *Union*) had charge of her construction in 1833 and also of her navigation. She was 100 feet long with a beam of 34 feet over her paddle-boxes, and so was a notable ship for the time. She sailed on three mornings each week from Aylmer, leaving at 7:00 a.m. Passengers had therefore to come by stage-coach from Hull and Bytown, staying overnight at the hotel that had been built by Charles Symmes by the Aylmer wharf. At the west end of the lake, the *Lady Colborne* at first docked at Fitzroy Harbour but from May 1837 she was able to berth at Victoria Island in midriver. The portage trail across the island had been rebuilt, leading to a small wharf on Chats Lake. In 1836 Captain Grant built the first vessel for this second phase of the journey above the Chaudière. This was the legendary *George Buchanan*, similar in design to the *Lady Colborne* but slightly smaller. When the river flow was suitable, she could sail through the Snow Rapids and reach Portage du Fort, but at other times she had to finish her upstream journey at the head of Chats Lake, for many years faithfully making the daily round trip to Victoria Island.

It is difficult today to appreciate what the daily service provided by these two pioneer steamers meant to the settlers who were slowly clearing land for their homes around the shores of the two lakes. There was as yet no postal service but the two boats used to bring the news from downriver, and even delivered newspapers to the occasional settler. It was through copies of a New York paper, thus brought to A. McDonnell at Sand Point, that news of the death of King William in 1837, and of the accession of young Queen Victoria, reached these isolated settlements. Their isolation was well shown when anything went wrong with either of the vessels. In June 1838, for example, a metal coupling in the main shaft of the *George Buchanan* broke. The engineer of the vessel was despatched on horseback to Kingston to get a new part, and service had to be maintained for five weeks by a large rowboat, fitted with sails, capable of carrying only three or four tons of freight.

Another of the famous river captains of the Ottawa took over command of the Chats Lake steamer in 1839 upon the retirement of the pioneer master, Captain Richards. The new man was Captain Daniel Cowley whose life almost spanned the century; he was born in 1817 and lived until 1897. For some years he had as a partner Jason Gould, whose cousin was known for his adventures in high finance in the United States. For a time Gould had an active interest in steamboating on the upper Ottawa, being a party to some of the complicated competition that featured transportation developments even in this isolated area in the 1840s and 1850s. Two new vessels, for example, were prefabricated in Molson's yard in Montreal during the winter of 1845–46 by a rival group, and dismantled into small sections which were hauled up over the ice of the Ottawa to be reassembled, one at Aylmer and the other on the Mississippi River at Hubbell's Falls. Later in 1846, however, the Union Forwarding and Railway Company was established, and it gradually brought order to the combined system. An early action of the new enterprise was to construct one of Canada's most unusual railways.

This railway provided an alternative to the rough portage trail between Lac Deschenes and Chats Lake over Victoria Island. It was located on the north shore of the river and had a length of about three miles; the sketch map on p. 150 shows its route, which can still be made out, with some difficulty, on the ground over which it ran. It was built with no appreciable gradients since its motive power was provided by horses. Accordingly, one had to mount a long set of steps to reach it from the new wharf which had to be built near the Quyon of today. The only known photograph of the horse railway on page 229 shows the *Ann Sisson* (a later vessel) berthed at this wharf and the then well-known white horse with its two little cars waiting to pull its load of passengers round the great rapids to join the steamer on Chats Lake, at another new wharf that had been built close to where the Canadian National Railway now crosses the Ottawa on a major bridge. Very few references with any details of this unique railway have been found, although some of the travellers up the Ottawa in the third quarter of the last century made passing references to it in published memoirs.

If one landed at Portage du Fort from the *George Buchanan* (when she was able to get up that far) one faced a rough eight-mile ride in a type of stage-coach until Bryson was reached, just above the great Calumet Falls. There one could board the steamer *Calumet* after it was built in 1862 by Captain Cumming and some associates. This would convey passengers to the foot of Morrison Island, whence another coach could be taken for Pembroke. Alternatively, and at times of low water, the *Calumet* would sail up the Culbute Channel, to the north of Allumette Island, as far as Chapeau where the stage would be taken for the drive across the island and

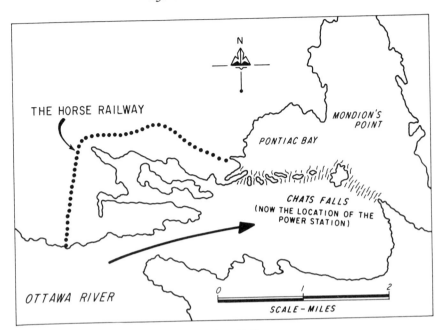

Route of the 'Horse Railway' around Chats Falls.

the short ferry trip to Pembroke. Long before this service was available in its final form, however, Cowley and Gould had decided to improve the old route up Muskrat Lake, that used by Champlain.

By 1849 they had improved the old portage road from a point on the south bank of the Ottawa, about one mile below Portage du Fort, to the foot of Muskrat Lake, the site of Cobden today. They started a stage-coach operation on this road and then built a small stern-wheeler which sailed the full length of Muskrat Lake and down the small Muskrat River to the rapids three miles upstream from Pembroke. Looking at this small stream today, it is difficult to imagine a steamboat sailing its waters, but this the *Muskrat* did, so successfully that in 1852 a second vessel, the *North Star*, was built to supplement it. The *Muskrat* was burned in the long hot summer of 1853 but service continued with the new vessel. In 1862 a third vessel was constructed, named by Cowley the *Jason Gould* as a tribute to his partner in the venture from which Gould had retired in 1855. This ship continued to give good service until the time came when all river passenger service was precipitately abandoned.

Steamship service continued to advance further up the river. In 1860

Captain Cumming built the *Pembroke* to supplement the service upstream from Pembroke that he had provided since 1854 with the little *Pontiac*; both vessels sailed as far as Des Joachims. A little later a further service was provided by a small vessel, the *Kippewa*, sailing from Des Joachims as far as Rocher Capitaine. After making the portage, one could then board the *Deux Rivières* to sail to the settlement of the same name. Great rapids made another portage necessary, above which one found the *Mattawa* waiting to take passengers up the remaining part of the great river as far as Mattawa. For a few years, therefore, it was possible to sail the full length of the Ottawa River, from Ste Anne's to Mattawa, on steamships, large and well-equipped to start with, then becoming smaller as the journey upriver proceeded. In view of the character of the rapids and waterfalls that had to be bypassed by the portage roads and trails, this must have been one of the most exciting journeys then available to travellers in North America.

One had to leave one's comfortable hotel in Ottawa early in the morning by a 'first-class omnibus' to catch the 8:30 a.m. sailing of the *Ann Sisson* at Aylmer. Breakfast was enjoyed during the leisurely sail on Lac Deschenes with several stops at the small settlements along the way. The ride around Chats Falls on the horse-railroad took about twenty minutes, at the end of which one would board the *Alliance*, due to sail at 11:00 a.m. Midday dinner was taken in the 'palatial' dining saloon of this Chats Lake vessel. If it was possible to get up as far as Gould's Wharf, one then took the waiting stage-coach for the twelve-mile ride through the forests to Cobden, there to board the *Muskrat* for the final sail to near Pembroke. Another meal, described as 'tea,' was taken on this small vessel, completing the unusual experience of enjoying three meals in one day in three different steamboats. Pembroke would be reached in the early evening. If one went further upriver after spending the night at Pembroke, one had to start at 1:00 p.m. next day on the *Pembroke* or the *Pontiac* for the sail to Des Joachims, where an overnight stay could be made in another of the riverside hotels then famous. The return journey from Aylmer to Des Joachims could be done in three days but most travellers took more time in order to enjoy fully the beauties of the great river, not a few going all the way to Mattawa as long as the service lasted.

The complete service did not last for many years. The railway was advancing slowly up the valley. The year-round service for passengers and freight that railways could provide was a convenience with which the steamboats could not compete. The extra revenue derived in summer months from the tourists of the day was small compensation for the loss of freight business to railways, first experienced when the Brockville and

Ottawa Railway reached the shores of the Ottawa River at Sand Point near Arnprior in 1865. These were days of massive railway building in Ontario and so it was not long before lines in the valley were advancing westwards. Once the railway reached Pembroke, the Union Forwarding and Railway Company gave up all hope of competing and abandoned all its passenger services, including the horse-railway, at the end of the 1879 navigation season. Some freighting still continued, using the river steamers, but this was a temporary reprieve; the company surrendered its charter in 1882. Only the haulage of logs by small tugs was left as a river activity. As we have already seen, this continues to this day, now under the Upper Ottawa Improvement Company's banner.

It is strange to reflect that all this activity on the Ottawa River above the Chaudière stopped completely about a century ago. Photography has fortunately left us some idea of what these early vessels were like and one later development gave to some valley residents still living a taste of the pleasures of river-boat travel. This was the service provided by the *G.B. Greene*, often described as the 'Queen of the River,' which was built for the Upper Ottawa Improvement Company in 1896. She was used primarily for hauling logs on Lac Deschenes but provided also occasional passenger trips out of Aylmer, notably evening excursion trips which became very popular in the years just before the First World War. She was seriously damaged by fire in 1916 but rebuilt in 1917. The old attraction had gone, however, and she was scrapped later that same year. Only one of the old upper Ottawa vessels now remains; she will appear in the last chapter describing the Ottawa today.

In surprising contrast to what happened to passenger traffic on the river above the Chaudière was the continuing development of steamship traffic between Ottawa and Montreal. With a fleet of fine ships of ever-increasing size, passenger service was maintained until 1910. Steamboat excursions continued until the mid-twenties, using some of the passenger vessels. Road and rail services finally displaced them until the 1960s, when river trips on a more modest scale were reinstituted from Ottawa. There is, therefore, a long and interesting story of this century of river passenger services between Montreal and Ottawa, the highlights alone being all that can now be recounted. We have already looked at the developments of the early years, halting in our record with the death of Sir George Simpson in 1860. The Ottawa Steamer Company continued its good service despite the loss of its president, Sir George's place being taken by Captain Robert Shepherd upon his return from a visit to England.

The *Prince of Wales* was one of the fine new steamers in the company's

An 'Alligator' boat in a boom near Arnprior on the Ottawa River.

Modern view of a 'pointer' boat at work on the Petawawa River, near the Ottawa.

The Ottawa River through a vista cut in the woods of Rideau Hall for Princess
Louise, wife of the Marquis of Lorne, Governor General of Canada, about 1880.
A steamer, timber raft, and pointer boat can be seen.

The first small lock leading from the Ottawa River to the original Carillon canal, as it is today, preserved in a small park adjacent to the Carillon power station. The excellence of the masonry can be seen. The lock, built in 1832, was abandoned about 1878.

The guard lock at Grenville looking towards the Ottawa River. The view shows the lock of the 1870s as it is today, with its gates removed. The original lock here was the narrowest on the whole Ottawa-Rideau system, and the cause of much concern to the Duke of Wellington.

Pleasure boats in the downstream lock of the reconstructed Carillon Canal – a typical scene in the 1950s and early 1960s before the canals were submerged beneath the waters impounded by the Carillon Dam.

Twin locks at Culbute, constructed of timber. This is one of the panoramic photographs (taken with a camera rotated on its stand by clockwork) taken in 1906–1907 along the full length of the Ottawa Waterway in connection with the study of the Department of Public Works summarized in the 1909 Report. The exposed timber was destroyed by fire a few years after the photograph was taken; as explained in the text, the locks had previously been disused for some time.

159

S.S. *Empress* leaving Ottawa to sail to Grenville; she was one of the regular mail steamers on the Ottawa to Grenville run.

fleet, placed in service in good time to carry the Prince of Wales on the first part of his journey to Ottawa in 1860. The *Queen Victoria* was the companion vessel above the Long Sault. These two ships, and their successors, maintained a daily service on the Ottawa until 1910. As the protracted negotiations leading to Confederation got under way, traffic to and from the new little capital city increased. Sir John A. Macdonald was said to have had a stateroom for his use held in reserve at all times. Indicative of the importance of the service was the change in the company's name, effected in 1864 by an act of the legislature, to the Ottawa River Navigation Company, as it was to be known throughout the remainder of its existence. In the same year, Captain Shepherd arranged to purchase the unique railway that had been developed as an alternative to the stage-coach service between Grenville and Carillon.

One result of the railway fever that gripped Canada in the middle of the nineteenth century was the resurrection of the idea of a railway up the north shore of the Ottawa River from Montreal. The Great Montreal and Ottawa Valley Trunk Line was the grandiose title adopted. Plans, financing, and associated construction ideas form an unusual chapter in the story of Canada's railroads, loss of the financier-contractor with £50,000 in gold in a wreck at sea, on a journey from England, being the most tragic feature. In the end, only the short line from Carillon to Grenville was completed and it was built to the 'provincial gauge' then in use, distance between the rails being 5 feet 6 inches instead of the standard spacing of 4 feet 8½ inches to which we are now so well accustomed. Isolated as it was from all other railways, the Portage Railway (as it was popularly known) maintained its broad gauge when others changed to standard, and was for many years the only broad-gauge railway in North America. It was opened for use in the summer of 1854, with one locomotive pushing or pulling two or three cars along its single twelve-mile track between wharves at each end.

Simple as it was, the Carillon-to-Grenville railway provided an efficient portage service between the vessels on the two sections of the river. It continued until the end of passenger services in the 1920s so that it is possible, as I have found to my pleasure, still to talk with senior residents of the valley who can remember using the little portage train in their youth. Unfortunately, it was completely dismantled when it fell into disuse and few relics of it remain, but photographs give us a good idea of what the train was like (see page 230). And we have quite a number of vivid descriptions of the journey by river between Montreal and Ottawa by travellers of the time, all of which show what a pleasant way this was of journeying, without the pressures on time so prevalent today.

A typical journey from Ottawa would start after a comfortable night at one of the hotels then famous – the Brunswick, 'the best $1.00 or $1.50 a day House in Canada,' or the Grand Union, 'equipped with speaking tubes throughout.' The white-hulled steamer would leave promptly at 7:30 a.m., the first-class fare from Ottawa to Montreal, including the railway trip, being $2.50 one way or $4.00 return, meals – and what meals they were! – being 50 cents each. Grenville was reached at 12:50, fifteen minutes being allowed for transfer to the portage train and 35 minutes for its 12-mile journey. The Montreal-bound vessel would be waiting at the Carillon wharf, scheduled to leave at 1:45 p.m. and to arrive at Lachine at 5:25 p.m. Here the more nervous or hurried passengers could disembark and finish their journey to Montreal by train into the old Bonaventure Station. More adventurous passengers could stay on the vessel, which then ran the Lachine Rapids under expert pilotage, reaching her berth in Montreal harbour at 6:30 p.m. During the evening the ship returned to Lachine up the Lachine Canal to be ready for leaving her berth there at 8:00 next morning.

It was still possible to enjoy travel like this at the turn of the century and even to take the 'Triangle Tour' all by steamship. This justly famous trip included the journey from Lachine up the Ottawa River to Ottawa, then the transit of the Rideau Canal to Kingston, and finally descent of the St Lawrence back to Montreal. The tour took four days and three nights but cost only ten dollars apart from meals and hotel rooms and berths. Similar delights, but on smaller craft, were available well into the twentieth century on some of the rivers tributary to the Ottawa and also, strangely enough, on Lake Temiskaming despite the abandonment of all river passenger services between Ottawa and Mattawa. The *Meteor* and the *Temiskaming* were familiar sights on the long lake during summer months, continuing their service to the many small points around the shores until the mid-twenties.

The largest vessel to sail the Ottawa was the *Peerless*, which was also the first vessel to have an iron hull. Built in England, she was match-marked, disassembled, and shipped in sections to Canada, to be reassembled in a new shipyard located on the Ottawa shore of the river close to the location of the Ottawa Canoe Club of today. She was 210 feet long with a 28-foot beam and was licensed to carry 1,100 passengers. She must have been a grand sight steaming at full speed. Like all the other river steamers but one, she was a side paddle-wheeler. The one exception was a small vessel built in 1899, named the *Victoria*, which was equipped with screw propeller propulsion; she provided a local service between Thurso and Ottawa. There was a variety of such local services, in addition to the 'mail steamers,' as the daily Montreal-to-Ottawa steamers were proudly called, one even being known for many years as the 'market boat,' making a thrice-weekly journey from Lachine with stops at almost all the small wharves along the way. For most of the nineteenth century, wood was the universal fuel. It was cut in the forests along the banks into standard lengths which were then neatly stacked at strategically located loading points. 'Wooding-up' was a picturesque scene for observers but hard work for the men engaged upon it, even though their long-practised motions made it look like an easy task.

With the turn into the new century, the beginning of the end could be seen as railway services continued to improve and even roads came into use for some riverside traffic. In 1907 Captain Shepherd sold his famous river company to the Central Railway of Canada. The new owners continued to operate the service, and the portage railway, until 1910. In this same year Captain Shepherd died at the age of 85, his last years spent in his hospitable home at Como on the Lake of Two Mountains from which he was able to watch the changing river scene.

All the vessels that had been so well known on the Ottawa gradually disappeared. Some were burned, fortunately with no serious loss of life despite their wooden superstructures. Some were sold for scrap; some went on to other duties. Longest lived of all was the *Duchess of York*, which served as an excursion boat out of Montreal until 1938, sailing under the new name of *Beloeil*. I can recall seeing her on several occasions when I lived in Montreal in the mid-thirties. Eventually, she was sold for final service as a pulpwood barge and so passed from the river scene. Some of the old Ottawa River vessels have achieved recent publicity as members of the Underwater Society of Ottawa have explored old wrecks, retrieving a variety of articles from some of the vessels that once made the Ottawa so busy a river.

The river was busy not only with passengers but also with the carriage of freight. Freight downriver until well into the present century was predominantly sawn lumber, carried on barges hauled by tugs, of which there have been several famous fleets on the Ottawa. Freight coming upstream was mainly supplies for the developing settlements on the river, culminating in a regular supply of fuel oil to the Ottawa region until this could be conveyed by pipeline. For many years, large quantities of sand and gravel were mined around the Lake of Two Mountains and taken to Montreal, but this traffic has now (fortunately) been terminated. The maximum tonnage ever carried was in the year 1882, when 790,400 tons of freight were delivered after passage up and down the Ottawa. In more recent years the tonnage carried has been negligible but it amounted to over 200,000 tons per year until the Second World War.

Barges could not make use of any convenient portage arrangements and so had to use the Ottawa River canals. Although the canals were built and initially maintained as military works, the British government soon came to wish that they could be transferred to Canadian ownership, control, and operation. As early as 1848 the first offer was made, but the Province of Canada pleaded lack of funds and so nothing came of it, maintenance (such as it was) being still carried out by British troops. Not until March 1857 was the necessary order in council passed, placing the canals under the Commissioners of Public Works of the united province. One of the reasons for the delay was the desire of the provincial government to know exactly what it was they were being asked to take over. A great civil engineer of the day, Walter Shanley, was therefore directed to make a survey of the Ottawa River canals. This he did in 1856, finding the condition of the locks 'in bad order, some of them indeed in a ruinous condition.' He recommended some immediate repairs and these were put in hand as soon as responsibility for the canals was transferred.

Shanley naturally dealt in his report with the limiting dimensions of the upper three locks of the Grenville Canal, complaints about which from commercial interests were now serious. Proposals for the rebuilding of these three locks continued to be advanced but nothing was done until the appointment in November 1870 of a special commission to review the overall canal situation in Canada. Rebuilding of the Ottawa River canals was a prominent recommendation of the commission, and one that was adopted. Even before the main report had been submitted, rebuilding of the three narrow locks was started (in October 1870), but eventually the entire system was reconstructed, with locks 200 feet long and 45 feet wide, and 9 feet of water over sills, considerably larger than the dimensions of the Rideau Canal locks.

Advantage was taken of the rebuilding operation to change the layout of the Carillon Canal into a 'normal' canal with two locks, advanced excavation methods making this task now one of no unusual difficulty. At the same time, for the benefit of logging operations on the river, a crib dam was constructed across the river at Carillon, raising the water level above to an extent that flooded out the slight rise in the single lock at Chute à Blondeau. Rebuilding was a complex operation since the canals had to be kept in operation throughout (annual tonnage averaging then well over half a million) but by 1882 the task was complete. The new arrangement consisted of the Carillon Canal with two locks giving a total lift of 14 feet, and the Grenville Canal with five locks providing a total lift of 43 feet. The single lock in the Chute à Blondeau cut was removed, being now superfluous.

These were the Ottawa River canals as known to older Canadians. It is the upper or guard lock at Grenville that can still be seen, although without its lock gates, as noted at the start of this chapter. The rebuilt canals served well for eighty years, always well maintained, the grounds around the locks always a joy to see in summer. As freight traffic declined in the last two or three decades, pleasure boating increased, the number of vessels locked through in high summer reaching over a thousand in the first year of operation of the new lock and increasing since then. The canals remained in full use during the construction by Hydro Quebec of the great concrete dam at Carillon. For its completion, during the winter of 1963, the new structure had to be carried through the Carillon canal, river traffic in 1963 using for the first time the single lock provided as an integral part of the hydro-electric dam. This has dimensions of 188 feet by 45 feet and its lift is 65 feet, the one lock replacing the seven locks of the combined canals. It is electrically operated, in great contrast to the hand operation of the old canal locks. As one watches it in operation and admires the simple overall design of the dam, lock, and powerhouse, it is only with difficulty that one realizes that over 800,000 horsepower is being generated in this single plant. It is natural for all who know the history of the Ottawa River to think of what the river might have been like if similar dams had been erected, with navigation locks, at all the main rapids up to Mattawa and then up the Mattawa River. For this was a very serious proposal that came within an inch of actually being undertaken.

The idea of being able to sail vessels right up the Ottawa Waterway, circumventing portages by canals, had been a dream of long standing. As early as 1829 Colonel John By had commended it to his commanding officer at Quebec after the idea had been placed before him by an early settler at Fitzroy Harbour, Charles Shirriff. The idea was prominent in military thinking of the time, more especially after a naval base had been established at Penetanguishene on Georgian Bay. Young officers of the Royal Engineers made a number of surveys, the first in 1819, up the Ottawa and through what is now Algonquin Park, searching for the best route. Reports were made but nothing was done beyond the construction of the Ottawa River and Rideau canals. Military interest in the canalization of the entire Ottawa Waterway long continued, there being a reference in a printed report of the (British) Joint Naval and Military Committee of 23 April 1896 to the fact that the command of Lake Huron, in case of armed conflict (with the United States!) was out of the question until the Georgian Bay Ship Canal (as the project became known) was constructed.

This long-continuing British interest in the defence of Canada against possible attack from the United States will be so surprising to many readers that it may be observed that a complete volume has been written on this one subject, *Britain and the Balance of Power in North America: 1815–1908*, by Kenneth Bourne. Those interested in reading more about this little-known part of Canadian history will find much of interest in this book. There is one interesting record, however, that the volume mentions only very briefly. In 1865 another of the several joint naval-military studies of defence measures was undertaken by Admiral Sir James Hope, commanding at Halifax, and General Sir John Michel, the commander-in-chief of British forces in North America. They decided to see the full length of the Ottawa Waterway for themselves, enlisting the assistance of the Hudson's Bay Company for the provision of the necessary canoes, *voyageurs* and guide.

The only known records of the journey are contained in the reports made by Sir John Michel to the Duke of Cambridge, then commander-in-chief of the British army. These are now in the Royal Archives at Windsor Castle. The following brief quotations from two of Sir John's letters are given by gracious permission of Her Majesty the Queen. Writing from Toronto on 22 August 1865, Sir John explained:

The Inland defence of Canada is as much naval as Military, and I deferred my tour until the arrival of the Commander-in-Chief, Sir James Hope, at Quebec, in order that we might together see the country. We have just finished the civilized part of our tour, and we are going to start from the French River at Nipissing Lake, leaving civilization, postal communication etc. for almost twelve days. I consider this portion of the tour of vital importance both in a military and naval point of view.

Sir John was able to report to the Duke of Cambridge on the successful completion of their journey, in a letter written from Montreal on 12 September, just three weeks later. After explaining that, accompanied by Admiral Sir James Hope and 'one or two engineers,' they had proceeded up the French River, across Lake Nipissing and then down the Mattawa and Ottawa Rivers, he goes on to say:

We proceeded in native Bark Canoes, which I procured from the Hudson Bay Company, taking with us one of their principal factors. For the 1st 150 to 200 miles, we did not see a living soul. All was one wild solitude. The rivers were broad and deep, interspersed with rapids, and occasionally fine falls: whilst the banks were rocky and covered with pine trees.

Shooting the rapids, with the water surging and eddying round us was very enjoyable, and there was quite sufficient risk to make it exciting. The system (when striking a rock, on one's rapid descent, and thus injuring the Canoe bottom), of having the canoe on shore ten minutes afterwards and of having her bottom plastered with bark, and cemented with gum, was to me quite a new feature in dockyard work: more especially as in half an hour, the canoe was again afloat, as sound as ever.

That delightful expression 'dockyard work' must surely have come from the admiral!

The letters from which these extracts come were the personal reports of Sir John Michel to his chief. His official report was entitled 'The Reports on the Ottawa and French River Navigation Projects,' and it was accompanied by a special memorandum on 'Our Military Position in Canada' – documents which are mentioned to indicate the importance which was still attached, in 1865, to defence measures against the Americans. So keenly did General Michel feel about the matters which he had studied carefully that, in his second letter to the Duke of Cambridge, he said that from the report His Royal Highness would see 'the reasons that have made me so enthusiastic on the subject of the French River project: reasons of so imperial a nature, that I shall deem it my duty with the Governor General's concurrence to urge the same with all the arguments and weight that lies in my power.' When it is recalled that this military exploration of the Ottawa Waterway was made less than two years before Confederation, its significance will be at once apparent.

Just as occurred with the Ottawa River canals, so also in the proposals for this great canalization project, what started out as a purely military work was soon seen to have profound civilian significance, which gradually came to dominate all discussions. This is the more easily understood when it is realized that the use of the Ottawa instead of the St Lawrence route meant a saving in total distance to Montreal of almost three hundred miles. From Thunder Bay to Montreal by way of the St Lawrence is 1,216 miles; by way of the Ottawa it is only 934 miles. This saving in distance, in the opinion of the many proponents of the Ottawa route for the seaway – for that is what canalization of the Ottawa would have been – far outweighed the disadvantage of the extra lockage necessary in order to get over the height of land at the portage into Lake Nipissing.

Civilian interest in the proposal started with the decision of the government of Upper Canada to have more surveys made in 1835. Lieutenant Carthew, R.N., and Lieutenant Baddely, R.E., were commissioned to make the first survey, their findings as to the suitability of land for settlement (in what is now Algonquin Park) being pessimistic in comparison with earlier enthusiastic suggestions. A commission (with Baddely, now a captain, as a member) was appointed in 1836 to broaden these studies of possible settlement and of routes between the Ottawa and Lake Huron. Of special interest is the fact that among the surveyors engaged by the commission was David Thompson, one of the greatest of all Canadian explorers, then sixty-six years old and nearing the end of his great career. The survey through the Muskoka Lakes must have been almost a holiday for him; but his survey of the route to the Ottawa was finished only in mid-December, the latter part of his journey (down the Madawaska River) being a real ordeal, owing to the early advent of winter, as the diary that he kept showed clearly.

The main result of all these surveys was to confirm that by far the most desirable route from the Ottawa River to Georgian Bay was up what we have been calling the Ottawa Waterway – the Ottawa, the Mattawa, Lake Nipissing, and then the French River. Experienced river-men and fur traders could probably have proved this beyond a doubt. Their familiarity with this remarkable natural route was inevitably shared with the new settlers who gradually penetrated farther and farther up the Ottawa. As Bytown grew in size and in importance as the main centre on the river, the possibilities presented by the Ottawa route for commercial traffic must have been a frequent topic of conversation. A great dinner was held in 1851 under canvas in the vicinity of Wood's Hotel, west of the Uppertown Bytown Market, to discuss the project. Leading citizens invited members of the government of the united Province of Canada, a prominent figure at the banquet being John Egan, M.P. It must have been a really successful dinner since it apparently resulted in the vote of $50,000 in the government's next estimates for a small canal project at Chats Falls. This was, however, only a concession to mounting local interest, since what was needed was an overall engineering survey, upon which sound planning could be based.

Walter Shanley, who made the first detailed survey of the Ottawa River canals, was requested to extend his 1856 survey up the full length of the Ottawa Waterway. His own words were: 'I voyaged the whole of the above mentioned portion of the route, some 260 miles, by canoe ... and I reached the end of my journey strongly impressed with the conviction that nature had thus marked out a pathway in the desert that the Genius of Commerce will, at no far off day, render subservient to its end; the navigable connection of the Great Lakes with "La Grande Rivière du Nord," I look upon as inevitable.' This was to be the conviction that brought the Georgian Bay Ship Canal to the very brink of actuality in 1911 through the devoted efforts of its successive advocates.

Shanley prepared an approximate estimate of the cost of constructing the entire project, based upon his fine reconnaissance survey, his total for a ship canal with a depth of twelve feet of water throughout being $24 million. This was so vast a sum for those days that it was, perhaps, not too surprising that in 1859 another overall reconnaissance survey was carried out, and another estimate prepared, by T.C. Clarke, another civil engineer. His estimate was only $12,057,680, but the difference between the two figures was readily explained by the different approaches taken by the two engineers to the formation of the necessary canals. Clarke relied on dams to raise water levels to necessary heights; Shanley depended more upon the excavation of channels to the maximum extent possible. As can be imagined, the difference between the two estimates, despite the quite rational explanation, was to be the basis of many arguments, providing initial fuel to the fires of controversy that continued to surround the Ottawa River project until the 1920s.

Public controversy about developing so fine a river as the Ottawa may seem strange at first thought, but it gradually became clear that the strong objections to the canalization of the Ottawa that were mounted throughout all the years during which it was under discussion came mainly from those favouring the development of the St Lawrence route to the Great Lakes. As early as 1865, for example, in a book purporting to be a general survey of all Canadian canals, it was stated: 'The Ottawa route will not enlarge the commercial relations of the Province [Ontario] as a whole and is injurious to the west. It can be regarded in no other light than as a local improvement.' This was a very mild statement indeed compared to some of the vitriolic comments that were printed in the pamphlets prepared by both proponents and objectors in later years.

The appointment of royal commissions in Canada to investigate impartially debatable public projects is sometimes regarded as a modern development. Only three years after Confederation, however, the new Minister of Public Works recommended the appointment of a royal commission to review the adequacy of existing canals in Canada and the desirability of constructing any new ones. This was but the first of several commissions and committees that were called upon to consider the Ottawa River problem, as it had indeed become, few of the final reports being helpful to the governments of the day in assisting with any resolution of the issue.

As interest grew, it became clear that individual efforts were of them-

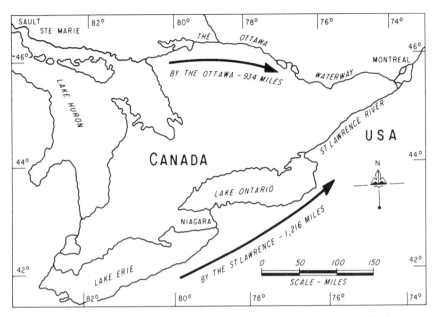

The two water routes from the West to Montreal; mileages from Thunder Bay.

selves insufficient; some corporate structure was necessary. There was therefore organized the Montreal, Ottawa, and Georgian Bay Canal Company in 1894, a former mayor of Ottawa, McLeod Stewart, being a leading participant. Thereafter, the name Georgian Bay Ship Canal was the generally accepted title for the great project – still a canalization project only, the possibility of developing power at each of the necessary dams being still in the future. The company was prominent in presenting evidence before a committee of the Senate of Canada, established in 1898 with the specific purpose of considering the Georgian Bay Ship Canal. One of the witnesses at the hearings was a Mr Meldrum, a senior member of the British firm of contractors, S. Pearson and Company of London. He stated that, having been approached by Mr Stewart, his firm was willing to undertake construction of the entire project if suitable financial guarantees could be arranged.

This brought the whole scheme into the realm of practical politics, the seriousness of those supporting it being made even more evident when a group of British financiers (known as the New Dominion Syndicate) bought a controlling interest in the company. A canal with a twenty-foot depth of water was now being proposed. So effective was the publicity put out by the company that even *The Times* of London had a long editorial extolling the advantages of the project, referring to it as a 'trump card.' More private surveys were made and proposals advanced to the government of the day, but it had already become clear that the public interest was so deeply involved that some action on the part of the government of Canada was essential. Accordingly, in 1904 Parliament authorized the expenditure of $250,000 on an entirely new survey. This was entrusted to engineers of the Department of Public Works, Arthur St Laurent being placed in charge under Eugene D. Lafleur, chief engineer of the department.

Mr St Laurent gathered together a remarkable group of fine engineers, the survey being organized under two able assistant engineers, one of whom – S.J. Chapleau – I had the pleasure of knowing in my first years in Canada. Sitting at his desk, I heard about the great work of thirty years earlier in carrying out a full survey of the entire route, preparing detailed designs of all dams, locks, and dredged channels, studying every conceivable aspect of ship canal construction and operation, and combining all the results into an integrated report. The final document was dated 20 January 1909; it was published in the rather dull-looking form of a sessional paper of Parliament. This volume of 600 pages is, however, one of the finest engineering reports ever produced in the history of Canada; it can be read with pleasure and profit even today, for its thoroughness and readability are exemplary. Right at the start come these blunt words: 'a 22-foot waterway for the largest lake boats (600 ft. x 60 ft., x 20 ft. draft) can be established for one hundred million dollars ($100,000,000) in ten years, and that annual maintenance will be approximately $900,000, including the operation of storage reservoir for the better distribution of the flood waters of the Ottawa River.'

Publication of the report made public discussion of the Georgian Bay Ship Canal much more realistic than had previously been possible. How the discussion did continue can best be imagined, this being near the close of Sir Wilfrid Laurier's Liberal government with its record of lavish financial support for railway construction all across Canada. Sir Wilfrid was even presented with a petition urging construction of the Georgian Bay project, signed by 110 members of the House of Commons. Suffice it to say that in preparation for the election of 1911 Sir Wilfrid committed his government to proceed with construction if the Liberal Party was returned to power. But this was the 'Reciprocity Election' and, although the Georgian Bay project was a prominent topic on the hustings, the election was lost on the issue of reciprocity and all hope for the project was an automatic casualty.

Sir Robert Borden became Prime Minister in the new Conservative government. He faced great problems from the start of his administration, not the least being the financial difficulties caused by the profligate expenditure on railways, and the threat of the First World War loomed up before he had been able to get the country's economy again on an even keel. Pressure for the building of the Ottawa River project continued, however, a large deputation from the valley going to see the Prime Minister on 14 March 1912 and an even larger delegation (1,500) from Montreal in 1914 to see the Minister of Public Works. Polite but noncommittal replies were all that the delegations received.

The pamphleteering continued, reaching the peak of vituperation. The outbreak of war, however, put a sudden stop to all such agitation, although the strangest of all the royal commissions involved with the Ottawa project was appointed in 1916; it never did submit a final report. And without any publicity, a start at building a great new Welland Canal (still in use today, as a part of the St Lawrence Seaway) had been authorized just before the outbreak of war, an action that really cast the die against the Ottawa Seaway, even though this may not have been realized at the time.

When active discussion was resumed after the close of the war, a new complication had been introduced, this being the possibility of developing power from the falling water at each of the dams proposed for the canalization project. Power developments at Niagara Falls had shown the world the remarkable potentialities of water power but on the Ottawa even this new concept was itself complicated by arguments between the government of Canada and the provincial governments of Ontario and Quebec about where the authority lay for development of interprovincial water power. And to compound the situation still further, the British financiers behind the company now transferred their rights to a new Canadian group in which the Sifton interests were dominant.

Debate between the proponents of public as compared with private power development was mounting in intensity. The stage was set, therefore, for a head-on confrontation when the charter of the Georgian Bay Company came up for renewal before the House of Commons, since the charter carried with it the right to develop power. Debate on the private bill authorizing a renewal of the company's charter commenced on 25 February 1927. The debate was long and acrimonious, the record filling some four hundred pages of Hansard. Committee procedure had to be changed so that the debate could continue in its hearings. Eventually the committee reported against the bill to the House of Commons on 7 April 1927. So the charter lapsed. This was, in effect, the end of the hopes of a century.

Quebec and Ontario reached a statesmanlike agreement for the development of power on the Ottawa, once they had been given the right to develop it jointly. But the only water-power dam that has been equipped with a ship lock is that at Carillon, despite the fact that the Ottawa is a navigable waterway and thus under the ultimate juri diction of the government of Canada. The dream of the Georgian Bay Ship Canal still persists, however, despite the neglect of navigation in the design of the dams. Deputations still come to Ottawa occasionally urging reconsideration of the project. In the late fifties an Ottawa River Development Association was formed with the avowed purpose of promoting the construction of a waterway twenty-seven feet deep from the St Lawrence at least as far as Ottawa. But with the completion of the St Lawrence Seaway and its commercial success, there would seem to be little possibility of any further serious consideration being given officially to a parallel Ottawa Seaway. And yet ... for I, too, have glimpsed the dream!

Was nothing at all, then, built above the Chaudière, despite all the talk and the arguments of a century? Plans were, indeed, prepared for a canal to bypass the Chaudière itself but nothing was ever done to implement them. We have seen how the sum of $50,000 was granted for canalization around Chats Falls and a start made at this remarkable project, probably the most political of all the canal works ever started in Canada. A canal just under three miles long (roughly parallel to the horse-railway) was planned, all the excavation to be in solid rock, six locks being necessary to pass vessels up or down the drop between the two lakes. A contract for the work was awarded in June 1854 and excavation did start. With the rather primitive rock excavation methods of those days, the difficulties can be imagined, especially since the material to be penetrated was unusually tough Precambrian rock. Complaints from the contractor started soon after the work had begun and continued with mounting urgency until the work was finally stopped in November 1856. By that time, almost half a million dollars had been spent for the excavation of a few hundred feet of the canal (which may still be seen, now remote in the bush near Quyon) and the opening up of a quarry to furnish stones for the masonry locks – but on the *south* bank of the river, politics of the time being what they were. Naturally, work was never resumed and so the great rock cut remains today as almost the only physical evidence of the hopes once entertained for making the Ottawa River a highway of international commerce.

Almost – but not quite, since in a much more remote area there is still another memorial to the politics of an earlier day, reflected in another abortive attempt to canalize a part of the Ottawa. It may be recalled that, as shown on the map on page 24, there were two water routes available around

Allumette Island. That generally used by the fur-trade brigades was to the north of the island, the Culbute Channel, featured by strong rapids to the west of Chapeau. These rapids impeded the navigation of steam vessels beyond Chapeau. Another of the visionary ideas for canalizing a section of the Ottawa was therefore to construct an impounding dam at the Culbute Rapids and install two locks adjacent to it so that vessels could be locked up to the level of the Long Reach and thus sail unimpeded up to Des Joachims. This project must often have been discussed in the Pembroke area since it is an obvious river improvement, which was featured in early plans for the Georgian Bay Ship Canal. It was not, however, until 1872 that the idea was resurrected, and then in connection with a bitterly fought general election in which Sir Francis Hincks attempted to retain the Pembroke seat which he had won in a by-election in 1869. Details of the political negotiations are, perhaps, best forgotten but engineers of the Department of Public Works were instructed to prepare plans for the necessary dam and dual ship locks.

The dam had to be 520 feet long; the locks were to be 200 feet long and 45 feet wide, with just three sets of gates since they were in tandem. A contract was awarded and the works were finished by November 1876 at a total cost of $235,808. This low figure is readily explained by the fact that all the structures, including the locks, were built of wood, hewn from trees in the forest around. The feelings of the residents of Pembroke at the possibility of being thus bypassed by all vessels using the new locks can be imagined. But a fixed bridge had been built somehow across the approach channel and so larger vessels were unable to use the locks until this had been replaced by a swing bridge. This was not done until 1880 and by that time the coming of the railway to Pembroke had provided the final answer, all passenger traffic on this part of the Ottawa having been abandoned in 1879 as we have already seen. Although used by a few small vessels for a few years, the Culbute Locks were really outmoded before they were finished. Official recommendations for their abandonment were made in 1888 and they were discarded in 1889. Derelict in the woods, the exposed woodwork of the locks was burned in 1912, surely the only example in history of navigation locks being destroyed by fire.

So completely are the remains hidden in the woods and so remote from the routes of any normal travel, that they are virtually forgotten. The timbers of the lock floors, however, are still in sound condition, having been always submerged, and the cribs of the dam are still to be seen. To stand there, in the quiet of the forest enlivened only by the roar of the nearby rapids is indeed an eerie experience, especially as one thinks of the century that has passed since such an enthusiastic start was made at building this small section of what might have been the Ottawa Seaway. Disappointment might well be a dominating thought but not if one turns one's mind to all that has taken place in the Ottawa Valley in this same century, even without the building of the Georgian Bay Ship Canal – to the cities that have grown up, dominated by the beautiful capital city of the Dominion, the great industrial plants that border the river shores, the majestic water-power plants that have tamed the wildness of the rapids.

Settlement of the Ottawa Valley is, in itself, an inspiring story to which we must now turn, keeping in mind that much of the development was possible only through the service of the river steamers down the years and the convenience provided by the Ottawa River canals, even though they were initially constructed for defence against attacks that, happily, never came.

# SEVEN

# Settlement on the Ottawa

The first European settlements on the Ottawa River were the early forts. The fort at Senneville, built in 1686, has already been mentioned; its ruins remain to this day. There was another one, however, of possibly more strategic importance, constructed on an island in the Lake of Two Mountains after it had been granted to Philippe de Rigaud, Marquis de Vaudreuil, as part of the Seigniory of Vaudreuil. Construction started in 1704. Almost all signs of the fort and its service buildings have gone and so it has been largely forgotten. Its foundations are crossed by a modern highway. Motorists heading west from Montreal on Highway 40 seldom notice that they are crossing the site of the old fort on the island with the lovely name of Île aux Tourtes, island of the turtle doves.

Prior to the construction of the great new road, Île aux Tourtes was a quiet rural islet, fitting well into the natural beauty of the lake, and displaying only to the expert eye a few signs of its former activity. It has now become little more than a convenient foundation for the roadbed and supporting piers of the highway. But in 1702 it was granted to Vaudreuil for the construction of a fort in the King's service, with associated rights of high, middle, and low justice and the privilege of hunting, fishing, and trading with the Indians. A Sulpician mission was established on the island under Abbé de Breslay, for which the King granted a pension of four hundred *livres*. It seems certain that a small chapel was constructed and this seems to have been used for Indian services well into the latter part of the eighteenth century. Both the fort and the mission had been abandoned, however, by 1726, the Sulpicians having already moved across the lake to

Oka, where another fort was established in 1721. Much dissension surrounded Vaudreuil's administration, especially with regard to the perennial problem of liquor. It seems probable that the Sulpician fathers made their move across the ice of the lake in order to remove themselves from this illicit traffic and other trials arising from contacts with travellers on the Ottawa. The mission they founded at Oka still continues, although under the Trappist Order since 1881. The seven little shrines that still exist, built between 1739 and 1749, are probably the oldest buildings now in the Ottawa Valley.

Île aux Tourtes achieved some fame when in May 1776 250 American prisoners of war were conveyed to it by boats across the lake from Fort Senneville. Their stay was brief; they were soon transported to military headquarters near Vaudreuil. There is a story that two men were left on the island and were later rescued by some of Benedict Arnold's troops, their condition when found being so serious that the Continental Congress made a formal protest to the British government – probably the only occasion in history when exposure to the famed mosquitoes of the Ottawa Valley resulted in diplomatic action. At an earlier date, the Abbé de Breslay fell while crossing the ice of the lake in winter from Île aux Tourtes to the island of Montreal. He injured his leg but survived, attributing his deliverance to Ste Anne, in whose honour he built a small church close to the nearby rapids, predecessor of the church at Ste Anne de Bellevue. Although, therefore, this early fort did not provide a continuous settlement as did Fort Frontenac at Kingston, it was important in its day; it was related to the start of Oka and its famous mission; and it led to the founding of Ste Anne's Church. But the turtle doves have long since gone; only the lovely name remains.

Permanent settlement in the Ottawa Valley started on the attractive Lake of Two Mountains, close to the Island of Montreal. From the earliest days of active fur trading there were a few settlers who built small homes along the main river but none of these appear to have led directly to the establishment of any permanent settlements. Even the five seigniories on the river, although all granted well before the end of the French régime, did not attract any significant settlement until around the end of the eighteenth century. Unlike the early British administrators, the officials of New France did not, in general, encourage settlement, in great contrast with the efforts of devoted Roman Catholic priests. As a result, many riverfront lots were surveyed only towards the end of the eighteenth century, and the nineteenth century had begun before any large number of settlers went up the Ottawa.

Settlement of the valley, therefore, is generally a development of the last century and a half with a steadily unfolding pattern, travel up the river being first by canoe and batteau; then by early steamboats, with some use of the primitive roads at the lower end of the valley; next by the early railways after they had pushed their way up the valley in the closing decades of the century, with an increasing use of the better roads that were gradually to be found around the major settlements. So complex is the overall pattern of settlement that all we can try to do is sketch some of the more personal aspects of the use of the river by early settlers, always remembering how interlocked the general pattern was with the development of the lumber trade and the associated growth of steamboat traffic.

Perhaps the most surprising feature is that the St Lawrence route (through Prescott) was the main means of access for most of the early settlers in the great plain between the two rivers, rather than the Ottawa route. Even Lanark County was first peopled by those who came up from the St Lawrence, often through Perth, although upriver from this justly famous county the Ottawa did become the route of the pioneers. Correspondingly, it was the banks of the St Lawrence that proved attractive to the United Empire Loyalists when they reached Canada in their great migration, and only relatively few journeyed on up to the Ottawa. There is, therefore, no very strong U.E.L. tradition in the valley but other loyalties were brought from afar, soon to be welded into a loyalty to the valley itself that is still a splendid contribution to the cultural life of Canada.

Let us now go back to the early settlements around the Lake of Two Mountains, remembering the pioneer establishment of Oka on yet another of the outlying seigniories, this one in the possession of the Seminary of Montreal. The settlement followed from earlier Indian encampments and always attracted Indians as residents; Thomas Keefer recorded that around 1850 the Iroquois and Algonquins were living there quietly together, separated only by the street between them. The Vaudreuil seigniory, granted in 1702, was surveyed for settlement as early as 1732 and some *voyageurs* came there to make their homes. Few records remain of their lives although it is known that Jean Baptiste Sabourin was one of two settlers who married girls who had been captured by Indians living at Oka in raids upon the Puritan settlements around Boston – a reminder that those days of settlement were not too far removed from the time of Indian warfare. The first English settler owned the lot next to the Sabourins. Other settlers followed, in such numbers that in 1805 the Bishop of Quebec sent up the river the first resident Anglican priest on the Ottawa, Reverend Richard Bradford. He made his headquarters on the north shore of the river, serving also the present districts of St Andrews and Cushing.

The area was still well forested in those early days; there is, indeed, a local tradition that one of the great pines on what was the Awde property (now Fogarty's) was taken across the Atlantic and used as a mast on one of Nelson's battleships. Other local products were barley, said to have been grown for the breweries in Montreal, and ginseng, which was processed as an early medicine. Even more remarkable, however, was the glass industry that developed here, starting about 1850, there being at one time three active glass-making plants. The local sand proved to be an excellent raw material. So important was the industry that the local post office was known as *Ottawa Glass Works Post Office* until about 1885, when the name Como was officially adopted. Some of the glass blowers came from the United States but returned after the end of the Civil War since cheap American glass then flooded the small Canadian market, putting all the Como works out of business.

Strong links with the river have always featured the Como area, first through the *voyageur* settlers and later through the century-long association with the Shepherd steamship family. Captain R.W. Shepherd was long a leading figure in the community. He was one of the founders of the first Anglican church in this district, St James's at what is now Hudson Heights; and he was the leading contributor, in time, effort, and money, to the start of St Mary's Church, Como. This little church was dedicated in September 1869 by the new Bishop of Montreal, who recorded that this was his first episcopal act: 'Our party, which numbered eight or ten ... left Montreal by train for Lachine, where we took the steamer, and at twelve o'clock arrived at Como. We had been detained for nearly two hours by a river fog, and found the congregation waiting for us ... Not one of our party was allowed to pay for our voyage, or for our journey by rail; such is the liberality one meets with in this country.' Even as the century neared its close, river traffic still was such that Captain Shepherd's daughter could recall that the river 'seemed carefree, alive and stirring. Puffing, sturdy tugs with bright blue barges in tow added romance to the water highway. A pulsating throb would sound far up the river. It seemed to reverberate through the Oka hills. The sound swelled into a rhythmic boom ... the tug, with its double row of barges might appear at any moment.'

At the head of the lake began the rough water dominated by the Long Sault that created such a barrier to upriver travel. Before the Carillon rapid was reached, however, the mouth of the North River was passed on the north shore. This led to the third of the river seigniories, that of Argenteuil, the name still carried by the county in this area. This was granted on 15 June 1682 by Count Frontenac to Charles Joseph d'Ailleboust. It started with a few settlers in 1785, two years after the first land surveying had been done on the Crown lands that adjoined the seigniory to the west. The first range, the lots on the north bank of the river, was naturally the most valuable. Settlement started here in 1788 but proceeded so slowly that Major Murray, the current owner, was in Montreal in 1801 trying to persuade immigrants to settle in his area. The region to the west had been designated as the District of Chatham, the river lots being known as 'The Front' of Chatham (an expression often encountered in the old records).

All the early settlers came from Montreal by boat, usually in batteaux, travel being so slow that it sometimes took them three or even four days between Montreal and St Andrews. In this way the Scottish settlers who formed the community of Lachute came to their new homes. There were already mills at both St Andrews and St Eustache when the first Lachute settlers arrived between 1803 and 1805, bringing with them their skills in weaving that are reflected in the industry of Lachute to this day. One of the early visitors to Lachute was Captain John By, who came in 1810 with Rev. R. Bradford to investigate the water-power potential of the Lachute Falls before he returned to Canada in 1826 to direct the building of the Rideau Canal. By was not impressed by the power potential at Lachute, although others proceeded to use it for industrial purposes. The fact that brick-making had started here before 1812 is some indication of the start of small industries in this pleasant area, notably the establishment between 1803 and 1805 of the first paper mill in Canada, at St Andrews. It was started by a group of New Englanders and later operated by James Brown, a stationer of Montreal. This was the beginning of one of Canada's greatest industries. Rags were used initially; the use of wood pulp developed later in the century.

These fledgling industries were well served by the new steamboat service from Montreal as soon as it was in regular operation, replacing the earlier packet service by batteaux. It was then possible also to reach the St Andrews district along one of the first roads up the valley. By the 1820s a line of covered stagecoaches was being operated from Montreal to St Andrews and on to Grenville, four horses to each coach, but so bad was the road that the journey took three days. The roads were mainly used for walking, records of marathon walks being not uncommon – for example, that of Dr John Bigsby from Hawkesbury to Montreal, previously described. On the other side of the river, a man named E. Pridham is said to have found it quicker to walk to Montreal from Grenville than to paddle down the river! He was reported to be able to walk from Pointe Fortune to Montreal in two days in summer and to return in three. He would have had to cross the Ottawa to use this route but pioneer ferries were probably in operation both above the rapids, at Grenville, and at their foot between Carillon and Pointe Fortune, soon after the first settlers came.

Roads on both sides of this section of the river were clearly an early necessity; corresponding to the road from St Andrews to Grenville, therefore, was one from Pointe Fortune to L'Orignal. A crude form of stagecoach used this road, poor as it must have been, in order to connect the first steamers on the upper and lower sections of the river. Just as soon as the portage railway was in operation, however, use of the portage roads lapsed and road transport did not become significant again for many years. Even the roadway that was cleared by the government of Lower Canada between Grenville and Hull about 1830 was but little used and reverted to bush, for the numerous stream and river crossings necessary, without the advantage of any bridges, made the journey along it as hazardous as it was tedious. Steamship was the preferred mode of travel until the coming of the railways.

It was at Pointe Fortune that John Macdonnell settled in 1813 after his experiences as a member of the North West Company. At the rapids he constructed a small canal and a lock, beside which he built a fine stone house combined with a grist- and sawmill. The basement of this structure was open so that boats could enter it. The cargoes to be shipped were placed on a platform in the basement so that they might be loaded directly into boats moored alongside. This could well have been one of the first 'modern transhipment terminals' on the waterways of Canada. Its construction indicates the close connection of John Macdonnell with shipping on the Lake of Two Mountains. He operated a service using batteaux, and later Durham boats, between Pointe Fortune and Vaudreuil in the first two decades of the century, until they were displaced by steamboats. He experienced many troubles with his enterprises but was made a colonel in the Prescott Militia and a judge in the Ottawa District, becoming a notable public figure.

Those who had to work their boats up the rapids were aided to a slight degree by some improvements that had been made to the northern rocky shore along the Long Sault. Some of the glacial boulders that were scattered all along this shore had been moved so as to form small 'canals,' some of these being inshore of the small islands that were to be found along the bank. Canoes and batteaux could be hauled through these channels a little more easily than in the open water of the river. Although they were later still further improved – almost certainly by the men of the Royal Staff Corps, since marks of drill steel were recently found on some of the boulders that had been split – these little aids to navigation may have dated from the early years of the century, if only because they were locally known as Treadwell Trenches. Nathaniel Hazard Treadwell was the owner of the fourth seigniory on the river, located on the south shore at the head of the Long Sault, the only seigniory to be granted in what became Upper Canada after 1791.

Treadwell was one of the numerous American settlers who came to the Ottawa around the turn of the century. Many of them, unlike Philemon Wright, gave up the hard life they found and returned to the south about the time of the War of 1812. Treadwell was no exception. The seigniory had been granted originally to Baron de Longeuil, but Treadwell, who had been born in Plattsburg, New York, where he had married, came to Canada in 1794 and purchased the seigniory for one thousand guineas. Active in opening up the land, Treadwell himself settled on the banks of the Ottawa at what is now L'Orignal. In 1812, however, he refused to take the oath of allegiance and was imprisoned in consequence for a short time at St Johns, Quebec, before being allowed to return to Plattsburg where he quickly built up a new milling business. His son, Charles Platt Treadwell, returned to Canada in 1823 and after prolonged negotiations repossessed his father's property and began to develop it as an integrated community. Well respected, the son was appointed High Sheriff for the district in 1834 and held this office until he died in 1873 at the age of seventy-one. Nathaniel Treadwell lost all his property at Plattsburg in 1830 and ten years later rejoined his son at L'Orignal, where he continued to live until his death in 1856. He was then described by the Montreal *Gazette* as combining 'the culture of a gentleman with the endurance of a backwoodsman.'

There exists a small plan of the Treadwell establishment as it was in 1833. Located on the Grand River, (the old name of the Ottawa being then still in use), it included, below a small dam on the mill stream, a two-storey stone grist mill and a sawmill on a stone foundation with a pail factory below. Other indications of the domestic economy of the time are the smokehouse used to dry staves, a stone arch for the potash kettle, and an outdoor oven for baking. This interesting record is contained in a small collection of Treadwell papers now in the archives of Queen's University. Most of the letters to and from Charles Treadwell related to land boundaries and sales, but repeated references to journeys on the river show that throughout his life it was the only means of transport up and down the valley.

Charles Treadwell was a man of many interests. He shipped his fine ground flour to different locations along the valley including Caledonia Springs, which was already being developed as a health spa. (In July 1849,

Treadwell shipped six dozen bottles of spring water from 'The Springs' to the Honourable John Beverley Robinson.) The rise and decline of Caledonia Springs is another of the little-known stories of the valley. For a short period, it appears that some sort of tramway was operated from the Ottawa River to Caledonia Springs to convey passengers from the river boats to the fine hotels that were being established to serve the Springs. No records have been traced that tell anything about this tramway but there are frequent references to coaches waiting for the arrival of the boat from Montreal in order to convey passengers to the health spa.

Perhaps of most significance was Treadwell's capacity for attracting fine people to settle on his lands. Thomas Mears of Vermont was another of the American settlers thus attracted to what is now Hawkesbury. He was a builder of boats and many other things, including a sawmill and a grist mill at St Andrews; he was one of those responsible for the first little paper mill. But he wanted to build other mills and so bought from Nathaniel Treadwell two islands and a large area of land at the head of the Long Sault, constructing between the islands a dam and a series of flumes, water from which operated a larger mill. In 1807 he sold this property, after three years of operation, to two brothers named Hamilton who had come to Canada, along with a third brother, from near Dublin, Ireland. One brother went back to Liverpool to raise funds for the big industry they hoped to establish, and did; a second one stayed in Quebec to arrange for the shipment of lumber; the third, George Hamilton, remained on the Ottawa where his name is still to be recognized in Hamilton Island, the large island just to the west of Sir George Perley Bridge at Hawkesbury.

This is the Hamilton we met when considering the early days of the lumber business on the Ottawa, for he was the founder of Hamilton's Mills and a truly great entrepreneur. He quickly developed a small town around his mills and a farm on which he grew winter feed for his teams of oxen and, later, horses. He was visited by Dr John Bigsby in 1819 when an outbreak of typhoid fever attacked his settlement. Worse was to come, for in 1822 he first lost his brother in England, the financier, with consequent money worries; a great spring flood carried away his main dam and many logs were lost; fire destroyed his house; and when he and his wife set off shortly by boat after this, with their three small sons, an accident caused the boat to capsize. The boys were drowned and Mrs Hamilton was saved only through the heroic efforts of her husband and the boatmen. George Hamilton was a man of great courage, however; he surmounted all these trials. His wife fully recovered her health and bore him another family of four more sons and two daughters. As Lieutenant Colonel of the Prescott Militia he played an active part in the suppression of the rebellion of 1837; but he contracted a cold in those troublesome days and in 1839 died from its effects.

Some idea of George Hamilton's character is given by the fact that he used to keep in touch with another early settler across the river at Grenville by a system of signals, believed to have been flags. This friend was Major MacMillan, the leader of one of the groups of Highlanders who came out to settle in the new land. He had taken up land at Grenville in 1810, the road to Grenville being known as the 'Scotch Road' for many years thereafter. It is

small wonder that it was once said that on the Ottawa in these early days one could have held a roll call of all the clans at Culloden.

The Hamilton family gave much to the Ottawa Valley, not least through the lifetime of service of George Hamilton's fourth son, Charles, to the Anglican Church of Canada. He became the first Anglican Bishop of Ottawa in 1896 and later, in 1912, the first Metropolitan (Archbishop) of Ontario. He lived until his eighty-sixth year, dying in La Jolla, California, in March 1919. This saintly man is still recalled with affection by older residents of the valley. His close connection with the lumber trade makes it entirely appropriate that the episcopal coat of arms for the Ottawa Diocese has as its main feature 'on a chief azure a ducal coronet or issuant therefrom an oak tree proper penetrated transversely with a frame saw proper.' (It might better have been a white pine tree.) One wonders how many loyal Anglicans, not to mention their fellow residents in the diocese, have ever noticed this symbol of the link between Church and the timber of the valley.

Sixteen miles upstream from L'Orignal on the north shore was the fifth and last seigniory on the Ottawa, that of La Petite Nation, so named because of the river flowing through the beautiful area embraced by the seigniory, the only one that looks today not unlike what it must have done when first granted to Bishop Laval in May 1674. It passed into the possession of the Seminary of Quebec from which it was bought in 1801 by J.H. Papineau, a wealthy notary of Montreal. Some development was carried out, mainly on an area at what is now Montebello, including the building in 1851 of a stone manor house which still stands. It was to this lovely place that the first owner's son retired when he returned from exile in France after the troubles of 1837 were over, and forsook the world of politics, his name being one that will always figure in Canada's history – Louis-Joseph Papineau, long the speaker of the House of Assembly of Lower Canada. A visitor records that in the 1860s

'He took an interest in all that was going on, and from the banks of the Ottawa surveyed the changes that were taking place around. He revelled in books. A tower of four or five stories high held a mass of information which a life-time longer than his could scarcely enable any one to digest. His mansion was a French château. There were chapels and servants' residences on his grounds which are undulating and tastefully laid out. Walks meandering through green parterres and primeval forest. There was a rivulet and there was a deer park in the vicinity. The peacock screamed, the fowls cackled, the cattle lowed, and all was peace, where, retired from men and the ordinary cares of man, the Honourable Louis Joseph Papineau was yet, until his 85th year, permitted to view human progress in a country which he had governed if not ruled, and to which he had drawn particularly European attention more than any person previously had ever done ... the Demosthenes of Canada, on the banks of the Grand River.

Papineau's library came to be famous. It was visited and used by Francis Parkman. The peace and quiet that pervade Montebello even today can almost explain the vehement protest that Papineau made against any change in the seigniorial system in Quebec. 'I am a great reformer in the matter of necessary political changes,' he proudly stated, 'but I am a great conservative in the matter of the preservation of the sacred right of Property.' And yet it was here that a later political activist, Henri Bourassa, the grandson of J.H. Papineau, spent some formative years, though born in Montreal (in 1868). He was elected mayor of Montebello at the age of twenty-one. In 1896 he was elected to Parliament as the Member for Labelle, the constituency of which Montebello was the centre. This was the start of another turbulent career in political life which seems far removed from the rural beauty of the Petite Nation seigniory. But when one heard Bourassa speak about Canada, as I once did, one knew that one was listening to a man whose roots were deep in the land. At that time I knew nothing of his connection with Montebello nor did I ever think that the day would come when I would be writing about the influence on him of an Ottawa River seigniory.

At Montebello, we are now on the long stretch of quiet water that extended from the head of the Long Sault all the way up to the Chaudière. Once the great barrier of the lower rapids was surmounted, travel on the river was easy for sixty miles, with another stretch of level water in Lac Deschenes once the Chaudière and the rapids above had been bypassed either by portage or, in later years, by the toll road to Aylmer. The first man to make this long journey of 150 miles from Montreal as a settler was Joseph Mondion, who brought his family in 1786 and established a little home on a low rocky point on the north shore of the river just below Chats Falls. But the isolation must have proved too much for him, since he sold his property to Montreal merchants just after the turn of the century and returned to civilization. His name, however, remains on the maps to this day, Mondion's Point being well known to sailors on Lac Deschenes.

Philemon Wright remains as the true pioneer settler upstream of the seigniories. He came in 1800, as we have already seen, with his family, and he stayed, the Wright name still being an honoured one in Ottawa and Hull. He was soon followed, however, since in March 1801 Abijah Dunning and his four sons settled at what is now Cumberland, having secured 800 acres in four lots. Very quickly they obtained 1,200 acres in the township of Buckingham and 1,200 acres in the township of Onslow, and thus began another valued family connection, which also continues to this day, with the Ottawa Valley between Hawkesbury and Ottawa.

The Dunnings found it hard going to clear the heavily wooded land round Cumberland and so moved down-river to a new location on what they called 'Treadwell's Seigniory.' Some of the family later moved to Vankleek Hill and finally to East Templeton, where the head of the family died at the age of seventy-five. One of the sons moved back to Cumberland and was active in the lumber business. Any such changes of location necessitated travel on the river, either by boat in the summer or over the ice in the winter. It was in these ways that all supplies were received from Montreal. Some of the prices charged at the early settlement of Cumberland are revealing. Tea was $1.50 to $2.00 a pound but salt only $2.00 a bushel. Board nails were 40 cents a pound, but gunpowder only $1.00 to $1.50 a pound. 'Jamaica spirits' (presumably rum) cost $4.00 a gallon.

There are no very large settlements between Hawkesbury and Buckingham even today, Thurso being one of the more recently developed. Lumbering is still an important activity. But in those early days, hopes were high for extensive settlement, as evidenced by the appointment in 1830 of commissioners to explore the country between the St Maurice and the Ottawa. A survey was made, which reported optimistically on the possibilities for settlement of this still sparsely populated region. Two young army officers and a surveyor, assisted by an Indian and some experienced woodsmen, formed the party which left the Grenville Canal on 28 September 1830, reaching Trois Rivières on 18 November after a final forced march. Little resulted from this study; transport was still the problem. And so settlement continued to be confined generally to the banks of the Ottawa and its major tributaries.

It may be recalled that John McLean was sent by the Hudson's Bay Company in 1826 up the Lièvre River to the Company's post at Lac des Sables, about fifty miles from the mouth. There he found a comfortable dwelling-house and a well-developed small farm. He stayed until 1833 and the post lasted until 1849, when it was closed and replaced by a small store at Buckingham. Justus Smith was the first settler here, coming from Montreal in 1823. The potential power from the great falls at Buckingham was a natural attraction and sawmills had a long history here, but by the turn of the century there were still less than five hundred families. It required the development of a major power plant and the associated manufacture of pulp and paper to bring the town to its present position. Long before this, however, the Lièvre had featured some interesting small mining developments; but the limitations of transport by water probably influenced the relatively short duration of these ventures.

Moving upstream to the Gatineau, we are reminded that Philemon Wright and his family and associates had been steadily developing their settlement at Hull since their arrival in 1800. They explored the Gatineau and started to take timber from it, the 'Gatineau Privilege' being an indication of its value. Tiberius Wright had developed a fine 2,000-acre farm at the first falls on the Gatineau, but he was forced to sell this in 1834. He made an agreement with an English gentleman who had fled to Canada after the Reform Bill of England threatened his way of life. This was William Farmer, after whom Farmer's Rapids and the modern power plant are named. Farmer was not a very practical sort of settler, however, being really an English Tory squire. In 1855 he gave up the battle and disappeared from the Gatineau and Ottawa scene, leaving his name behind him.

We have now reached the sites of Hull and the capital city of Ottawa. It is difficult to imagine what a wonderfully beautiful but singularly effective barrier to travel on the Ottawa the Chaudière used to present. The clutter of nondescript buildings that are such a lamentable legacy from Victorian days, even though well maintained and containing today sophisticated equipment, almost completely screen what was once a mighty waterfall. Hurrying across the Chaudière bridges gives one no opportunity for even a glance at what little can still be seen; but if the automobiles be left for once and a walk taken instead, especially at the height of the spring flood, the sight of the water coming through the curved control dam is still inspiring. The exposed limestone rock ledges that can still be seen give at least a glimpse of the majesty of the falls in their natural condition. If we go into the small parking lot outside the Hydro Quebec Station on the Hull side of the main steel truss bridge, we can see one of the elegant masonry arches of the original bridge across the Ottawa, the first of all the bridges that were eventually to span the river. It was started in 1826 but there were plans for the development of settlements on both banks long before this.

The War of 1812 had alarmed the British government in several ways, one of these being the number of Americans who had settled in Upper Canada. As soon as the war was over, therefore, the Earl of Bathurst, Secretary for War and the Colonies, proposed emigration from Great Britain to ensure a loyal population in Canada, a matter about which there had been some doubt during the war. A proclamation was posted in Edinburgh, Scotland, early in 1815 offering those who wished to emigrate free passage to Canada and one hundred acres of free land in either Upper or Lower Canada, together with supplies for the first six months. Four shiploads sailed in the late summer of that year, most of the emigrants on board proceeding up the St Lawrence to Prescott or Brockville, thence travelling by trails through the bush to the areas set aside for settlement. Perth, established in 1816, was the main new centre.

Surveying of the townships in the Ottawa-St Lawrence plain proceeded rapidly and other sites for permanent settlements were considered. It was clear to the military authorities that for sites closer to the Ottawa, travel up that river would provide a shorter route than up the St Lawrence. I have always wondered if those who made decisions based on this geographical fact had themselves ever had to come up the Long Sault. Be that as it may, four hundred men of the 99th Regiment of Foot, upon being disbanded at Quebec in the early summer of 1818, elected to take up the offer of lands on the Jock River at what is now Richmond. They and their families were transported in Durham boats and batteaux up the St Lawrence to Montreal, thence up the Ottawa, with what problems and trials at the Long Sault we have already considered. But they passed this great barrier and landed safely at the Chaudière on a small peninsula, thereafter called Richmond Landing. The families camped here while the men went ahead to clear a road (the Richmond Road of today) and the land for the first simple shelters that were erected. The families then followed and the town of Richmond was established.

The Richmond Landing is therefore one of the historic spots of the Ottawa region. A fine view of it and of the foot of the adjacent Victoria Island can be obtained from the rear windows of the National Library Building. Unfortunately, it will then be seen that these historic areas have not been preserved but were used in 1972 as a dumping ground for excavation waste from the building of the Portage Bridge which now bisects the island, the home of some interesting pioneer industries of Ottawa. In the interest of log movements, the water level above the falls has been controlled at its natural high-water level through the construction in 1907 of a concrete dam with a long spillway structure.

A good look around the southern end of the Chaudière will show a large area of level land extending to the foot of Bronson Avenue and Preston Street. Originally the site of a cluster of old industrial buildings, Le Breton Flats (as the area has long been known) has now been cleared by the National Capital Commission. Future plans for the area are still uncertain, but there was a time when it could have been used to surprisingly good effect. This was soon after the first settlers had left their camp at the Landing and passed over this area on their way to their new homes in Richmond. The area was an ideal site for the erection of storehouses for the goods that would have to be brought up from Montreal by boat, prior to being carted along the Richmond Road to the new town. This was urged upon the governor, the Earl of Dalhousie, at a dinner he attended in Richmond on 27 August 1820 soon after he arrived in Canada in June of that year to start his long service to this country.

Lord Dalhousie readily agreed and ordered that the necessary land should be secured for the Crown from the owner, Robert Randall. Had this been done, the immediate needs of the Richmond settlers would have been met; and of far greater importance, when the Rideau Canal came to be built a few years later, its entrance could have been across this flat area, up the hill at the foot of Bronson Avenue and thence in a straight line to what is now Dow's Lake. This would have saved time in construction and money since it is a shorter route than that which had to be used. The present route is scenically beautiful but, of more importance, the alternative route would have made practicable an ascent for boats over the Chaudière, into the

Ottawa River again, and so into Lac Deschenes, as an integral part of the entrance to the Rideau Canal.

All these opportunities were lost when it was found that one of the first land speculators in Canada had stolen a march on the governor and purchased the land for a relatively small amount, thereafter demanding a sum almost eight times as much before he would sell it to the government. The name of this gentleman was Captain John LeBreton. He had a distinguished war record before coming to Canada; because of this, there are some who have tried to make out that he has been an unfairly maligned man. Since, however, his perfidy has affected the entire development of the city of Ottawa, as well as navigation on the Upper Ottawa River, to an extent that cannot now be fully imagined, it will be well to set the record straight. Fortunately, we have a full account of what happened in Lord Dalhousie's own words.

They are contained in a letter written from Quebec on 9 May 1827 by the military secretary to the governor and addressed to Mr. Le Breton, who kept up a running legal battle, with additional appeals to authority, for well over a decade after his failure to 'make a fast buck.' Colonel Darling, the military secretary, states that the governor 'would not have thought it worth while to return any answer but for the purpose of having a true statement on the subject.' He is to convey the following statement 'drawn up by himself [Dalhousie] on a perfect and clear recollection of the whole of the transaction.' This is what the governor said:

In 1820 I made it my first duty on my arrival in the Province to visit it as extensively as the period of the season permitted. I passed up the Ottawa and crossed the Country from Hull through the Military Settlement then just begun. At Richmond Major Burke with a party of the Half Pay Officers there (as many as the house could hold) dined with me; the chief subject of the conversation was the means of promoting the public prosperity in that newly settled track. It was evident to all, that a Government Depot for stores and supplies was highly important at the Richmond Landing, so called, on the Ottawa; to establish an accessible point of communication and a certainty of supplies for the large population likely to assemble in that new Country.

The land belonged to a Mr. Randall, an absentee who could not then be found. No improvement had been made on it, and it was probable that the purchase might be made for a trifling sum. I gave instruction to Major Burke as Superintendent and in the presence and hearing of all at table, to take steps to effect the purchase, or to watch any advertisement of the sale of it, but to report to me before he concluded.

Captain Le Breton was then present; heard my sentiments and in my idea, as a Member of that settlement; as an officer and a Gentleman was in honour bound to give his assistance – He did not do so; he availed himself of the information and set about a speculative purchase to make a profitable bargain and then offer it to Government.

I heard nothing more on the subject until when Lieut. Col. Cockburn informed me that the Richmond Landing had been sold; and that Capt. Le Breton was in Quebec to offer it to Government. It was stated to me that he had bought it for £400, and offered it at £3,000, but in all probability might yield it for £2,000 – I desired to see Captain Le Breton personally, and, he came with Colonel Cockburn up to my writing room – I asked him if he seriously proposed such a demand – He said he did – and justified himself, I forget in what terms. I, at once, and very angrily told him, I would not permit so scandalous an imposition on H.M. Government; and, I gave him all my reasons for so thinking – 1st – a breach of confidence in availing himself of the information which passed at my table – 2nd – it was not becoming in a British Officer to catch at such a speculation – 3rdly – the difference from £400 to £3,000, or even £2,000, before he himself had paid his price, was indecent and shameful imposition.

From that one interview I formed an unfavourable opinion of Captain Le Breton, and I have seen no cause to alter it since – I know nothing of his character, I thought then and think still that due notice of the Sheriff's sale was not given, and although the Solicitor General did report to Sir P. Maitland that it was done in due form, the later Memorials of Mr. Randall himself incline me to think the sale was not legal, and therefore Mr. Le Breton's title altogether bad, and the purchase of the lot an illegal transaction. I do not believe one word of Mr. Le Breton's assertions that he could have obtained from Mr. Fraser at £15 the lot for which that gentleman obtained £750 from Government.

With regard to the family of Firth, I did say I would support the family if illtreated by these illegal proprietors; and I will do so still, at my own private cost ... No further answer will be made on this subject if continued. 7th. May 1827 – [signed] Dalhousie.

Much of this recital has a strangely modern ring to it, as Canadians see urban land costs mounting astronomically. And it is strange to think that Ottawa has honoured this gentleman down through the years with a perpetuation of his name, not only to describe the Flats which are now so valuable a part of central Ottawa, but also as the name of an important street. When the final disposition of the Flats is decided upon they could well be renamed, possibly after Lord Dalhousie who did so much to lay the foundations of the Ottawa of today. For he did not make the same mistake twice. He arranged to procure for the Crown much of the high land on the Ottawa side of the river to the east of the Chaudière, including the ravine that was later selected jointly by himself and Colonel By as the alternative location for the entrance locks of the Rideau Canal.

Before this, however, the governor had conceived the idea of a fortified settlement on the high ground now occupied by the Parliament Buildings, then thickly wooded, that would serve as protection to the Richmond and Perth settlements should an attacking force come up the Ottawa River. This fear is an accurate reflection of the state of alarm that still existed even ten years after the end of the War of 1812. Lord Dalhousie therefore directed Major G.A. Eliot of the 16th Regiment to proceed up the Ottawa to the Chaudière in 1824 in order to survey the area he had in mind, now procured for the Crown from a Major Fraser of Trois Rivières. Major Eliot recommended that a village should be laid out on what is now the Lower Town area, but the swampy nature of the ground prevented him from surveying it as he wished. He recommended two main batteries on Parliament Hill and a smaller one on Nepean Point.

Before the government could take action on this interesting report, the decision had been reached to proceed with the construction of the Rideau Canal. Lieutenant Colonel By landed at Quebec on 30 May 1826. After preliminary work in Montreal, he came up the Ottawa in September. The governor came also, all these journeys involving passage of the Long Sault so that they were not joyrides. On 26 September they jointly agreed upon the location for the entrance to the canal, the governor confirming this in a letter that he wrote that day while still in Hull. This was the start, under the active direction of Colonel By, of this great construction project.

On the Hull side of the river, Philemon Wright had got his settlement well established. On the south side, however, the virgin forest was still almost untouched, as records of those days make clear. There were only six 'houses' and a few small log cabins in what are today the townships of Gloucester and Nepean. In one of these, near the falls, Ralph Smith was concocting the first whisky to be distilled in the area. Isaac Firth was operating his small inn, widely known as 'Mother Firth's' after his courageous wife who, as Miss Dalmahoy, had come out alone from Edinburgh all the way to the Chaudière as early as 1818. The only connection between the two banks was, however, by water in summer and over the ice (where the river was frozen) in winter. A bridge was clearly an urgent necessity. The islands and rocks of the Chaudière made such a structure possible since simple approaches could be built of wood or masonry, only the main central channel requiring a large bridge span. Colonel By planned the general lines of the bridge before leaving for Montreal; work started in the late fall of 1826. Four masonry arches of about eighty-foot span were necessary, two across smaller channels on each side of the main gap, as well as minor approach works which included a log bridge across a small stream on the south bank long known as Pooley's Bridge, after Lieutenant Pooley, one of By's trusted assistant engineers. Work on the masonry proceeded well into the winter, one arch being completed despite an initial failure and extremely cold weather. Work resumed in 1827 and all the masonry was completed that season.

The problem of spanning the 200-foot central gap must have been the subject of much discussion. Eventually it was decided to try shooting a line across and Captain Osterbrooks of the Artillery brought up a brass cannon for this purpose. The first try, using a half-inch rope, failed since the rope was damaged by the firing and broke. A second attempt with a one-inch rope succeeded. With this frail link, successively stronger connections across the gap were hauled into place, and eventually chains. The main bridge structure was to be a timber truss with additional support from suspended chains. This was hazardous work and several men lost their lives during construction, the worst accident occurring in April 1828 when the work was almost complete. A chain failed, throwing eight men into the river, one of whom drowned. Colonel By decided on larger chains; work was resumed; and the structure was finally completed in September 1828 – the Union Bridge, as it was so properly called, since it was the first land connection across the Ottawa and so between Lower and Upper Canada. The Countess of Dalhousie was the first lady to cross the frail structure, on yet another visit that the governor paid to the Chaudière, so interested was he in the works under his command. In view of the absence in those days of any real criteria for structural design, the bridge must be counted as very creditable even though it can so easily be criticized in the light of modern knowledge. It was sketched by a number of artists, including the famous Bartlett, so that we know what it looked like. Its limited capacity soon became evident and so traffic had to be restricted to pedestrians, but even this service across the river must have been a real boon to the early settlers and workers on the canal. This first bridge collapsed on 18 May 1836, only two hours after the last pedestrian had crossed it.

In view of what the existence of the bridge had meant to the two communities, Lord Durham was petitioned for an 'iron suspension bridge' and this was authorized. The design was prepared by Samuel Keefer, who had been appointed as the first chief engineer to the Commissioners of Public Works of the United Province of Canada. His design for the Union suspension bridge can well be regarded as one of the early masterpieces of

Canadian civil engineering. It was, as can be seen from the photograph (page 111), elegant in appearance. It was well maintained by the Department of Public Works until 1876 when it was taken over by the city of Ottawa, and still served admirably despite the great increase in the volume and character of the traffic it carried, for it was still the only bridge across the Ottawa. Tolls were charged from the outset: one penny for each pedestrian and for each head of cattle, horses, sheep and pigs, but two-pence for every cart, waggon, carriage, or sleigh. The toll house had previously got a bad name, so bad that in August 1835 Sir John Colborne sent to the Governor, Lord Aylmer, a 'Presentment from Mr. Justice Sherwood, presiding at the Assizes in the Bathurst District' which stated:

The Licensee or Collector at the Toll House on the Union or Suspension Bridge erected over the Ottawa River is a Grievous and public Nuisance to the great danger of His Majesty's liege subjects, and the actual supposed death of some already from the uncertainty of the Boundary Line dividing the province of Upper and Lower Canada, the said Toll House Keeper does not yet consider himself amenable to the laws of either province and sells spirituous liquors without a license, that the Tollhouse is a common rendez-vous for Raftsmen and other persons, that it presents a continuous scene of riotous and disorderly conduct and few if any are allowed to pass along the said Bridge without being insulted or assaulted and some bodies that have been found below are supposed to have been thrown over the said Bridge.

The Union Bridge lasted until 1889, when it was replaced by a far less elegant steel truss bridge. This was damaged in the great fire of 1900 but immediately repaired, continuing in use until the larger steel truss spans of today were installed in 1919. The Union Bridge remained unique until 1880 when the Prince of Wales Bridge was built across the river at Lemieux Island, upstream of the Chaudière, to give the then new Canadian Pacific Railway access to Ottawa. The Alexandra, or Interprovincial, Bridge at Nepean Point followed in 1901; it was when first erected the longest cantilever steel span in North America. The Champlain Bridge near Remic Rapids is relatively recent, having been completed in 1928. The beautiful MacDonald-Cartier Bridge below Nepean Point opened on 15 October 1965, is a yet more recent crossing of the river.

When the first Union Bridge collapsed in 1836, a scow was immediately pressed into service as a temporary ferry. This was succeeded by one of the most unusual craft ever to sail on the Ottawa – a one-horsepower ferry boat, actually operated by a horse installed in a special driving cage. It was provided by a John Bedard and gave good service until the opening of the Suspension Bridge on 17 September 1836. Unfortunately, no picture of this unusual craft has yet been located so one must imagine a combination of a ferry scow and the common horse-mill used on pioneer farms for threshing. Other ferries gave crossing service above and below the Union Bridge, perhaps the most famous being that between what is now Rockcliffe and Gatineau Point. It has been in service for 130 years since it was started in 1843 by James O'Hagan of the Point, who operated it until 1870. The access road to the south bank of the river from the high ground of New Edinburgh was built before the ferry started and was called Rockcliffe, giving its name to the present municipality of Rockcliffe Park.

It was, however, the Chaudière that continued to dominate the river scene for Ottawa and Hull, with its unique bridge and little mills, its natural beauty and its great timber slides. When the possibility of developing power from falling water began fully to be appreciated, about mid-century, the water-leases at the Chaudière were seen to be of unusual potential. Industrial development led to the disappearance of almost all of the natural beauty of the great falls as more and more mundane buildings were erected. As sawmilling grew, every available piece of land around was used for the stockpiling of sawn lumber, not only at the Chaudière but also at Rideau Falls, since here also industrial plants were developed to use the power available. The photograph on page 111 gives merely an impression of the crowded industrial scene at the Chaudière in the latter part of the nineteenth century.

We must recall, however, that until the coming of the first railways from Montreal about 1860 (for the initial Ottawa and Prescott line provided only a very limited service), all traffic to and from the Chaudière settlements was by way of the Ottawa with its steadily growing fleets of elegant steamships, powerful tugs, and gaily painted barges. In the building of the Rideau Canal, Colonel By had the problem of having to bring all his men and all his supplies, as well as the ironwork that had to come from Montreal, up the Ottawa past the Long Sault, still not bypassed by the Ottawa River canals. The slow progress on these small works must have been a real frustration to him, especially since he would know that very shortly after he had finished his great work, the other little canals would be completed.

Some settlers still came to Ottawa by land across the plain from the St Lawrence, but most arrived by way of the river. It is difficult today to realize that when the original Parliament Buildings were started in 1860, virtually all travel was still by water. Colourful or historic scenes were regularly to be witnessed at the steamer docks. On a cold October evening in October 1864, for example, Sir John A. MacDonald and his immediate colleagues escorted ashore other delegates from the Quebec Conference which had concluded so well on 27 October. It was dark and so they saw little of the city but they were taken out on to the river again the next day on the steamer *England*, specially provided by Ottawa's Mayor Dickinson, so that they could enjoy the approach to the city by water which they had not been able to see on the evening before.

With Ottawa adopted as the nation's capital, the city became the site of the official residence of the governor general. All the early governors general, therefore, with their ladies and their staffs, came up to their new home by steamer; some have left pleasant records of their enjoyment of the river. Possibly the most unusual use of the river was that made by Lord Monck who, as R.H. Hubbard has reminded us, was distressed by his 'greatest burden of office, the miserable road between Rideau Hall and Parliament. Only in winter, when the snow had filled up its many holes, did it become bearable. To avoid it in summer, he arranged for a six-oared boat with a canopy and a crew "dressed man of war fashion" to row him up the Ottawa from the cove below the house to a stage at the foot of Parliament Hill.' If ever a future governor general gets too frustrated with the traffic he has to disrupt on Sussex Drive, he might well revert to the idea of a royal barge on the Ottawa for making his ceremonial journey to Parliament.

In her interesting *Canadian Journal*, the Countess of Dufferin records that on her last day in Ottawa, 7 May 1878, 'we had to get up early and be at the boat at seven ... the large guard of honour was drawn up at the top of the cliff and at the water's edge were the friends. A number of young men – the bachelors – were waiting for me on board with a bouquet and a silver holder; then the ship began slowly to move away, and there were long cheers and waving of handkerchiefs till we were out of sight. Ottawa looked lovely as we left and never shall we forget our happy six years here and our innumerable friends.' There is really nothing to match the joy and sorrow of a departure by water. The Marquis of Lorne and the Princess Louise, although able to travel by rail to a limited degree, were also lovers of the river, as was shown by a special cutting that was made through the trees on the grounds of Rideau Hall in order to give a view of the river from the great house. An engraving made at the time shows clearly a river steamer, part of a timber raft, and a pointer in action (p. 155).

The most remarkable viceregal association with the river, however, occurred just before the end of the century when Lord Aberdeen was governor general. Lady Aberdeen also kept, and had published, a journal of her stay in Canada. One Wednesday afternoon in April 1896 (the 22nd)

Lady Aberdeen decided to take an outing by crossing the Ottawa River with her small carriage on the Gatineau Ferry. She decided to drive along the river road. Here they encountered

a man loading his cart with wood a little ahead of us and Cowslip one of the ponies gave a little swerve – not more than a foot or two, but it was a foot or two too much, for he lost his footing and Buttercup was necessarily dragged along and before we knew where we were, the ponies had disappeared into the river and the carriage half overturned followed and the waters closed over them. I found myself on my back in the water – Boy [Captain John Sinclair, her secretary] was looking over me for a moment and smiled and said 'It's all right.' I tried to smile back again and then remembering that I had been told one ought to float in such emergencies I stretched out my feet and B. jumping over me (so as to be on right side of current) supported me from behind somehow. John Keddie a coachman ... tried to support me on the other side. But B. was out of his depth and found me very heavy and my head got under water which was not at all pleasant (and he says he thought things looked very nasty then) and I began to wonder how long one could remain conscious under water and whether the people from the cottages behind would come in time. B. began to swim, and somehow got to a shallower place and regained his footing and then hoisted my head up and then got me on my feet somehow ... Just then the men came along with their boat and we got in and were soon standing on the shore.

Lady Aberdeen goes on to record her distress at the loss of her two ponies, making light of her own danger and discomfort in wet heavy winter clothing. They walked back to the ferry, after calling on the curé to 'ask him to prevent any sensational message from being sent off from the telephone office.' They crossed back to Rockcliffe in a small boat. After a rest, Lady Aberdeen presided at dinner with Sir Wilfrid Laurier as guest, joining in an evening reception for senators and M.P.s who came to say good-bye, the session finishing on the day following.

Almost exactly one year later, 'a special steamer went over from this side at 2.30 to Gatineau Point ... A great concourse was assembled outside the church on the river's bank when we arrived, for Father Champagne allowed no one to go into the church until we arrived and all the members of the St Jean Baptiste Society acted as stewards and kept a pathway for us.' The service started – it lasted from 'about 5 minutes to 3 and we came out at ¹/₄ to 6' – and the special bell that had been cast in London as a thank-offering for Lady Aberdeen's escape from drowning was duly dedicated by the Archbishop. It is still there, adding its own special note to the peal which, when it is heard by citizens of today, might remind them of a very great and courageous lady who was once almost a victim of the flood-swollen waters of the Ottawa.

We have already seen how the first settlers in what is now Richmond used the Richmond Landing for their families while the Richmond Road was hacked out of the bush. The men of the 99th Regiment were not, however, the first to land at the Chaudière prior to tracking inland, since some months earlier (in June 1818) a group of three hundred Scottish farmers, led by John Robertson of Breadalbane, made the same journey en route to a new settlement that had been granted to them in Beckwith Township. They came generally from Loch Earn and Loch Tay in the Scottish Highlands. They landed somewhere near Nepean Point; again the families waited while the men blazed a trail through the woods. They clearly suffered much hardship, some baggage being lost by fire and some men being overcome by the unaccustomed heat of summer – heat that still surprises visitors from Great Britain. Some left their families in what accommodation was available in Hull while they went ahead to build houses for their new homes. Their settlement was long known as 'The Derry,' a name still to be heard in the valley.

Since it is so easy to forget what the valley was like in 1818 – a century and a half ago – it may be helpful to repeat an incident that appears to be well authenticated. One of the Scottish settlers in The Derry, James McArthur, came up with the main group to his new home in Beckwith Township by way of the Ottawa River. In Montreal he had parted from a close friend who had also come over from Scotland, John Anderson. Anderson decided to use the St Lawrence route in order to reach his land grant, which was also in Beckwith Township and also in the seventh concession. He therefore came up to Prescott and walked into Perth, thence to the new settlement. The two men then lived on the same concession, within a mile or two of one another, for two years without ever finding out that they were neighbours.

These were civilian settlers, given land grants but not on such a generous scale as that available for officers and men discharged from the British army. Rank made a difference, lieutenant colonels (in some areas) being given 1,200 acres, majors 1,000 acres, with decreasing amounts down to the 100 acres granted to privates. Land grants such as these must have been one of the attractions to the distinguished gentlemen who settled in 1819 in what is now March Township, their settlement being named Horaceville, although now known as Pinhey's Point after the one civilian amongst the retired military and naval officers who established this outpost of England in the wilds of Canada.

Captain John Banning Monk, late of the 97th Regiment, was the first to arrive at the site selected, about ten miles upstream from Britannia on the west shore of the river, a site suggested for settlement by Sir John Colborne as an alternative to joining with others at Perth. Monk left his wife in Hull while he built the first cabin at the new clearing, then bringing her up to land at 'Mosquito Cove' as an introduction to her new home. Hamnet Kirkes Pinhey followed later in the same summer; others who joined them included Colonel (formerly Major General) Lloyd, Captains Cox, Weatherly, and Landall, and Lieutenant Read of the Royal Marines. All were interesting men; some had interesting families, none more so than Captain Monk, one of whose ten children became known as 'The Prophet of March,' an early proponent of world peace, a vivid portrait of whom by Holman Hunt of the Pre-Raphaelite school is in the National Gallery of Canada. Hamnet Pinhey, however, is the best known today of this remarkable group of settlers; some of his descendants have continued to reside at what is left of the original settlement, while others have contributed greatly to life in the Ottawa of today.

Following the initial simple cabins, these new settlers built for themselves splendid masonry houses. Possibly the most remarkable was 'Bessborough,' built by Colonel Lloyd, a really fine residence, unfortunately destroyed by fire in 1870; a few ruins still remain. 'Helensville' was the name of Lieutenant Commander Benjamin Street's house; it, too, was destroyed in the 1870 fire but a reconstruction (now in use) indicates something of the fine original. 'Horaceville' was the Pinhey house, possibly the best known name since it was adopted as the name for the local post office and was the subject of one of Bartlett's views of early Canada. This is indeed a place of ghosts, for here English gardens were planted with roses, lilacs, and apple trees, all brought up the river from England; here ladies rode in sedan chairs and the gentlemen enjoyed their wines, their port, and claret, also from England. They hunted foxes and entertained royally, but today even the roadway that used to link together the houses has disappeared. Here the Earl of Dalhousie was received and entertained, as were many other famous travellers up and down the river.

So high were the hopes for the future of the settlement that the gentlemen submitted a petition to the governor urging that their settlement should be the 'Capital of Upper and Lower Canada established on the River.' This was almost an anticipation of the decision later made by Queen Victoria and is indicative of the great hopes that so many of the early settlers entertained for the future of the great valley in which they had settled. Hamnet Pinhey, however, must have known in his later years that their dream was not to be, for before he died, probably in 1856, he saw the change from Bytown to Ottawa. His life on the banks of the Ottawa was in great contrast to his early exploits as a carrier of official British despatches to the King of Prussia through the French lines, a service to the nation that resulted in his being given a land grant as if he had been a commissioned officer. His move to Canada resulted naturally in his assumption of the leadership of this most unusual of all the early settlements on the banks of the Ottawa.

Horaceville was in some ways unique. Few, if any, of the other early settlements were started on such a grand scale only to fade away as the years went by. All along the river, however, there are to be found indications of earlier settlements that have been superseded by the thriving valley towns and cities of today. We cannot look at more than one or two but we must make a brief stop as we travel up Lac Deschenes, in imagination and so many years ago, at what has long been known as Maclaren's Landing. Here may still be seen some remains of the old wharf that was for long an important stopping place for the lake steamers. David Maclaren was a hardware merchant of Glasgow who settled in 1825 in Torbolton Township. He had given his name to the landing, near which some of his descendants still live, before moving on to Wakefield in 1844, where he bought the Fairbairn grist mill. His son, James Maclaren, was the founder of the important Maclaren industries of Buckingham.

Just below Chats Falls, in a small bay near the foot of the falls and close to the mouth of the small Carp River, there was an obvious site for a settlement. It was so selected in 1819 by a young man, Alexander Shirriff, on behalf of his father, Charles Shirriff, whom he welcomed with his family the year following to what is now Fitzroy Harbour. Charles Shirriff was a shipbuilder and merchant from Scotland who had emigrated to Canada in 1817 with a fortune of £50,000, settling in Cobourg. Lord Dalhousie offered him 5,000 acres on the Ottawa, in keeping with the efforts that he was making to develop the valley; it was to select the area that Alexander Shirriff came up the river. A fine establishment was quickly developed. The Shirriff house is featured in yet another of the engravings that Bartlett made on his trip up the Ottawa in 1838. The settlement remained, as did some members of the Shirriff family. It prospered and was an important port of call for the steamers on the lake, until the horse-railway with its associated wharf on the Quyon side of the river started its operations. Even the consequent decline in the fortunes of the harbour did not lead to its final disappearance, as sometimes happened elsewhere. Fitzroy Harbour remains as one of the many agreeable smaller towns of the valley, serving now the power station that generates power from the great falls.

The years around 1820 saw the beginnings of many of the small settlements in this part of the valley, early settlers in some cases being ex-lumbermen who preferred the hard work of farming the new land to the hazards of labour in the woods and on the river. This is reflected in an interesting way in one of the letters of David Maclaren that have been preserved, and to which I was introduced by Dr George Glazebrook, who has quoted from them more fully in his own book, *Life in Ontario*. Writing to his wife on 2 August 1837 from Quebec, where he handled timber duties, McLaren says with reference to the economic difficulties of that year: 'This is a trying season for lumberers ... Many of the rafts that have come down are *laying-up* here until it can be seen what the *fall* will do, and others are stopped above and laid up at different places on the way. It is hardly possible to raise money to pay off the hands ... It must be desperation which drives people to lumber, and madness that continues them in it.' But people did continue in it most profitably, including David Maclaren's own son.

Many of the townships in Lower Canada that were surveyed at this time did not front on the river, but paved the way for the clearing of the good farm land around Shawville, in the Township of Clarendon, the name given later to the Anglican deanery that served the district in more recent years. A moving account of the early days in Clarendon was given in Christ Church Cathedral, Ottawa, on 24 June 1965, at the service when this deanery was legally transferred from the Diocese of Montreal to that of Ottawa. The speaker was Archdeacon Naylor of Montreal. Despite his physical infirmity, this beloved churchman kept the vast congregation enthralled for almost an hour with his reminiscences of early years in this part of the valley, based on his own recollections and those of his father, who was Rector of Shawbridge for over thirty years. He told, for example, of the first confirmation held in the Clarendon area in the 1850s, with seventy-five candidates gathered from the new homes where there had so recently been virgin forest. The Bishop of Montreal came up the Ottawa by steamboat but a breakdown occurred eight miles from Ottawa so he had to be put ashore on a raft, and rode on horseback to Hull. There he took the stage-coach for the journey to Aylmer, where he boarded another steamer (the *Lady Colbourne* in all probability) which landed him at Sand Point on the west shore of Lac Deschenes, which he had to cross by canoe. He spent the night as guest of a farmer and continued on horseback next morning, arriving at the little outpost church one day late. But somehow over fifty of the candidates managed to reassemble; the confirmation service was held; and then the bishop returned down the river by the same varied modes of transport.

That reference to the stage-coach from Bytown to Aylmer shows that one more improvement to travel up and down the Ottawa had been made. Philemon Wright cleared the first rough track through the forest between the foot of the Chaudière, on the north bank, and the first convenient landing point at the south end of Lac Deschenes. It was to this landing that Wright's nephew, Charles Symmes, moved in 1827 after a violent quarrel with the old squire. He laid out a townsite and in 1832 built a fine masonry hotel close to the landing. This building still exists. It is one of the capital region's most historic buildings but, like so many other treasures of the past, is in serious condition and has not (yet) been preserved as it should be in the public interest. Bartlett featured it prominently in one of his fine views of the Ottawa Valley. It was a strategic inn so long as the steamboat service operated on Lac Deschenes. 'Turnpyke End' was the first name given to the little lakeside settlement but it was renamed Aylmer in honour of Lord Aylmer, Governor-in-Chief of Canada from 1831 to 1835. The steamship era gave Aylmer its heyday but it is still an important and pleasant community, now providing homes for many workers in Ottawa. The road from Aylmer to Bytown was steadily improved but it was not until 1849, when a company was formed to macadamize it, that it became really worthy of the name of road. The company, at one time called the People's Forwarding Company, charged tolls and these were not abolished until well into the twentieth century; one of the old mileposts has been preserved and may be seen near the start of the driveway to the Champlain Lookout.

The Ottawa River canals, after 1834; the Bytown-Aylmer (Britannia) road after 1820; the horse-railway at Chats Falls after 1840; and some well made plank roads around some of the upper rapids, notably those at Portage du Fort – these were the only improvements made to assist all who travelled up and down the Ottawa River in its great days as a waterway. Only the Britannia Road, such as it was in 1825, was available to ease the journey of the first group of settlers who were to go beyond Chats Falls when they started on their long journey up the Ottawa, after leaving Greenock on 19 April of that year. They had been met at Montreal by the thirteenth chief of the Clan McNab and his personal piper. Their spirits must have soared as they heard the pipes on shore but it would be a long time before they would recover the joy of that first day in Canada.

Archibald McNab had come to Canada in 1823 and was granted by the Executive Council of Upper Canada a large area of land, starting with twelve hundred acres, on the south bank of the Ottawa above Chats Falls, the grant specifying how McNab was to administer this land for the new settlers he promised to bring from the Scottish Highlands. He had other ideas, considering himself to be a laird, and it would be 1841, and after a succession of increasing difficulties, before the settlers were able to secure a copy of the original grant. Upon their arrival, they were allowed to select their lots, and then each man had to sign a 'ticket' which made him almost a vassal of McNab.

The first group took twenty-eight days for the journey from Montreal to their new home, the duration of the trip giving some idea of the difficulties they had to surmount on the way. Clearing the land was a herculean task and they soon discovered that the conditions under which they had to live, and such matters as the promised free supplies, were not quite what they had been led to expect. It is a long sad story, a blot on the wonderful tale of the Ottawa, and it distresses a Scots-Canadian author to have to deal with it. But it is a part of the story of the river and so must be briefly related. These fine Highland people had to live in poverty, peons of the great chief who himself lived in grand style. Dissatisfaction existed from the very outset of the settlement. Meetings were held but it was not until Alex Miller was imprisoned at Perth for debt in 1839, after leaving the township without the laird's permission, that the troubles really came into public view.

Lord Sydenham sent Francis Allan, a Crown land agent, to investigate the settlers' grievances. His report was a sorry record of Chief McNab's machinations, concluding with the statement: 'McNab has conducted the affairs of the township in the worst possible manner for the interests of the settlers or the country.' McNab by this time had moved his residence from Kinnell Lodge on the Ottawa to Waba Cottage on White Lake. After the sudden end to his long reign, he still further enraged some of his settlers by flamboyant mill construction; but this was declared a public nuisance and had to be removed. He won a pyrrhic victory in a libel suit about articles on his misguided reign on the Ottawa, but he was a ruined man. He left Canada for Scotland and died in France in 1860. Kinnell Lodge has long since disappeared although Waba Cottage may still be seen. All that remains is the name of the township that was the scene of this feudal tragedy.

That the settlers' difficulties were not confined to the Scots of McNab Township is shown by this statement that appeared in the *Bathurst Courier and Ottawa General Advertiser* (later the *Perth Courier*) about 1844:

The great tide of emigration flows up the Ottawa as far as Bytown, but although there are steamboats plying on the river for about sixty miles farther up, there is seven miles of an extensive land carriage (Bytown to Aylmer) before these boats are reached, and as emigrants are pretty much sickened with the toil and expense of embarking and disembarking by the time they reach Bytown, they are generally inclined to consider the easiest method the best for the present, and therefore proceed through the Rideau Canal to Kingston, there to see and perhaps experience misery and destitution equal to that which induced them to leave their native land ... All the workable land for hundreds of miles in that direction is already purchased, and the expense, toil and time necessary to reach the Western or Huron Districts renders it nearly as formidable an enterprise as a second crossing [of] the Atlantic.

Such sad statements are but typical of many that show that the discouragements of early settlers in the upper Ottawa Valley were widespread. Although the settlers probably did not realize it at the time, much of the difficulty, apart from the problems of transportation, was due to the local geology. Once Chats Falls was passed, much of the land covered originally by the unbroken forest consisted of very thin soil overlying the ancient rocks of the Precambrian Shield, in great contrast to the fertile plains in the lower part of the valley provided by the deep deposits of marine clay or the sands and gravels of glacial outwash deposits. Many a settler on the Shield must have seen some of the soil cover actually washed off the underlying rock by the first thunderstorm, once he had done his back-breaking clearing. It is no wonder that so many became discouraged and moved on to other areas.

It is easy to see today, with the benefit of hindsight, that some of this Shield country never should have been cleared at all but left perpetually under forest cover. Much of it has now reverted to forest, but one cannot pass by the evidences of all the abortive clearing that once was carried out on such land without remembering the courageous and indeed heroic efforts of the pioneers up the valley. The wonder is that so many stayed and that so much fine settlement resulted. Fortunately, there were good areas of fertile land near the river and not all of the Shield country had treacherously thin soil cover. Not only did settlement continue but it laid the foundations for the fine and prosperous Renfrew County of today – the 'River County' as it may well be called, stretching from the tip of McNab Township just downstream of Arnprior for almost one hundred miles up the river to beyond Deux Rivières where it meets the District of Nipissing. Only Pontiac County in Quebec can compare with Renfrew County in dependence on the river, both in its earliest days and still to some degree today.

Renfrew County has fortunately had a lover of the river as its most recent historian. Clyde Kennedy has written engagingly about all aspects of the county's development and history, and not least about its river settlements. Through his own archaeological studies, he has been steadily extending our knowledge of the prehistory of this part of the valley. He has told of the dual start of Arnprior, first in 1832 when George and Andrew Buchanan built a grist and sawmill but abandoned the site after one of the inevitable quarrels with the McNab; and the second time in 1857, when the booming of a cannon signalized the start of a new town by Daniel McLachlin, who had come up the Ottawa to establish his home on the 400 acres he had bought. His three sons were the McLachlin Brothers, soon to become another of the famous companies engaged in the Ottawa timber trade.

One would expect to find that the town of Renfrew was perhaps the original settlement, but the honour of having the first post office (opened in 1832) in the county belongs to Castleford, originally established at the First Chute of the Bonnechère but then moved to the bank of the Ottawa. The Honourable Francis Hincks was one of the founders of Renfrew, selling some of the land he had bought at the Second Chute in 1855 to John Lorn McDougall on condition that he build a mill. McDougall did so with such good effect that the mill building is still standing today, in splendid condition. This was the real beginning of Renfrew, incorporated as a village in 1858, although some settlers had been in the vicinity since the 1820s.

More closely tied with lumbering was the start of Pembroke, when Peter White, prospecting for good timber limits, built a log cabin at the mouth of the Muskrat River in 1828 and decided to make this his home. A native of Edinburgh, he had served in the Royal Navy with Admiral Yeo prior to lumbering in the Ottawa Valley, which led to his explorations and the start of what is now the city of Pembroke. He served as the local magistrate for forty years, dying only in 1878 after seeing great changes come to his town, including the entry of the Canada Central Railway, an event that was to change forever the pattern of life in the valley.

Up and down the hundred miles of Renfrew County's frontage on the Ottawa there are small settlements, individual farms, and even some abandoned clearings about which many a tale can be told. We can permit ourselves only one such tale, the story of the Opeongo Road. In the 1850s the government of the United Province of Canada was most anxious to get more people on the undeveloped lands in what we would now call the southern part of the province. It embarked on an ambitious programme which included the building of three 'Great Lines of Roads' as they were called, through undeveloped country, with the offer of a hundred acres of free land adjacent to the roads for each new settler. The Ottawa and Opeongo Road was one, the Addington and the Hastings roads the other two. Clearly misled by over-optimistic reports on the hinterland of the

Ottawa Valley, the government had a line for the road surveyed in 1852–53, starting at Farrell's Landing on Lac des Chats, about two miles west of the mouth of the Bonnechère River. The road ran inland through Renfrew and then about midway between the Bonnechère and Madawaska Rivers. Despite early hopes, the Opeongo Road never got further than about five miles from the present village of Madawaska and so never did reach Opeongo Lake. Remains of the logs used to form the corduroy road surface may still be seen in places, as can also the ruins of some of the log cabins built by optimistic early settlers along the road.

In September 1855 T.P. French was appointed Crown land agent for the Opeongo Road. He wrote a remarkable booklet that was published with the official approval of the provincial Commissioner of Crown Lands, Hon. Joseph Cauchon, and the President of the Executive Council, Hon. P.M. Vankoughnet, who was also Minister of Agriculture. Entitled *Information for Intending Settlers on the Ottawa and Opeongo Road, and its vicinity*, and thirty-six pages long, it was published at Ottawa, Canada West, in 1857, although Mr French dated it at Mount St Patrick, where he had made his initial headquarters. The author gives sound advice about crossing the Atlantic, and the food supplies that must be taken aboard ship, and then describes travel in Canada:

The journey from Montreal to Ottawa may also be made either by Rail or Steamboat at these prices, viz.: By Mail Steamer – going through in one day. Cabin, and three meals, 10s.; Steerage, without meals, 5s. No cabin. By Rail – going through in about seven hours. First class, 20s. Second class, 15s. Emigrants, 10s. From Ottawa the journey to this Agency may be made by land, or partly by land and water, and as there are no public conveyances on the land route, the other is by far the best. It is 9 miles from Ottawa to the Village of Aylmer, and Stages are continually running between these places, that carry passengers at 2s. 6d. each. From Aylmer a Steamer starts at 7 a.m. on Tuesdays, Thursdays and Saturdays, and passengers by it are put ashore at the Bonne-chere Point, or at Ferrall's Landing, 2 miles nearer Renfrew, about 3 p.m. The Fare being: Cabin, with breakfast and dinner, 12s. 6d. Steerage, 7s. 6d. Steerage, without meals, 5s. 0d.

This bland description of the journey we now know so well, with no reference to the transshipment necessary at Chats Falls, is typical of the optimistic tone of the whole brochure, clearly written by an enthusiast who seemed genuinely to believe that he was helping emigrants to come to a

Canadian Garden of Eden. The weather? 'as healthful as that of any other portion of the globe.' The soil? 'is a sandy loam, in some places light, but in others rich and deep ... a good deal of rock and loose surface stone is also to be met with, and while it must not be denied that such often proves a source of much annoyance to the farmer yet they do not prevent the proper cultivation of the land, nor form any great obstacles to the raising of excellent crops.' And the land of Canada? 'LIBERTY, in the most extended sense of that soul-stirring word, prevails in Canada. We have here a happy and harmonious blending of the best parts of the Monarchial and Republican forms of Government.'

If I quote further, it will be thought that I am ridiculing Mr French. He was an enthusiast, and enthusiasm was necessary in his position. What the heartbreaks were for some of those who travelled the Opeongo Road with such high hopes we shall never know. But despite the actual conditions that clearing of the land so soon revealed, many new Canadians did make their start in this land by going up the Opeongo Road as had been hoped and planned. Prominent among them were Polish settlers of Wilno, some perhaps of the three hundred immigrants who came up the Ottawa in 1864 (possibly by one of the early trains as far as Sand Point), to be followed by others at the turn of the century, resulting in what was, at the time, the largest Polish settlement in Canada. There are today about two thousand Polish Canadians around Wilno, the old wooden crosses near the great modern church paying mute testimony to their pioneers.

If we now think of the general progress of settlement throughout the valley, we find that it is reflected in an interesting but quite natural way by the retreat of the Hudson's Bay Company up the valley. This has been conveniently summarized by Courtney Bond in another of his helpful contributions to historical records of the Ottawa. Soon after the great merger, all the Ottawa River posts were placed under George Simpson, who made no bones about the fact that he wanted to reduce the labour of the long canoe journeys, using the Ottawa route only for express journeys to the west. But the Ottawa River posts had still to be served. John McLean was sent up to the post at Lac des Sables on the Lièvre as late as August 1826. The post at the Lake of Two Mountains was never profitable but was kept operating mainly for prestige purposes. New buildings were erected at Fort Coulonge in 1827, and at Lac des Allumettes and Chats Falls in 1828. Late in the same year a new post was established at Mattawa.

Trade was uncertain along the river, however, the advance of lumbering and the clearing of the land for settlement gradually changing its character. The post at Chats Falls was the first to be closed, in 1837. The post at Lake of Two Mountains was finally closed in 1848 and the next year that at Lac des Sables was moved to Buckingham, and used as a store. The decision to close Fort Coulonge was made in 1844 when the great Company farm was sold; the post itself was open until 1855 when it, too, was sold. Lac des Allumettes, known after 1848 as Fort William, lasted until 1869 when it was also sold, local Company business being then carried on from an office in Pembroke. The post at Mattawa lasted, surprisingly, until 1908–9 despite the coming of the Canadian Pacific Railway in 1881. But the famous post at Temiskaming ceased to be active before the end of the century, closing down in 1902–3.

Twenty-seven years later I happened to be working in the Temiskaming area on a new power project which included a transmission line crossing of Lake Temiskaming, located at The Narrows for convenience. When inspecting the erection of the great towers, I was attracted to the log buildings, which I knew to have been used by the Hudson's Bay Company. I was, however, most surprised to find some old Company papers in a corner of one of the buildings, even then in a poor state of preservation. It was a strange experience to read the laboriously hand-written sheets with work on high-tension transmission towers going on almost overhead. The papers were duly passed to the Company archives.

My keen interest in the Ottawa Waterway must date from that discovery for it was then that I first heard of another of the pioneers of the Ottawa. This was the Reverend Father Charles Alfred Marie Paradis, a member of the Oblate Order, son of a carpenter in Saint André de Kamouraska, to the southeast of Quebec City. He served for some years as an art teacher at Ottawa College but after his ordination was sent by his Order in 1881 to the missionary district of Temiskaming. A Sulpician Father, the Reverend Louis Charles de Bellefeuille, had journeyed to Temiskaming in July 1836, his companion, Father Dupuis, building a small chapel near the Company post. It was not until the coming of the Oblate Fathers in 1863 that the mission became a permanent one, even then still very small. It required the enthusiasm of the young Father Paradis to display to the superiors of the Order the settlement possibilities of what he used to call 'my Temiskaming.' The result was the establishment in 1884 of the Temiskaming Colonization Society.

It was in this same year that there took place the last of the great Ottawa canoe journeys of which report has been made. The main record of this journey is an illustrated manuscript now in the provincial archives of Quebec. Its title page carries the inscription: *De Temiskaming à la Baie Hudson; Rapport presenté à l'Honorable Sir Hector L. Langevin C.B.,*

*K.C.M.G., Ministre des Travaux Publics, Ottawa, par C.A.M. Paradis Pr. O.M.I. Missionnaire.* The manuscript is accompanied by a number of charming watercolours, each in a decoratively drawn frame, all the work of Father Paradis. And the title is explained by the fact that this was, in effect, a repetition of the journey of de Troyes – up Lake Temiskaming, over the Abitibi portage, and down to James Bay, the main difference being that the journey started at Pembroke instead of Montreal.

It was an unusual pastoral visit, led by Monseigneur N.Z. Lorrain, Bishop of Cythera and apostolic vicar of Pembroke. Father Paradis was one of the party (and one cannot escape the feeling that the trip might have been made at his suggestion), as was Father J.B. Proulx, who published an unillustrated record of the journey in 1886. With two other companions and a crew of seven Temiskaming Indians led by one Okoushin, the party used a birch-bark *canot de maître* of the traditional style, naming it *Zephire*. It was a summertime journey so the travellers were much bothered by flies but all went well; they reached Moose Factory and later Fort Albany quite safely, being kindly received and entertained by the officers of the Hudson's Bay Company at whose posts they stopped. They even enjoyed a race between Fort Abitibi and Fort Temiskaming on the return journey with a gaily decorated Company canoe carrying Mr D.C. McTavish, a bourgeois of the Company who was moving to a new posting.

The journey must have quickened Father Paradis' enthusiasm and stirred his dreams, for we find him suggesting the construction of a dam across the Ottawa River at Mattawa in order to raise the level of the river by thirty-two feet in order to drown out the first of the rapids on the way to the lake. The remaining rapids were to be eliminated by dredging the shoal that created them, thus lowering Lake Temiskaming by twenty-six feet – complex engineering feats that he treated lightly in his desire to 'form a grand chain of communication to divert a vast trade down the Ottawa River to Ottawa.' His rather limited engineering talents were demonstrated when, some years later, he accidentally drained Frederick House Lake during some mining operations. He did not stop at engineering but invented his own fly dope, calling it *La Maringouinifuge* and obtaining a certificate of commendation from the saintly Bishop Lorrain, who testified that it 'was most effective in protecting myself and my companions against the stings of mosquitos, black flies and midges.'

Clearly, Father Paradis was a man of parts; but it was a Father P.E. Gendreau who was made president of the Colonization Society. The society abandoned Father Paradis' visionary projects but as an alternative solicited from the government of Canada a subsidy to support the building of a colonization railway as a portage around the worst of the rapids. Two small sections of light railway, or tramway, were built but the construction of the C.P.R. branch to the new town of Temiskaming in 1894 soon made them redundant and they disappeared. But the hopes of seeing the Ottawa converted into a busy waterway remained, and still remain. They form a vital part of the Ottawa story.

# EIGHT

# The River Today

The dream of a Georgian Bay ship canal remains a dream, but the mighty river still flows by majestically to join the St Lawrence and roll on to the sea. The river has been tamed but the enduring things remain. Floods in the spring and low water in the fall are reminders of the constancy of the seasons. The everlasting hills rim the north bank of the river, pointing always to the fascinating geology of the valley, the mysteries of which are steadily being unravelled by geologists both amateur and professional. The forests provide cover for the extremely varied plant life that has always been a feature of the valley, and for the innumerable insects, some of which make themselves known to travellers every passing year in the same irritating ways. Other insects, however, add immeasurably to the beauty of the woodland scenes as even the early travellers were able to record, hard pressed though they might be by the difficulties of their journeying. And the flashing wings of birds at all seasons of the year add life and beauty to the river scene and provide interest for many observers. Up and down the valley, therefore, there are still – as there have been since first the river was used as a waterway – varied delights for the naturalist.

Such a man was the Reverend John Kerr McMorine, a well-known preacher of the gospel in the valley, first as a minister of the Presbyterian Church but, after 1867, a priest in the Anglican Church. He became a Canon of St George's Cathedral, Kingston, and Rural Dean of Frontenac before he retired in 1909. A native of Upper Melbourne in the Eastern Townships, he grew up in the Ottawa Valley, graduated from Queen's University in 1864, and served in a number of valley towns and townships from 1864 until 1877, when his roving spirit took him out to the mission then established at Thunder Bay. He was an active and beloved pastor who early developed a love of botany, so that wherever he travelled he collected specimens of new plants. This resulted finally in a collection of more than 1,200 different specimens, representing 111 families and about 780 species. Most of these were collected in seventeen townships of the valley, many along the Ottawa River, in McNab Township and also at La Passe and Gould's Landing, the start of the Muskrat Lake route. Most of the collection can be seen today in the Department of Biology at Queen's University, but 141 specimens are included in the herbarium of the Department of Agriculture in Ottawa.

There have been many men and women who have similarly studied the natural history of the Ottawa Valley, few perhaps making such extensive collections but many writing up their findings to a greater extent than did Dr McMorine, for he wrote but little about his hobby. The eighty-six volumes of the *Canadian Field Naturalist* (the oldest journal of its kind in Canada) contain many papers about the fauna and flora of the valley. Local groups of enthusiasts continue to enjoy the special delights that the banks of the great river provide for the observant naturalist. J.M. Gillett, for example, has identified no less than 1,355 species of plants within a radius of thirty miles of the Parliament Buildings in Ottawa, about one-quarter of which are normally alien to such a region, lying as it does between the deciduous forest zone to the south and the boreal forest zone to the north. He has identified no less than eighty-six species in one afternoon's outing to Haycock Island in Lac Deschenes, indicative of the remarkable flora to be found along the river.

No less than 275 species of birds have been recognized in the Ottawa area, the large number due in part to the water birds found along the river. One need not be an expert bird-watcher to enjoy this aspect of wildlife, since the river is crossed by at least one of the great north-south flight routes used by migrating birds; these provide memorable sights for all to see. On a never to be forgotten fine afternoon in May, my wife and I were walking near the golf course of Montebello, high above the river, when we heard an unusual noise. We could see nothing until we looked above our heads. There, quite low, was an immense flock of Canada geese in typical V formation but flying very slowly. We sensed that they were looking for something and this was confirmed when the leading bird dropped very quickly and soon disappeared into a swampy area in a small bay on the river. The others followed as if commanded by a stentorian sergeant-major; soon all were at rest, sheltering again on the waters of the Ottawa.

And on summer evenings there is still to be seen the loon skimming the waters, breaking the silence with his mocking cry. Memories of silent evenings by the river, thus enlivened by this zoologically senior of all Canadian birds, must be among the treasured recollections of many a valley lover.

It took a stranger within our gates, however, fully to record the delights of bird-watching on the Ottawa. When the Right Honourable Malcolm Macdonald was British High Commissioner in Ottawa, he resided at Earnscliffe, one of early Ottawa's great houses, located on the high river bank just to the east of Rideau Falls. 'One day in July, 1944, I paddled my canoe into Brewery Creek and found it a pleasant haven inhabited by some interesting birds,' he has told us. (Brewery Creek is a channel of the Ottawa running through Hull and joining the Ottawa again just opposite Earnscliffe.) 'Sea birds, river birds, lake birds, marsh birds, shore birds and land birds all came to it sooner or later. I watched them from the middle of 1944 until the end of 1945. My observations were scrappy, for work kept me in an office all day and I could only cross the river for an hour or two in the early mornings, before breakfast, and occasionally for a short while in the lunch hour or in the evening.' Despite the 'scrappy' observations, this distinguished diplomat wove the record of the birds he saw into a charming book, now unfortunately out of print, leaving it as a delightful legacy for the citizens of Ottawa with whom he developed such close links. From it these quotations are taken.

In eighteen months, I saw 160 different species in the estuary. ... I did not count birds which I saw outside it, wishing to confine the study to bird life within this area ... Nor did I bother to paddle my canoe to the creek at dead of night, otherwise I might have added a Whip-poor-will ... I believe that a keen observer could see about a dozen more species than I have recorded [in this book]. ... I wonder how many inhabitants of Ottawa realize that more than 170 species of birds can be found during the year in a small area on the edge of the city. It is charming to know that so near the East Block, where civil servants prepare Acts of Parliament, the love life of the Spotted Sand-pipers is also being enacted; that within spitting distance of diplomatic cocktail parties in Rockcliffe Park many kinds of Warblers, Vireos and Finches also hold their social gatherings; and that not far from the mumble of legislators' oratory on Parliament Hill can be heard too the querulous scream of the Yellow-bellied Sapsucker.

Brewery Creek is passed over just as one leaves the exit from the

Macdonald-Cartier Bridge to join Quebec Highway No. 8 going east but, with the traffic seemingly always to be found at this junction, few motorists have time even to glance at the creek when crossing, while pedestrians keep away from this point if they can. The creek was once the site of a brewery. Mr Macdonald relates:

The creek has not forgotten the hilarious distinction which [the brewery vats and presses] once lent it and in pious and nostalgic gratitude celebrates the fact in its charming bibulous name ... Although the place is little more than a mile from the centre of Canada's capital city, its aspect is wild. Its shores are a mixture of rocks, mud and reeds. In spring it includes one or two marshy inlets which dry up later in the year ... Willow trees flourish by the water's edge.

This description applies generally to the area that includes Leamy Lake and its creek, extending over to the west shore of the Gatineau River. Now park land, it should be kept in this natural state, despite occasional publicity about plans for its 'development' for commercial purposes. All who cast envious eyes on it should be required to read *Birds of Brewery Creek*, which was written 'in the hope that the citizens of Ottawa may take an increasing interest in this pleasing aspect of the capital's life' – a challenge from a lover of Ottawa that must not be forgotten.

Fortunately, vital areas in the Ottawa district are now largely in the good care of the National Capital Commission, protected – in intent at least – for public use and enjoyment for all time. Elsewhere in the valley the provincial governments of Ontario and Quebec have made a start at conserving a few other valuable natural areas. In large measure this has been as a direct result of land rearrangements following the flooding of shoreline land in the valley by the construction of major dams for hydro-electric development. And it is these same dams that have completely transformed the turbulent river of yesterday into the series of major lakes of today, the power of the falling water previously wasted in the raging rapids that were such an impediment to travel on the river being now converted into electrical energy in vast generating plants, true temples of power, examples of modern engineering at its best. Not only has the river itself been thus tamed but its major tributaries also, the total capacity of the power plants in the Ottawa basin now exceeding four million horsepower, all within the watershed of the one river, and it but a tributary of the St Lawrence. It is doubtful if anywhere else in the world is there any comparable example of the natural power given by the falling water in one river system being developed to such an extent for 'the use and convenience of man,' to use once again the famous old phrase.

This is not a book about engineering; rather are we concerned with the Ottawa River as one of the great waterways of the continent, in its histori- cal role and as it is today. The complete transformation of the main river by the construction of major water-power plants has all occurred within the last forty years and mainly within the last twenty. In earlier days there were a number of small power plants constructed generally on tributaries of the Ottawa, apart from those at the Chaudière, but it required the development of high-tension transmission of electrical energy over great distances, as well as settlement of jurisdictional questions, to pave the way for the developments that have given us the river as it is today.

All the essential data about the main river plants are given in the table that follows so that those with an engineering bent can see for themselves how the power of the Ottawa is being generated. Only a few capacities will be given as we explore together, very briefly and in outline only, the way in which the river has been tamed. Figures given in the table represent the capacity of the plants in 1974; many have been considerably extended from the initial installations as demand increased.

The story of power development on the Ottawa begins at the Chaudière. We have already noted that in the middle of the last century leases were granted for the erection of mills to use the power of the water falling over the Chaudière Falls. These were, however, what is called direct-driven mills, the falling water driving the water-wheel which in turn, either di- rectly or through mechanical gearing, operated sawmills or grist mills. Soon after it became possible to use water-wheels for driving electrical generators, then transmitting the resulting power through cables, an instal- lation was made of this new type of mill at the Chaudière, a small unit operating as early as 1902. Older mill installations were gradually con- verted and today all the power development that can be permitted has been made in the seven small plants, the flow through which passes through the turbines from intakes above the control dam, discharging in different channels below the falls. It is surprising to find that more than 80,000 hp are today being generated at the Chaudière. The character of the original leases for water rights naturally makes the Chaudière power plants a unique feature of power development on the Ottawa. In a different way, so also is the Bryson plant now owned and operated by Hydro Quebec. Built in 1925, it features a concrete dam filling the narrow gorge of the Grand Calumet Channel to the east of Calumet Island, all of which lies wholly in

*Water Power Developments in the Ottawa River Basin*

| Development | Built | Last Addition | Installed Capacity (hp) |
|---|---|---|---|
| *On the Main River:* | | | |
| Rivière des Prairies, Montreal | 1929 | 1930 | 60,000 |
| Carillon | 1962 | 1962 | 840,000 |
| Chaudière (7 plants) | 1902 | 1955 | 87,170 |
| Chats Falls | 1931 | 1932 | 224,000 |
| Chenaux | 1950 | 1951 | 168,000 |
| Bryson | 1925 | 1949 | 78,400 |
| Des Joachims | 1950 | 1951 | 496,000 |
| Otto Holden | 1952 | 1953 | 272,000 |
| Above Lake Temiskaming (4 plants) | 1923 | 1967 | 447,000 |
| Other | — | — | 1,000 |
| **Total on Main River** | | | **2,673,570** |
| | | | |
| *On Tributary Streams:* | | | |
| *The Lièvre* | | | |
| Masson | 1933 | 1933 | 136,000 |
| High Falls | 1930 | 1936 | 122,500 |
| Dufferin Falls | 1958 | 1959 | 50,000 |
| Buckingham | 1901 | 1939 | 30,800 |
| | | | |
| *The Gatineau* | | | |
| Farmers | 1927 | 1947 | 120,000 |
| Chelsea | 1927 | 1939 | 170,000 |
| Paugan | 1928 | 1956 | 285,000 |
| | | | |
| *The Madawaska* | | | |
| Stewartville | 1948 | 1948 | 84,000 |
| Barrett Chute | 1942 | 1942 | 56,000 |
| Mountain Chute | 1967 | 1967 | 224,000 |
| | | | |
| *The Montreal* | | | |
| Lower Notch | 1971 | 1971 | 306,000 |
| 4 other plants | 1910 | 1930 | 18,340 |
| | | | |
| *Other Tributaries* | | | |
| About 30 plants | — | — | 110,686 |
| **Total on Tributary Streams** | | | **1,713,326** |
| **Grand Total** | | | **4,386,896** |

the province of Quebec. Enlarged in 1949, this station can now generate 78,400 hp. Power development on the tributary rivers to the Ottawa could similarly proceed without any legal difficulties having to be solved in advance.

On the main river, the conclusion of the protracted negotiations for the building of the Georgian Bay Ship Canal led directly to consideration of power development on the Ottawa, for which the government of Canada had issued some early development rights. This led to long legal discussions since the provinces of Quebec and Ontario regarded the available power on this interprovincial river as under their jurisdiction. The plant at Chats Falls was a special case and so, once the legislation covering the Canal Company's rights had been allowed to lapse, negotiations for a power plant there started between Ontario Hydro and the Ottawa Valley Power Company. Work on the dam started in 1930 and in 1933 the first power was delivered.

Little would be gained by any attempt to summarize the legal discussions and proceedings regarding power development on the rest of the interprovincial part of the river. Suffice to say that the two provinces were granted control and in 1943 they reached a historic agreement about the allocation of the main power sites so that each could be developed in the most efficient manner without regard to the provincial boundary. So short of new power was Ontario Hydro at that time that it started surveys for the design of its plants almost immediately. Construction of the second-largest plant on the river, that at Des Joachims (496,000 hp), started in 1946, the official opening taking place in June 1950. The Chenaux plant at Portage du Fort (168,000 hp) followed in November of the same year; and finally the plant at La Cave, just above Mattawa, later renamed in honour of Dr Otto Holden (for many years chief engineer of Ontario Hydro), was in operation by June 1952, its capacity being 272,000 hp. Each of these projects involved a major construction operation. The resulting dam raised the water level above it to an elevation determined by the level of the tailrace of the plant next above it upstream.

Under the terms of the interprovincial agreement of 1943 and its subsequent minor amendments, Quebec was to develop the power sites at Rocher Fendu and Paquette Rapids, power at the latter site being equally divided with Ontario, and at Carillon. To date, only the Carillon project has been constructed by Hydro Quebec but it is by far the largest power plant on the river, with an installed capacity of 840,000 hp. Work on this splendid plant started in 1959. With its fourteen great power units, each generating as much power as the entire Des Prairies station, it was completed in 1964.

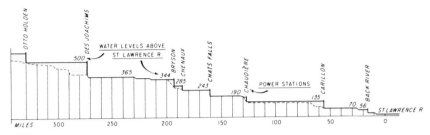

Profile of the Ottawa River as now developed for water power.

Located between Montreal and Ottawa, it gave many city dwellers a unique opportunity of seeing how such a large project is carried out, one of the best laid-out major construction projects that I have ever seen.

Only when the dam and powerhouse were complete could the flood gates be closed and a slow start made at raising the water level above. Planning for this had been in progress for several years: land to be flooded had been cleared of trees and many buildings had been relocated; some roads had been rebuilt. The central section of the Sir George Perley Bridge at Hawkesbury-Grenville had to be raised by 9½ feet to give the necessary clearance above the new water level. Lovely old trees at the Seigniory Club, Montebello, had to be cut down before the flooding. In these and a thousand other ways, the building of the Carillon plant affected the valley all the way from Carillon to Ottawa.

The rushing, turbulent river has thus been tamed. But while the major rapids have now been flooded out, fortunately there remain a few stretches of swift water that can still give us some idea of what the Ottawa used to be like. At Ste Anne de Bellevue and Vaudreuil, the swift water remains as it always was, except that the bridges cross the two channels. The ship lock at Ste Anne's parallels the rapids there but does not diminish them. The Lake of Two Mountains and what may be called Carillon Lake, vast expanses of quiet water, bring us up to Ottawa. There the Chaudière, as we have already had to note, is cluttered with a miscellany of buildings, only the curved overflow dam with its sluices giving us any impression at all of what the falls used to be like. Immediately upstream, within the boundaries of Ottawa, there are small rapids still to be seen just above Lemieux Island (the Little Chaudière Rapids), again at the Champlain Bridge (the Remic Rapids), and near Britannia (the Deschenes Rapids). Small though they are in comparison with the greater falls of the past, they are yet most pleasant features of the river in the Ottawa area. Then come Lac Deschenes, Chats

Lake, and the unnamed lake above the Chenaux plant, giving smooth water up to the tailrace of the plant at Bryson. On the west side of Calumet Island, however, the river still remains as it was (apart from one small control dam), but it, too, will be flooded when eventually the Rocher Fendu plant is constructed. Here are rapids, but no roads, and so they remain virtually unseen. After this we have still water again all the way to Mattawa.

Is the Ottawa still a waterway? It is indeed, in some ways more so than ever before, although busy with craft far different from those of the pioneers. Each of the 'lakes' has its own complement of pleasure craft, both sail and power propelled, with the necessary dock and wharfage facilities, some in the form of modern marinas. Since the power-boat industry is reputed to be one of the fastest growing in the North American affluent society, these inland lake fleets of pleasure craft, together with the facilities to service them, may be expected to increase steadily in size as the years go by. Each fleet is, naturally, confined to its own waters, apart from those on the Lake of Two Mountains and between Carillon and Ottawa. Here we still do have a through waterway, connecting at Ste Anne's with the St Lawrence system which, through Sorel and the Richelieu River, gives access to the Hudson River in the United States and so to the Inland Waterway of the Atlantic coast and all connecting channels. At Ottawa is the entrance to the Rideau Canal, passage through which gives access to Lake Ontario and so to the New York State Barge Canal at Oswego; and, by passing up the Welland Canal, to the Chicago Drainage Canal and thence to the Mississippi system with all its interconnected mid-continent waterways. Intrepid voyagers in suitably equipped vessels can eventually reach the Gulf of Mexico, the Panama Canal, and the West Coast of the continent. This is no dream of an enthusiast. Every year Ottawa is visited by welcome guests from the United States, some of whose vessels have travelled from these far places to the 'Golden Triangle,' as the Montreal-Ottawa-Kingston-Montreal route has often been described since the days of steamship travel on these waters.

Special mention must be made of one vessel that may be seen sailing on Lac Deschenes, out of the Britannia Yacht Club. This is the *Blackjack*, a brigantine owned and sailed by Captain Tom Fuller, a well-known contractor of Ottawa with a naval record during the Second World War of unusual distinction. The ship is now fore-and-aft rigged on the mainmast and square-rigged on the foremast, and splendidly equipped. All this would not call for mention were it not for the fact that the *Blackjack* used to be the *C.B. Pattee II*, the last of the steel-hulled steam-driven ships of the river fleet on Lac Deschenes. The remodelling has been most expertly done. No lover of the river can watch the *Blackjack* under sail without recalling the days that have gone, the days when she was but one of a fine group of ships sailing this part of the waterway.

Visitors to Ottawa have the opportunity during summer months of a brief sail on the river, starting from almost the same place as did the steamers of decades ago, but using the cruise service that is now well established both on the Ottawa River and the Rideau Canal. The tug boats of the Upper Ottawa Improvement Company above the Chaudière, and of the Canadian International Paper Company below it, still add their own activity to the river scene as they haul booms of pulpwood downstream to the mills. Even this apparently mundane activity enjoyed an unusual burst of publicity in 1973 when attempts were made by a flotilla of small boats on Lake Temiskaming to prevent 60,000 cords of pulpwood from being hauled down the lake to the Ottawa for use in the Gatineau Mill rather than in the mill at Temiskaming, which was threatened with closing.

The river was also used for some years by tugs hauling a very different kind of load – barges full of excellent sand and gravel – out of the Lake of Two Mountains to the Montreal docks for use in the building of that great metropolitan area. Beyond this, however, commercial use of the Ottawa is now limited but not negligible. When major construction projects are undertaken on or adjacent to the river, water transport again comes into its own as an economical and convenient way of handling unusually heavy loads. During the construction of the new bridge over the Lake of Two Mountains, across Île aux Tourtes, the contractors built at the site a giant barge. It measured 160 feet long and was 50 feet wide. It was needed later for similar use at the Boucherville bridge-tunnel project, downstream from the centre of Montreal. The barge was too large to go through the lock at Ste Anne's and so it was navigated through the rapids by Norman St Aubin, a veteran river-man. Barges that did fit into canal locks have been used by the Dominion Bridge Company to move heavy structural steel sections and prefabricated elements from their plant at Lachine to Ottawa for the MacDonald-Cartier Bridge, the Portage Bridge, and also the new grandstand at Lansdowne Park, all with safety and economy.

Between the great days of lumber haulage on the Ottawa and the handling of such occasional and exceptional loads, there is one small additional chapter that brought to a close the continuous use of the river for regular commercial purposes. The Ottawa Transportation Company continued in operation, on a small schedule, until 1941 when its charter was finally surrendered. In its later years, it carried coal and oil from Montreal, the oil being delivered into large storage tanks, now gone, which were located on the Richmond Landing. Oil shipments to Ottawa continued until after the Second World War years in a fleet of small, specially designed tankers owned and operated by major oil companies. They worked to a regular schedule, a typical round trip for the *Supertest*, for example, being to leave Ottawa at noon one day, arriving back with a full load from Montreal just twenty-four hours later. Even this use of the river was finally rendered obsolete by pipelines through which all oil supplies for the capital city are now delivered.

The waterway is still available, therefore, for unusual shipments that can be made only, or most conveniently, by water, but these are bound to be the exception, as are also the occasional uses of the river as a through route by canoes. The canoe pageant that formed so interesting a part of Canada's Centennial celebrations in 1967 was the highlight of all recent uses of the Ottawa by canoes. All the crews from the west, using simulated North canoes, crossed Lake Nipissing after coming up the French River; they made the difficult descent of the Mattawa and then paddled down the Ottawa all the way to Montreal. Naturally they had to portage their canoes and loads round each of the great power dams but they were spared the heavy loads that the early *voyageurs* had to tote. They had ready assistance and much free advice from the public, who were attracted to this imaginative reminder of past uses of the Ottawa River. A little-known Centennial project on the river was the canoe journey from Ottawa to Montreal by Mrs Agnes Dexter, a lady then in her seventieth year, accompanied by her daughter. Averaging about fifteen miles a day, the two venturesome ladies reached Como without any trouble but were there persuaded to leave the river because of high winds. And almost every year one hears of, or sees, a few adventurous young people paddling up or down the Ottawa, despite the dams, inspired by what they have heard about the journeys of the pioneers.

There is yet another way in which the Ottawa continues to provide a waterway – through the several cross-river ferry services that remain. One of the mysteries of the Ottawa River is why so few eastern Canadians seem even to know about the ferries, let alone use them as short-cuts between the few bridges that span the river, or as breaks from the tedium of motoring along crowded highways. The ferry service from Oka to Como is in continuous service every year as long as the Lake of Two Mountains is clear of ice, the crossing with a modern diesel boat taking about ten minutes. They can be ten minutes of real delight for all who like the water, giving most satisfying views of the lovely shores of the lake as well as a reminder, to all who are in the least historically minded, of what the lake used to be like.

Since this ferry operates entirely within the province of Quebec, its operation comes under the jurisdiction of the Quebec Transport Commission. Although the two provinces, Ontario and Quebec, have developed interprovincial power on the Ottawa, the government of Canada still maintains control of interprovincial bridges and ferries. As the Glassco Royal Commission discovered in the course of its wide-ranging inquiry into governmental operations, the Ferries Act, dated from 1868, among other things regulated until recently interprovincial ferry services – matters of prime importance in earlier days. Time has changed, but this law required that the grant of a licence to operate local ferry services between places on the opposite sides of the Ottawa River 'shall be made under the Great Seal, and shall be issued by the Governor in Council.' When, therefore, any reader of this book boards an Ottawa River ferry, other than at Oka or Carillon, he may well recall that he is doing so under the highest legal auspices of the land. Upstream of the Lake of Two Mountains, the next sail can be either at Pointe Fortune or Carillon. This is a relatively short crossing but it has the great advantage of being just downstream of the Carillon dam and powerhouse, of which splendid views are obtained throughout the crossing.

The next crossing, similarly direct, is between Lefaivre (Ontario) and Fassett (Quebec), and then one from Montebello wharf across to a small landing on the Ontario side from which the main highway can readily be reached. This is a particularly beautiful stretch of the river, which even the necessary cutting down of some of the great trees has not spoiled. All the ferries are well-constructed vessels capable of carrying a number of automobiles, a modest charge being made for each crossing. Some operate to a regular schedule but more usually the boats will oblige any prospective passengers, on either side of the river, if they make evident their desire to cross. Next is the crossing between Thurso on the Quebec side and Clarence, near Rockland, on the Ontario side, the distance from the main roads on both shores being quite short so that this is one of the more active ferries. So popular is this service that in 1962 a small canal, 625 feet long (really a big ditch) was excavated right through Clarence Island that lies directly between the two ferry docks, and around which the ferry boat used to have to navigate. Now it travels directly with an appreciable saving of time.

The island is shown on all recent maps as Clarence Island but older residents know it as Fox Island, as they know also Clarence Creek as Fox Creek. Further inquiry shows that the point of land immediately downstream of the Clarence landing was known as Fox Point, although not so marked on recent maps. And the Fox involved proves to be one of the almost forgotten pioneer settlers on the Ottawa, perhaps the first man to establish a permanent settlement upstream of the Long Sault, certainly antedating Philemon Wright. But his settlement did not endure as did Hull. James Fox was a native of Dublin who emigrated to New York in 1770, was drafted into the Revolutionary army and was with the contingent sent to capture Montreal, where he deserted. He married a French-Canadian girl named Mary Desang in 1780 and, having been told by friends about the Ottawa, came up the river a little later with his wife and new son and two or three servants in a single canoe. Mistaking the course of the main river, they camped for some days near what is now Montebello but went on again upstream, stopping near Rockland but finally selecting a site slightly downstream as their permanent home. This is the spot now known as Fox Point. Mary Fox died in 1816, aged sixty; James Fox lived seven years longer, being seventy-seven when he died; their joint grave was the first in the Clarence Cemetery, the years marked on a small monument. Their son became a local figure of note and had a large family, the late Dr Sherwood Fox – once president of the University of Western Ontario – being a descendant. They traded in furs at first but this did not last and their later years were spent similarly to many early settlers, living off the land with some lumbering and some farming.

Old Mr Fox used to relate a story about an even earlier settler at Butternut Point near his home, a French count who chose to stay in Canada after 1763. On his death, his countess married their clerk and, as Madame Perault, once rescued a young British army officer from Indians who had brought him bound to her trading post for torture. Waiting until the Indians were away hunting, she decoyed the women and children away and rescued the young man, dressed him in woman's attire and put him to bed, warning the Indians when they started their search that she had a very sick lady who could not be disturbed. Such was the courage of the pioneers; what other untold tales of similar adventure the Ottawa River must hold!

A few other settlers appear to have joined the Foxes but no permanent village developed for some time. In 1822, however, came the first of a family still well known in the Ottawa Valley. John Edwards, a native of Morayshire in Scotland, was a shipwright who had emigrated to New York in 1819, came to work in the naval dockyard in Kingston but eventually decided to settle on the Ottawa. After selecting the neighbourhood of Fox Point, already being called Clarence, he walked back to Kingston and organized a group of families who, with their belongings, sailed from Kingston down the St Lawrence and then up the Ottawa, in a naval batteau lent to them on condition that it be returned when they were finished with it. They reached Fox Point safely despite the ascent of the Long Sault and all settled at Clarence.

John Edwards was a devout Baptist and organized a meeting-house at Clarence in 1825. He travelled up and down the river by canoe every summer Sunday to hold services in the small scattered settlements then beginning, and was instrumental in the founding of at least six Baptist churches in the valley. On one of his canoe journeys the steersman guided his frail craft too close to one of the early paddle-wheel steamers. Edwards was tipped out so close to the ship that he was caught up by one of the paddle wheels, carried round for two revolutions while grasping one of the blades, and lived to tell the tale. He assisted in the establishment of Baptist education in Canada, persuading Reverend John Gilmour of Aberdeen to come out to Canada. He was thus indirectly responsible for yet another university president – Dr G.P. Gilmour of McMaster University, a direct descendant. One of his sons started in the lumber business with a steam sawmill at Rockland, and W.C. Edwards and Company became one of the famous firms of the valley, the family tradition continuing today in the firm of D. Kemp Edwards and Company.

Continuing upstream, we find the next ferry running between Masson and Cumberland, at the end of a long but clearly marked road leading down from the Quebec Highway No. 8. The landing wharf is within sight of Ontario Highway No. 17, so the ferryboat can often be seen by any motorists who can spare a second to glance at the river. Again the crossing is direct and relatively short, but my wife and I will never forget one trip we made on this ferry that made us wonder if we were ever going to see land.

It was on a stormy night late in November; we doubted whether the ferry would still be running. But when we came out of the darkness into the light of the Masson wharf, the captain said he would take us. It was very dark, with no moon or stars, and a strong wind from the east was blowing up the river. The temperature had been dropping all evening, as it can on those early winter nights, but we did not realize how quickly the freezing point had been reached. We blocked our car in the centre of the steel deck and then set out into the pitch black of the night, a small searchlight the only light showing in addition to navigation lights on port and starboard. The wind must have suddenly increased for waves were soon dashing over the boat and onto the car, the water freezing as it struck the metal body, so cold had it become. The ferryboats are not exactly designed for rough seas, and it was a rough sea indeed that evening. After what seemed to be an age, the little searchlight picked out something in the darkness; we slowly approached the wharf and berthed, but only with the greatest difficulty. The deck and our car were coated with a layer of ice which we had to chip off; and as we did so the captain, obviously relieved to have made port, said he was going to stay there for the night.

In great contrast to this crossing are the many fine sails that we, and many other lovers of the river, have enjoyed on the Quyon ferry, running between the Quyon wharf and a stage called Mohr's Landing. The latter is the most isolated of all the ferry landings, Fitzroy Harbour being the nearest town; the road connections are not particularly well marked. But it is well used: this is the only ferry on the Ottawa that schedules two boats in service together when the traffic demands it, despite the fact that the crossing is but little longer than most of the direct routes from bank to bank. It is, however, not only an efficient and convenient ferry but, in our view, quite the most beautiful, the wooded banks of the river today being very much as they must have been when the early *voyageurs* reached this turn in the lake (it is located at the upstream end of Lac Deschenes) to be faced with the great Chats Falls in all their glory. The falls have gone, their sound stilled for all time. Fortunately, the rather mundane powerhouse and dam cannot quite be seen from the ferry so that if one faces the Ontario shore and disregards the cables of a transmission line crossing the river, it is a wholly sylvan scene that meets the eye. Our only complaint about the Quyon ferry is that the crossing is always over too soon; but then we have long since been lovers of waterways rather than highways. It must be the general worship of speed that has driven other ferries from the river. We can remember the service between Fort Coulonge and La Passe, now no more. Others will recall the sturdy boat that plied between Norway Bay and Sand Point on Chats Lake.

We are thinking of the river as it is, however, and not as it was. Use of the ferry services can be most warmly recommended but they show only very small sections of the river of today. How can the river best be seen by those who do not have the opportunity of travelling on it by private boat? There remain the roads and the railways. Surprising though it may seem, there are still sections of the Ottawa that can be seen from the coaches of railway trains but not from any road. This exploration of the waterway will not seek to be a tourist guide with long, impersonal, listings. Rather let me try to act as a counsellor, indicating the roads that may best be used for seeing the river, mentioning just a few of the more unusual places to be seen, but generally leaving each reader to make his own way in his own time on personal journeys of discovery. It will probably be convenient if we consider the valley in three main sections – from Ste Anne de Bellevue to the first bridge crossing at Hawkesbury-Grenville; then on from there up to Ottawa and including the capital area; and finally that part of the river above the Chaudière, with a natural subdivision at Pembroke.

Coming from Montreal, one should first make a brief stop at Lachine in order to see the old warehouse of the Hudson's Bay Company, a fine old stone building suitably marked, now used by a religious order. This means using the old lakeshore road, No. 2, although brief mention should be made of the usual way of dashing out of the city and off the island on the new highway, No. 40. The latter does afford a wonderful view of the Lake of Two Mountains as the main part of the great bridge is crossed, but only a brief glance at Île aux Tourtes. Thereafter the road is located some distance from the river, a few sections only of which can be seen in the distance in the vicinity of Rigaud. Once the Ontario border is crossed the river is increasingly far to the right as the new road turns inland to avail itself of the flat terrain of the great inter-river plain all the way to Ottawa. This is an advantage for all who wish to hurry from city to city but the interest provided by the older routes has been lost.

When we reach Hawkesbury, we can cross the bridge to Grenville which is named after Sir George Perley, a distinguished local public figure of the interwar years. As the bridge is approached its odd hump-backed appearance will be noticed. This is not an indication of initial poor design but rather of its flexibility, which permitted the superstructure of the bridge to be raised and one span replaced by a steel truss span when the Carillon power development was constructed, in order to give the necessary clearance beneath it for navigation – another reminder that the river still is a waterway, at least in this section. Raising the water level not only drowned out the magnificent rapids of the Long Sault, the upper part of which could be seen so well in earlier days from the lookout just east of Hawkesbury on the old river road, but changed appreciably the appearance of the river bank near the Ontario end of the bridge, once the location of sawmills and other local industry. Advantage has been taken of the change to lay out an attractive little park in which an interesting small museum is to be found and adjacent to which is a public wharf for power-boats.

If time permits, it is worth parking one's car after leaving the Quebec end of the bridge in order to walk back a short distance, since a good view can be obtained of the old Grenville Canal as it passes under the bridge. Despite the rise in the water level of the river, the canal is clearly visible on both sides of the bridge, its tree-lined banks giving some indication of the pleasant bypass that it used to provide around the turbulent rapids. Resuming our journey by road, however, we must make a sharp turn to the right at the foot of the incline from the bridge and start to retrace our journey back to Montreal, although now on the Quebec shore. Surprisingly, a railway station will be seen on the left a short distance from the bridge, on a line seemingly stopping nowhere. The station is that for Grenville; the line is a branch of the Canadian National Railways. It used to cross the road (as can still be seen) and proceed to a bridge across the river into Hawkesbury, with connections beyond. This bridge was one of the unusual ventures of the Canadian Northern Railway, having been built in 1899, but traffic over it was never heavy. Rather than reconstruct it when the water level in the river was raised, the decision was taken to abandon it. The Grenville branch is, however, still used as far as the isolated station by the road; a weekly train from Montreal on Fridays and a return train on Monday mornings being still provided as this is written. These details would not call for mention were it not for the fact that the last six miles of this CNR branch line use the same right-of-way as did the old portage railway.

We pass through Cushing and Greece's Point, as does the railway – pleasant, well settled riverside communities, but there are signs of the change in this part of the valley caused by the Carillon Dam. Some new sections of road have had to be built, at higher elevations than previously. Once Greece's Point is passed, the road is entirely new, having been reconstructed on top of the long, low dam that had to be built here to form part of the reservoir rim as the alternative to flooding a large area of land to the north.

The drive along this embankment is an interesting experience for all who know the river. A few projections from the still waters of the raised river indicate where the canal used to be. In the distance the headworks of the Carillon development can clearly be seen. On the left is the railway, now well below the elevation of the road and, towards Carillon, on a new right-of-way. A stop is recommended just before the road swings round to the left, for here, at the foot of the bank to the north, may still be seen the little feeder channel to the original Carillon Canal, coming from the North River. Its continued existence is part of one of the more interesting old-and-new features along the Ottawa. To the right of the road, as we resume our journey, the fine landscaping that Hydro Quebec has carried out at this end of the Carillon Dam may clearly be seen, the start of a great project for an extensive Dollard des Ormeaux Park.

As the dam and powerhouse come into view there will be noticed on the top of a knoll in the park a large assemblage of rectangular blocks of concrete. It must be made clear that these are not, as some visitors think, a number of pieces of concrete left over from the construction operations, but rather an ultra-modern artistic tribute to the heroism of Dollard des Ormeaux and his young companions, in rather striking contrast to the small but dignified memorial to them that was erected long ago in the village. Before the village is entered a stop may well be made at the parking lot near the power development. Some will wish to see this magnificent example of modern Canadian engineering but readers of this book may prefer to walk off to the left, to see the remains of the old masonry lock wall now incorporated into the concrete approach wall to the vast new navigation lock, and, more particularly, to look down into the remains of the first lock of the original Carillon Canal, fortunately fairly well preserved. Standing on the point of this little park with the old lock on one side and the new power station on the other, one has to be insensitive to a degree not to feel the stirrings of historical interest. This stop, however, is but a prelude to one of the greatest historical delights of the Ottawa Valley.

At the end of the village street, just after one passes the ferry landing, there stands a fine well-preserved masonry building. This is the museum of the Argenteuil County Historical Society, and a visit is really obligatory for all interested in the Ottawa River. The building is a British military structure erected in 1829 for service as a barracks for troops at the canals while they were still under the control of the British army. It has been excellently preserved and but little restored, so that to walk its solid floors is to get an immediate feel for the past. Leased to the society, it now contains a most interesting collection. Models of the Ottawa River steamships are there, as also displays of ladies' costumes of an earlier age. There are some relics of the portage railway, the most important of which few visitors notice, for it is the old conical smokestack of the locomotive, now stored beneath a wooden porch on the river side of the building. The society is one of several that bring together, in main centres along the valley, those interested in its history. Special tribute must be paid to the members of the Argenteuil Society, notably Dr G.H. Rigby and Miss Helen Lambart, for all the work they did in recording as much as possible of the old Ottawa River canals and the older buildings associated with them before all disappeared beneath the rising waters behind the Carillon Dam.

Our journey continues through St Andrews with its broad streets reminding one of the gracious living of an earlier age, and the plaque commemorating the first paper mill of Canada. Instead of turning up to Lachute, we continue on Highway 29 which again becomes the river road, leading through Oka and past the other ferry landing of the Oka-Como

**S.S.** *Ann Sisson* at Quyon Wharf. The white horse and the two little cars of the horse railway can just be discerned on the platform at the right that carried the railway some distance above the wharf; it was reached by a long stairway. The photograph was probably taken in the 1870s.

The broad-gauge train that operated between the steamer wharves at Grenville and Carillon during the third quarter of the nineteenth century. The locomotive faced upstream so the little train is on its way to the Grenville wharf.

The S.S. *G.B. Greene* at a wharf on Lac Deschenes, early in the twentieth century.

Modern marker at the Vase Portage near North Bay, adjacent to the main road (No. 17), in place during the 1960s but now removed.

Mouth of the Vase River in Lake Nipissing with memorial cairn. The site has been developed by the city of North Bay as a pleasant park, also named after Champlain.

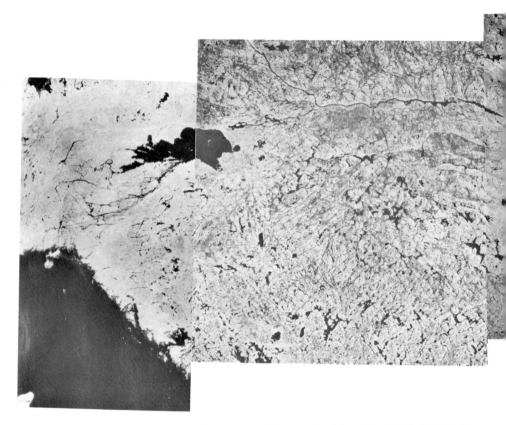

View of the entire Ottawa Waterway as photographed from the Earth Resources
Technology Satellite (E.R.T.S.) at a height of over 500 miles. From Lake Huron
on the left to Montreal on the right is over 430 miles.

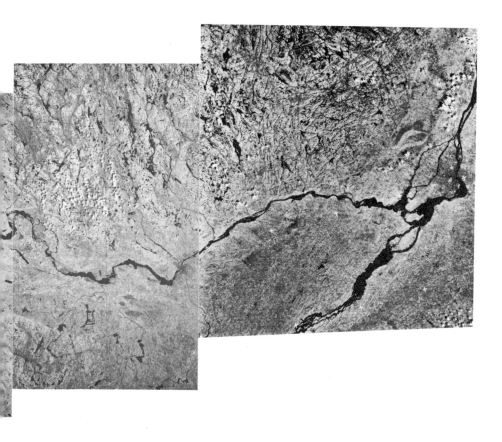

The cofferdam in place for the first phase in constructing the Carillon Dam and power-house. The view looks upstream: the cofferdam is keeping river water out of the area to the left in which the left half of the dam will be built. The Ottawa River canals on the right are soon to be submerged above the Dam.

crossing, La Trappe and the famous monastery, with fine glimpses of the lake, and finally we pass through St Eustache with its bullet-marked church, a sobering reminder of the troubles of 1837, before we are again on the Island of Montreal. The crossings of the Rivière des Milles Îles and the Back River or Rivière des Prairies, two of the four outlets of the Ottawa River from the Lake of Two Mountains, show well the greatness of the river.

More dramatic are the other two outlets, at Ste Anne de Bellevue and Vaudreuil, with the rapids and swift water so clearly to be seen from the two suites of bridges that carry the old main road and both railways first to Île Perrot and then on to the mainland at Vaudreuil. A visit to the riverside church at Ste Anne repeats the old ceremony of the early *voyageurs* before they set off up the river on their journeys to the west. We now know well how crucial to navigation up the Ottawa is the single lock close to the shore at Ste Anne. Looking up the lake from this fine masonry structure shows clearly the strategic position of Île aux Tourtes. An even better view of the lake and its islands can be obtained if access to the well-kept grounds of the Domtar Research Laboratories can be gained. The importance of the old fort at Senneville, its ruins now to be seen only from the water, can well be appreciated from this vantage point.

Crossing to Vaudreuil, we must make a sharp turn in the town onto the original road to Ottawa which followed the river bank throughout almost its entire length, as was so natural in early roads. Through old Vaudreuil, Como, Hudson Heights, and Choisy the road stays close to the water so that some splendid views of the lake are to be enjoyed – and they can be, since this is a road on which one must travel at relatively slow speeds. With a slight diversion at Rigaud, the same old road can be followed into Pointe Fortune, still a charming riverside community although now dominated by the adjacent Carillon Dam. The ferry still operates, however, its route being below the dam; but the continuation of the old road through Chute à Blondeau that used to give such fine glimpses of the rapids in the river has gone. One must now turn up a road away from the river to gain access again to Highway 17 along which our journey up the river can continue, past the junction leading to Hawkesbury. Beyond this point the road returns fairly close to its original route (still followed in places) so that it again becomes a real river road.

There is no need to detail the many fine views of the river that one obtains in making this sixty-mile drive; they speak for themselves. Near Rockland and Cumberland the road runs right on the river bank, affording wide-ranging views of the river and its other shore. Proximity to the river has brought its own penalty to the road since some small landslides have taken place, notably just to the west of Cumberland, in all probability as a result of the recent change in the level of the river from the Carillon development. Correspondingly, Highway No. 8 on the Quebec shore is also a river road for almost all of its length to Hull, rarely very close to the river bank but in many places high enough in elevation to provide good views of the river and its valley. The South Nation River, with its meandering entry to the Ottawa, is the main tributary to be crossed on the south shore but on the Quebec side there are crossings of the Rouge, the Petite Nation, the Lièvre, the Blanche, and the Gatineau to remind the traveller of the many feeders of the Ottawa that drain from the lakes of the Precambrian Shield, which makes itself so evident by the escarpment that closely follows the north bank of the river.

There are to be seen many evidences of the lumbering that is still active in the woods to the north. Almost all who use this road, however, will pass through Thurso without realizing that the pulp mill there and the associated furniture factory are supplied with hardwood brought from the woods along one of the few private logging railways still operated in eastern Canada, built originally by the Singer Sewing Machine Company although now owned by the MacLaren Company through one of its subsidiaries. Ferry landings will be passed at Fassett, Montebello, Thurso, and Masson. Just to the west of the main part of Montebello, the dignified entrance to what is now the Château Montebello will be passed. For many years a private club, this magnificent property is now operated as a hotel so that the public may enjoy not only the excellent service in the 'biggest log cabin in the world' but also the delights of the river view from the well-kept gardens and a visit to the original manor house of Louis-Joseph Papineau. And those who visit the lovely little Anglican chapel adjacent to this historic house may be moved, as I was when first I saw it, to copy down the inscription engraved on a bright plaque on the left wall.

The Capital region of Ottawa-Hull is dominated by the Ottawa River, the Gatineau River bounding it on the northeast, the Rideau River and Canal adding their own charm to the central part of Ottawa. The flight of locks in the heart of the city serves as a constant reminder of the silver link that the Rideau Waterway provides between Ottawa and Kingston, although now with little to remind visitors of the original military purpose of the canal. But a visit to the Bytown Museum, housed in the original old masonry workshop building amid the trees, halfway down the flight of locks, will soon bring this history vividly to mind. Developed and maintained by the members of the Historical Society of Ottawa, the Bytown

Museum is one of the real highlights of the valley for all who wish to savour something of its history.

The bridges are a vital and integral part of the civic scene. The elegant lines of the Macdonald-Cartier bridge blend remarkably well into the beauty of its setting. Gaunt and unattractive as the cantilever frame of the Interprovincial – or more properly the Alexandra – Bridge may be, it has its own claim to fame, for, as previously noted, when constructed in 1900 it had the longest cantilever span in North America. It is still a notable engineering structure, still useful, and fortunately still available for the day when Ottawa-Hull will construct the rapid-transit rail system that the capital area can be seen even now to need.

We have already had occasion to look at the Chaudière. Unattractive though the Alexandra Bridge may be, it is still a thing of beauty when compared with the disfigurement that has, over many long years, completely spoiled the great cataract of the Chaudière. We cannot blame our forefathers since they merely did what came naturally in Victorian times. But Ottawa-Hull citizens of today may well ask themselves if more could not have been done up to now to restore at least some of the beauty of this most famous of all the falls of the Ottawa. There have been plans but all have so far proved abortive. Industry cannot be expected to do more than offer its co-operation to public agencies. The move of part of the Eddy plant facing the Parliament Buildings shows that this co-operation can be anticipated without much question. But without the public voice being heard, nothing will be done. Already the interesting remains of the Wright log-chute on the Hull side have been desecrated. The remaining arch of the first bridge across the Ottawa has been so surrounded by modern structures that very few, even in Ottawa, know that it is still there, still graceful in its original setting, still sound masonry. The old Bryson log-chute, adjacent to Victoria Island, scene of so many regal and viceregal adventures, has been replaced by a utilitarian slide for modern use, efficient but certainly not beautiful and with nothing to indicate the historic nature of its predecessor.

Victoria Island offered an opportunity for redevelopment as a historic park, with some of its interesting old buildings still intact, the adjacent log-slide and the Richmond Landing at its side. A plan for this was prepared but never even publicized, let alone implemented. A great new public building was to have been erected on Le Breton Flats, the landscaping for which would have provided rare opportunity for some recognition of the historic past of this area. The old Thomson Mill building has been renovated and converted into a restaurant, already well known in Ottawa; but, apart from this, little effective restoration can now be done at the southern end of the Chaudière because of the construction of the latest and the only questionable one of the bridges across the Ottawa, the so-called Portage Bridge. Much can still be done at the Chaudière, even though less than is historically desirable. It is greatly to be hoped that the public conscience on this matter can be so aroused that the responsible authorities will be moved to take action before it is too late. Power plants and some industrial buildings must remain but glimpses of the real Chaudière could be regained.

Immediately above the Chaudière is the pioneer railway bridge of the valley, that built in 1880 to give the Canadian Pacific Railway access to the Quebec side of the river. Actually there are two bridges, the first from the Quebec shore to Lemieux Island, the second from the island to the Ontario shore, the latter now paralleled by the bridges leading to the water filtration plant on the island. The third most recent of the Ottawa bridges, built in 1928 and replacing minor bridges that had linked the mainland with Bate, Cunningham, and Riopelle Islands, has an incomparable setting with the islands at its southern end and the Remic Rapids beneath it, always an interesting sight for first visitors to Ottawa, especially if logs have been run in the river leaving the invariable stray logs wedged in rocky corners, mute testimony to the hazardous but skilful work still carried out every season by Ottawa river-men.

Making a right-hand turn when Highway No. 8 is reached again, one should follow the highway as far as Val Tetreau, the community that lies just at the start of the splendid Driveway up into Gatineau Park. Another right turn should be made immediately opposite the exit lane from the Driveway, down Rue Begin, and this should be followed to its junction near the river with Rue Bourget. Here the automobile may be deserted temporarily for a journey back in time. The attractive little park is named after Jean de Brébeuf, a statue of whom stands at the upstream end of the park, the inscription a constant reminder of his martyrdom on 16 March 1649. He passed this spot on his Ottawa River journeys and camped nearby. If we now walk to the downstream end of the park, we can see a large boulder decorated with crossed paddles in metal. These point the way to a pathway along the very edge of the river, half a mile in length, leading to a deep pool at the foot of the Little Chaudière Rapids along the side of which we shall be walking. On the way there are steps to descend, steps in solid rock, some formed of well-worn boulders. Well worn they are indeed, for this is the original second (or little) Chaudière Portage route exactly as it was used by the pioneers, and yet within sight of the Parliament Buildings of Canada, less than half a mile away.

Along the portage trail there will be found a plaque bearing this inscription:

This commemorates the second (or little) Chaudière portage which extended from the West end of Brébeuf Park to the Deep Bay half a mile downstream. Over this portage passed first Champlain in 1613 and until the middle of the last century nearly all the Canadian explorers and fur traders on their canoe route from Montreal through Lakes Nipissing, Superior and Winnipeg to the Athabasca country and the Rocky Mountains. Brûlé, Radisson, Groseilliers and LaSalle in the seventeenth century; La Vérendrye, Alexander Henry the elder, Peter Pond, Alexander Mackenzie in the eighteenth century; Daniel Harmon, Alexander Henry the younger, David Thompson and Simon Fraser in the last century – all trod this path. The crude stone steps and rock causeway a few paces to the east of this marker were constructed by the voyageurs to help them carry their heavy loads of furs and trading articles past this rapid [now mostly drowned out by the Chaudière Dam]. The Portage remains in its original state and other sets of steps may be noted further along the path. This portage was declared a National Historic Site by the National Historic Sites and Monuments Board of Canada on June 8 1954. This marker was erected in October 1955 by the Men's Canadian Club and the Women's Canadian Club of Ottawa.

Ottawa is indebted to these public-spirited clubs for thus marking so historic a site. Disfigurement of the plaque and occasional minor vandalism show that some people do pass along this historic trail but I have not spoken to more than half a dozen citizens of Ottawa-Hull who have walked the portage. Many residents of the capital area have never even heard of it and are incredulous to know that, so close at hand, there is such a vivid reminder of the great days of canoe travel on the Ottawa. The swift water itself is glorious to see, again so close to the city's centre, as are also the Deschenes Rapids, easily reached by a short side trip from the main road to Aylmer.

Aylmer itself can still remind the observant visitor of its great days as the 'port' on Lac Deschenes. The location of its busy wharf can readily be discerned, since hard by still stands – but only just – what is left of the Symmes Landing Inn, the Symmes Hotel so well known to early travellers, the taking-off point for early-morning journeys up the lake on the *Lady Colborne* and other steamers.

Before we embark upon the last part of our exploration of the Ottawa

Waterway, we may take a side trip up the Gatineau Parkway as far as the Champlain Lookout. On a clear day, the view up the valley is rewarding, almost all of Lac Deschenes being visible. The change in the nature of the landscape at Chats Falls will be evident, a reminder of the way in which geology has determined the land forms of the valley. Close at hand is an even clearer reminder, since adjacent to the lookout the ancient rocks of the Precambrian Shield plunge down beneath the flat clay plain, the junction being readily visualized as an ancient shoreline. The ancient rocks do indeed continue beneath the more recent Paleozoic rocks, so widely exposed as the local limestones and sandstones, over which lies the sediment, laid down in the Champlain Sea, known as the Leda Clay. As we set out up the valley, therefore, the varying geology that we see explains much of the different landscapes.

Perhaps the best way to start is to use Quebec Highway No. 8 again, carrying on through the town of Aylmer. The road is narrow so that driving must be unusually slow but this will enable fine views of Lac Deschenes to be enjoyed the more, there being a particularly fine vista just before the railway station at Breckenridge is passed. The road turns away from the river soon after this but glimpses of the water can still be seen across the fertile fields. As we pass through Luskville, we are close again to the escarpment provided by the edge of the Shield, this being a particularly dramatic exposure.

The road has been reconstructed from a point just east of Quyon, another community that should be visited, if only to use the ferry. For those who have the time, exploration of the side roads leading down to the river just to the west of Quyon, with ordnance maps in hand, will enable them to find the route of the old horse-railway and, after a climb over rocky terrain, the abortive excavation for the ill-fated ship canal around Chats Falls. The river road can be followed upstream and this will permit a visit to the iron mine at Bristol, now a gigantic excavation. All the ore, however, is moved by railway, so that it has no direct connection with the river. Norway Bay, long a famous summer resort, can also be visited before a return is made to Highway No. 8. The fertile land around Shawville will show why Clarendon Township was so favourite a location for early settlers even though it is a little difficult to remember, as we drive along the modern highway, that they came to it by way of the river, now far to our left.

At Bryson, however, we are back with the river again, and a visit to the dam and powerhouse will give a good idea of what the gorge here used to be like, a formidable obstacle to canoe travellers. Calumet Island can readily be visited from here and a variety of scenes of the river enjoyed from its quiet roads. Beyond Bryson the river is now another lake, the water impounded by the dam which floods back all the way to Allumette Island. This provides some lovely views from the road, at Campbell's Bay and beyond Fort Coulonge. This famous settlement is still the site of lumbering operations so that, at the appropriate times, logs can be seen floating down the Coulonge River where the road crosses it, having come through the Grand Chute at the falls about three miles above the town. Just beyond the bridge, the road turns and reveals a splendid covered bridge, still in use, preserved through the active interest of local residents. Booming of the logs takes place just downstream of this bridge so that it is a pleasant place to stop and dawdle on a sunny day when the logs are running. Several large sand and gravel pits close to the road are useful reminders of the great glacial rivers that deposited this material.

The road continues round the head of the lake provided by the Bryson Dam, thereafter following the Culbute Channel (so well used by the *voyageurs*) just after passing Waltham, which is the end of the C.P.R. line that we have been paralleling up the valley. We must take the right-hand road at the junction here, the main road going to the left to Allumette Island and so over to Pembroke, so that we may parallel the Culbute Channel passing the bridge at Chapeau as we continue on to Sheenboro, then turning left for a brief visit to what is left of Fort William. And this is the end of the road up the valley on its Quebec shore. This is a fact that few Canadians realize until they actually travel the valley roads and then come to realize that from this point westwards the Quebec shore of the Ottawa River is virtually the same as it has been for centuries, just the same as it was when the early explorers and *voyageurs* paddled these waters. Fort William is another of the boom headquarters for the Upper Ottawa Improvement Company, a quiet and secluded spot but still a place of memories.

As we retrace our steps to Chapeau, the splendid character of this most isolated road will be noticed, the result of a major reconstruction job of the early seventies. Why this road should have been given this fine treatment, rather than the heavily travelled section of No. 8 between Hull and Quyon, must remain one of the minor political mysteries of the valley. Over the bridge and up the hill at Chapeau, we have a few miles of pleasant travel on Allumette and Morrison Islands, now fertile farm lands with good bush lots which were, as we may recall, homes of the Indian residents of the valley many years ago, and well known indeed to the early river travellers. A further bridge over the main channel of the Ottawa brings us to Ontario Highway No. 17.

This is the road we would use in coming up the Ontario side of the valley from Ottawa, after a brief excursion along the roads of Torbolton and Fitzroy Townships permitting visits to such places as Baskin's Wharf, MacLaren's Landing, the Quyon ferry landing, and Fitzroy Harbour, all with their own views of the river. Once Ottawa is left, the main road affords no opportunities for seeing the river until after the crossing of the Mississippi River as Arnprior is approached. We cross the Madawaska at the entrance to the town, the placid appearance of the river as it approaches its junction with the Ottawa giving no indication of its original turbulence, now tamed by the power plants along its course. Brief reference must be made to the delights of the valley of the Madawaska, well worth a side trip certainly as far up as the great Mountain Chute hydro-electric plant. In Arnprior itself there is, again, an engaging little museum to enjoy, this one located in the old Post Office building, donated to the city by Mr. D.A. Gillies, of the Gillies family of lumber fame, a notable resident of the valley who died only in November 1967. He served as a clerk on the last raft of squared timber to be sent to Quebec by Gillies Brothers, in 1905.

Instead of continuing along No. 17, we will use the county road from Arnprior that runs along the river bank through Braeside and past the Gillies Brothers establishment, and through Sand Point and Castleford, with a succession of varying glimpses of the river. Just past the point at which our road joins the county road coming north from Renfrew, a steep hill leads down towards the river. A stop should be made at the crest of this hill since here is one of the finest of all river views from any of the valley roads, the gorge-like scene ahead being one that, apart only from the presence of the road, must be very similar to what it was before the white man came to the valley.

If we go down the hill we shall soon come to the Chenaux power station, another fine example of Canadian engineering well worth a visit if time permits. Continuing along the road, we shall cross the new bridge that here spans the Ottawa, coming round to the north end of the powerhouse, then crossing two other channels of the river, with fine views below, along the crests of the spillway structures.

The village of Portage du Fort stands at the end of the dam, a pleasant quiet place long famous in the story of the river. At its eastern end there is a white marble war memorial, noticed by visitors to the village as they pass by. We must stop, however, and look at the reverse (or river) side of the monument, for there we shall see this inscription, engraved in a slab of the white marble of which the whole monument is built:

To commemorate the visit of LADY HEAD, who made the tour of the Upper Ottawa in a bark canoe in September 1856.

The name 'W. McFarlan' appears below the inscription – presumably the name of the craftsman who carved this unique memorial. Lady Head was the wife of Sir Edmund Head, Governor of the Province of Canada from 1854 to 1861. No record of this interesting journey has yet been traced, but Dr. J.A. Gibson, joint author of the biography of Sir Edmund Head, tells me that the tradition of this journey still persists in the family. Although Lady Head was an artist, no sketch or painting that she may have made on this journey is known. The journey was, however, in keeping with the devotion of Sir Edmund and his wife to the country they served so well at a critical period in its history.

We must now retrace our journey to Renfrew, another active valley town, if only to visit the fine museum that has been developed here by the Renfrew and District Historical Society in the really splendid old building that once was the mill of John Lorn McDougal. The mill was built in 1855 but its conversion to a museum started only in 1969, following the development around it of the M.J. O'Brien Park, to mark Canada's Centennial of 1967 and to honour the name of Renfrew's most famous recent resident. One cannot even attempt to summarize the remarkable collection of varied historic items contained in the museum; it really must be seen, in the most appropriate setting of the old mill building.

Continuing our journey, we must give up river road travel between Renfrew and Pembroke, since Highway 17 follows roughly the Muskrat Lake route first used by Champlain. There is nothing to mark the start of this route at the Ottawa but about 2½ miles before Cobden is reached, a historic plaque and cairn indicate the place where Champlain is thought to have lost his astrolabe. At Cobden we see the south end of Muskrat Lake and we follow this to its outfall as the little Muskrat River, now so small a stream, except in spring flood, that it is difficult indeed to imagine its having been in regular use by a steamboat service – as it was.

So into Pembroke, past the junction with the road leading from Quebec Highway No. 8, with a stop at the next museum, the Champlain Trail Museum of the Ottawa Valley Historical Society. Housed in two small old buildings, one a schoolhouse from 1838, the collection includes a number of exhibits illustrating phases of the lumbering industry that has always meant so much to Pembroke. Some of these are so large that they are displayed in the attractive grounds around the museum, another local venture demonstrating the appreciation of the legacy of the past that is fortunately widely found in all parts of the valley.

Pembroke is served by the two main transcontinental railway lines up the valley and so we may remind ourselves of the views that they give of the Ottawa which are not obtainable from the roads we have been using. The C.N.R. line has followed an odd route, generally quite a distance from the river but with two major crossings due to its unusual location. The first bridge is just above Chats Falls, taking the line over into Quebec, and affords a good view of the river close to the upper end of the old horse-railway. The line crosses back into Ontario by a long bridge just to the west of the Chenaux power station, the two bridges having been built respectively in 1914 and 1913. Thereafter, although glimpses of the river can be obtained at one or two locations, the C.N.R. line on its way to the west becomes an inland route all the way to North Bay.

The C.P.R. line, also because of its origins, has an unusual route out of Ottawa but comes close to the river just west of Arnprior and thereafter is, for most of the way, a riverside line as far as Mattawa. After Castleford it turns inland, as did our highway route, going through Cobden with good views of Muskrat Lake. Beyond Pembroke, road and railway run parallel for about ten miles but then, between Chalk River and MacKay, the C.P.R. also becomes an inland line. It runs along the river bank again, however, at Stonecliff and thereafter provides a succession of splendid views of the river, from which it is never far separated. At Deux Rivières, road, railway, and river are all close together but afterwards the road turns inland and thence to Mattawa the railway alone follows the Ottawa, always close to the shoreline. So wide is Holden Lake (as the reservoir above the Des Joachims plant is officially called) that one can hear travellers on the transcontinental train, *The Canadian* asking, "What is this lake?", but at Klock the first signs of flow in the narrowed channel of the river can be seen. Here, sitting in the comfort of one of the finest trains ever to run on North American rails, one can look out across the few hundred feet of flowing water to the steep wooded Quebec bank of the Ottawa and see it exactly as did the pioneer *voyageurs* when they paddled up and down the great waterway.

Travelling by road, we leave Pembroke, still on Highway No. 17, heading west for one of the most attractive drives in eastern Canada, 132 miles of first-class road through beautiful country all the way to North Bay.

Petawawa with its great military camp is passed through soon after leaving Pembroke, the sand exposures to be seen all around indicating the usefulness of this area for its special purpose even as they can also remind us of the great delta in which this sand was long ago deposited. Canada's famous atomic research establishment will be passed at Chalk River, followed by the new associated town at Deep River, a development of the last twenty years which has a fine river frontage. At Rolphton is the pioneer demonstration atomic power plant with a lookout that gives a splendid vista of the Ottawa – Oiseau Rock in the distance and the sand spit of Point Baptême also to be seen, with its memories of initiation ceremonies for all novice *voyageurs*. A stop must be made to see the Des Joachims dam and power plant which have so completely transformed this part of the river.

If one crosses over to the small village of Rapide Des Joachims, located in Quebec but with access only from Ontario, glimpses of the river bed downstream will give some idea of what this turbulent section of the Ottawa used to be like. (Children from Des Joachims cross the river to go to school in Ontario, an interprovincial educational venture that has led to occasional minor problems!) Upstream of Des Joachims we have just the river to enjoy, with fine views at Bissett Creek and Deux Rivières across to a small mill of the Consolidated Bathurst Paper Company, smoke from which is usually the only sign of life on the Quebec shore. Gaps in the uniformly rolling topography of the Shield on this northern shore betray the valleys of rivers, the main one being the Dumoine. I never fail to find it interesting that, from the convenience of so good a modern highway, one can look across to such a vast expanse of virtually untouched forest land, admittedly not with its original crop of trees but now so well managed on a perpetual-yield basis that one may be confident that it will long remain wild country.

Mattawa is one of the key points in our exploration of the valley. Its location still is dramatic, and for all to whom history has meaning the junction of the small Mattawa River with the Ottawa must be a place of pilgrimage. The Ottawa is here crossed by a C.P.R. railway bridge, constructed in 1911 but reconstructed in 1950 to allow for the rise in water level (even here!) created by the Des Joachims dam. Pedestrians are not supposed to cross this structure but if one can take a boat across and then climb the steep bank on the Quebec side one gets the best of all views of the famous river junction.

The historic significance of the junction is indicated by the existence of the little Explorers' Park at the point of land between the two rivers, and by suitable plaques nearby, close to the post office building. The simple bronze plaque of the Historic Sites and Monuments Board of Canada reads:

Main canoe route to the Great Lakes, Plains, Rockies and beyond used by Indians, and by explorers, Traders and Missionaries, French and English. Upon its traffic was founded the early commercial prosperity of Montreal.

The dignified effect of this plaque is somewhat diluted by very obvious duplication in the form of a much longer inscription on one of the standard signs of the Ontario Archaeological and Historic Sites Board a mere one hundred feet away. Here is one place where Dominion-provincial co-operation was needed badly, the site being so obviously one of national historical importance. But even such bureaucratic insensitivity cannot affect the profound impression that a visit to this confluence of two rivers will leave in the minds of all Canadians who see it, as they think of the many intrepid men of the past – only some of whom have been mentioned in these pages – who have here turned up the Mattawa or come down from its turbulent passage into the broader waters of the Ottawa.

Apart from the existence of a small power plant adjacent to the town of Mattawa, the Mattawa River is but little changed from its original state, as all those who have in recent years ventured upon it in canoes will know well. The journey from North Bay to Mattawa can still be made by canoe, and guides are available (at Mattawa) to assist the inexperienced with this still hazardous journey. Nothing of the river can be seen from Highway 17, however, except at one point a little more than eight miles west of the town. Here a simple sign indicates the way into the Samuel de Champlain Provincial Park. This is an area of 5,805 acres set apart for recreational purposes and most carefully planned as a wilderness park. It includes Moore Lake and Long Lake, the former on the route of the Amable du Fond River as it flows to join the Mattawa between two of the four rapids that are included within the park boundaries. Enough roads have been provided to give access to camping and picnic sites but most of the area has been left as it was, apart from the trails that have been cut to make walking more convenient. One of these is along the banks of the Mattawa and to take this walk, after seeing first the swift water of the rapids upstream, is to be vividly reminded that the canoe journey up the Ottawa Waterway was far from the leisurely one of today.

A similar reminder is given if one stops a few miles before entering the city of North Bay where the modern highway crosses the old portage route out of Trout Lake and into the tiny Vase River, the final portage before Lake Nipissing. This is not too clearly marked but it is well worth the trouble of exploring before the city is reached, as is also a visit to the captivating little park that now stands at the mouth of the Vase River on the shore of Lake Nipissing. Apart from its historical importance, this spot would be just another recreational area. Fortunately, it has been well marked and even though the children happily splashing about in the waters of the park enjoy merely the present, the visitor will realize that he is again standing on historic ground.

North Bay, well known in Canada as an important railway centre, provides us with the culmination of our modern-day exploration of the Ottawa Waterway. It will be recalled that the historic canoe route led along the south shore of Lake Nipissing into the head of the French River, which was descended, through all its rapids, until Lake Huron was reached about fifty-five miles from Lake Nipissing. The French River is still a wilderness stream, untouched by modern highways except for one crossing by Ontario Highway No. 69 between Bigwood and Bon Air. It is, at the same time, a river well known to anglers, its pristine condition making it a justly famous fishing area. Along its banks and on its islands are to be found summer residences of those who wish to spurn city life during summer months. The difficulty of reaching these summer homes and fishing camps is a part of their charm.

Access to such outposts on the upper reach of the French River, above Chaudière Rapids, is given during summer months by a small diesel vessel, the *Chief Commanda*, which sails every day except Tuesday from North Bay, across Lake Nipissing, between the Manitou Islands, and then for twelve miles down the quiet waters of the French River until it has to turn back just before the rapids are reached. The shores of the river and of the many islands that are passed, apart only from the existence of buildings and the occasional evidence of a power line, are virtually the same as they were three centuries ago. A sail on this trim little ship, therefore, is a sail into history. True, it serves four small wharves and delivers supplies, at which times it will be almost surrounded by modern power-boats from the cottages around, but it requires little imagination to forget these features of today and to picture the great *canots de maître* being paddled along these same rocky shores, into the lake, past Cross Point and the deep bay to its east, and over to the little Vase River for the start of the tough journey down the Mattawa, down the Ottawa, to Montreal.

The reference to fishing in the French River must have made readers who are devoted anglers wonder if any note would be made in this volume of the fact that there are fish in the Ottawa River. The time has come; there are fish indeed! As recently as July 1972 a young man of Deschenes, Raymond Martel, distinguished himself by catching in the Deschenes Rapids a sturgeon weighing 107 pounds, a fish that was 5 feet 10 inches long. And any who doubt the importance of angling in the Ottawa Valley should have their doubts removed by the fact that at White Lake, near Arnprior, one of the few full-scale bait farms of North America is owned and operated by Morris Stewart, producing worms and minnows by the hundred thousand.

A survey carried out in 1969 between Rockland and Hawkesbury, along the Ontario shore, found that 386 anglers had been catching fish at an average rate of 1.78 per hour, a figure that looks as though it could be just another fish story were it not well authenticated in an official report. Ice fishing is still active every winter on the Lake of Two Mountains, a total catch of seventy thousand pounds being taken in the winter of 1965–66. And there are, even today, about two hundred commercial fishermen along the Ottawa, generally in its lower reaches, with a capital investment in their equipment of $80,000, who took fish to the value of $118,443 in the year 1968. In 1972, however, a research project, undertaken jointly by the National Research Council and the University of Ottawa, had to be started to investigate the amount of mercury in fish caught in a three-mile stretch of the river, such was the alarm at the pollution that had fouled this great river. Pollution by sawdust and sawmill wastes was bad enough in its way and in its day, but the pollution of more recent years by the effluents from industrial plants and by the indiscriminate discharge of sewage from all the cities, towns, and villages along the river, is a national disgrace.

Public opinion has, fortunately, at last become aroused. In June 1970, for example, there was held at Carleton University, Ottawa, a public conference on the matter, organized by Pollution Probe, which was one of the several activities that have helped to focus public attention on this pressing problem. Local newspapers up and down the valley are doing their part to awaken the public conscience to this social problem that affects the entire valley. Inevitably, there have been statements that were perhaps too emotional; some enthusiasts have been carried away by their righteous and rightful concern and led to make impossible suggestions for correction. But there is a problem, and a very real one, that demands the concern of all residents of the Ottawa Valley if they are to be true to the heritage which their river represents.

In Chapter Five some indication was given of the serious problem that the disposal in the river of the waste products from the Ottawa sawmills presented at the height of the sawn-lumber industry. With the decrease in the volume of sawn lumber produced, and when the controls insisted upon were put into effect, this particular problem of river pollution disappeared from public view. But the sunken logs, the accumulated sunken waste, and in particular the sawdust are all still in the bed of the river, to be encountered whenever engineering works have to be carried out in the river bed, such as the construction of piers for a new bridge. The decaying organic matter is encountered by the scuba divers who have been making such exciting and significant dives in the Ottawa. It generates methane gas, very slowly, to a degree that is not normally hazardous. In fact, some readers may have heard of the experience of ardent winter fishermen who, in earlier days, used to recognize the small domes formed in the river's ice cover by methane escaping from the river bed, and built their little shelter over one of these. They bored a one-inch hole through the ice, which they then sealed with an old tin can in the upended bottom of which a hole had been punched. When the methane escaping from the can was lit, a simple but effective 'natural' heater was obtained – probably the only benefit ever to result to anybody from this type of river pollution.

Pollution from industrial plants and urban sewage has no such interesting overtones. It is a grim and nasty picture. Calling the Ottawa River of today 'one continuous open sewer' is the sort of exaggeration that makes some people dismiss the whole matter as emotional overplay. An official description, however, states that, in 1971, 'Water quality impairment in the river is evident from the Town of Temiskaming to Deux Rivières, a distance of 60 miles, and from the cities of Hull and Ottawa to the Lake of Two Mountains, a distance of 80 miles;' and this is saying almost the same thing in polite technical language. It is such a restrained but factual picture of the overall situation that should be, must be, known throughout the valley. Let it first be recognized that the problem is not new, even if public recognition of it has occurred only in the last few years. Towns and cities have been dumping their raw sewage into the Ottawa and its tributaries ever since the start of settlement. Ottawa, capital city of the Dominion, dumped all its sewage, without any treatment at all, into its glorious river from the time of its foundation until 1962. Citizens of Ottawa, therefore, are in no position to point a finger at any other municipality for what it is not doing.

Paper mills started their waste discharges about the beginning of the century. Fortunately, or perhaps unfortunately, the great river was big enough, and then turbulent enough, to take care of these foul additions to its flow. The aeration created by the many rapids on the Ottawa had the effect of purifying much of the foreign material that had been dumped into the river above them. But the rapids have been tamed. Nature's own purification system has been almost eliminated, while populations along the river banks have rapidly increased and production of mills has grown, with consequent increase in industrial waste discharge. This is the combination that has led to the critical situation of the early seventies. Ironic is the fact that the intake screens of the great hydro-electric plants that have tamed the rapids are amongst the victims of the pollution of the river, and cleaning the screens has become a serious maintenance problem.

As early as 1954, the Quebec Anti-Pollution League published a report by Dr Lucien Piché on the serious condition of the Ottawa River. The Ontario Department of Health followed with a report based on studies of the river in 1956. In 1960, Dr A.E. Berry, first general manager of the internationally known Ontario Water Resources Commission, testifying to the Mines Committee of the Canadian House of Commons, urged the necessity of joint effort by all the governments concerned if the Ottawa River problem was to be solved. The commission carried out a most detailed survey of the situation between 1961 and 1965 but it was not until 25 August 1967 that a joint announcement came from the premiers of Ontario and Quebec to the effect that a combined attack on the problem was to begin by the o.w.r.c. and the Quebec Water Board, the initial estimate of cost for this major effort being $250,000. Work started early in 1968. An interim joint report was issued in July 1969. Volume 1 of a first major report was published in 1971. Quotations already given, those which follow, and the facts so briefly summarized here all come from this notable document.

The Department of the Environment of the Government of Canada has, since its formation, indicated its interest in and concern for the Ottawa River problem. It has suggested somewhat increased estimates of cost for the necessary remedial works. Reliance on the joint Ontario-Quebec Report, however, will be desirable since it was the first public document to give, in detail, the overall picture of the problem and to suggest quite specific remedies. The report confirms, for example, that Ottawa River water is used in enormous quantities – 200 million gallons per day (mgd) by industrial plants, and 103 mgd of water of its tributaries; 56 mgd for the public water supplies of 15 municipalities, Ottawa-Hull taking 46 mgd; 66 mgd for cooling purposes at the Chalk River and Rolphton atomic plants; and even 1 mgd for irrigation. All this is in addition to the use of most of the normal flow of the river for power generation as it passes through the water turbines of the great hydro-electric plants. Some recreational and tourist establishments, serving seven thousand people, are located on the main river, as are something like five thousand summer cottages.

If all this water were returned to the river in even approximately the same condition as when extracted, there would be no real problem. But it is not. 'The greatest damage to water quality results from the discharge of substantial volumes of untreated pulp and paper mill wastes including large quantities of suspended solids (bark, wood chips and fibre), soluble organic components, colour and odour causing materials, toxic components and in two instances the deleterious effect of previously discharged organic mer-curial compounds.' This part of the damage to the Ottawa is being caused by no more than ten industrial plants. With appropriate public demand, governments can frame regulations to have this damage eliminated. The damage caused by municipal wastes, however, comes from thirty-eight urban communities (with very minor contributions from individual dis-charges).

In 1971, only eight of the thirty-eight communities provided adequate treatment of their sewage discharge; sixteen provided none at all, this representing the waste from about 116,000 people. Of the twenty municipalities in Quebec on the main river, only three had secondary treatment plants and one a primary plant this being the tiny pioneer effort at Deschenes, established in 1963, showing a good example to the valley which, unfortunately, was not followed. Of the eighteen Ontario municipalities, seven have primary treatment, five secondary, and five use septic tanks. Only one has as yet no treatment but, together with four other municipalities using septic tanks, it has new sewage treatment facilities under development through the Ontario Water Resources Commission. The Hull area will have a secondary sewage treatment plant in operation by 1976. On the Ontario side, Nepean Township was the pioneer with a primary plant in operation in 1962; it was soon inadequate for the rapidly growing population it served but it was a start; it is now administered by the Ottawa-Carleton Regional Municipality. This was the overall situation in 1971, a beginning having been made at grappling with the problem, but only a beginning. Sewage treatment plants (and that is the name, not the mealy-mouthed euphemism of 'water pollution control plants') must be developed to serve adequately all municipalities which discharge their wastes into the Ottawa and its tributaries.

This will cost money and lead to increased taxes, municipal or provin-cial, but in any case coming out of the pockets of residents of the valley. All residents should, therefore, be acquainted with the conclusions of the two responsible provincial bodies that have studied the situation with the best technical and scientific skills available: 'It is technically feasible and economically justifiable to satisfy reasonable standards of water quality [in the Ottawa Valley] without extensive consideration of numerous alternatives.' And the solutions:

Immediate priority should be given by the pulp and paper industry to the installation of treatment facilities to accomplish the removal of settleable suspended solids no later than December 31, 1973. These programs should further provide for the elimination or reduction of all pollutants in waste effluents as soon as possible and in no case later than December 31, 1977. ... other industries should provide adequate waste treatment for the elimination or reduction of all pollutants in waste effluents as soon as possible and in no case later than December 31, 1975 ... [and] municipalities should provide adequate sewage treatment including disinfection of treated sewage discharges as soon as possible and in no case later than December 31, 1975.

Here, in outline, is a specific programme that will restore the Ottawa River to the state in which it should be. The cost? The 1971 report estimates that for the necessary capital expenditures, the industries on the river must expend between $40 and $50 million by the year 1977, adding between $5 and $10 per ton to the cost of their major product. Municipalities in Ontario and Quebec must spend from $22 to $27 million by the year 1975, and probably from $28 to $33 million more for the additional facilities that will be needed before 1990, in view mainly of population increase that can even now be anticipated. In summary, something of the order of $90 to $100 million must be spent by the year 1990 if the Ottawa River is to be restored to a reasonable standard of water quality.

Is this too much to pay for saving one of the great rivers of North America? This is the question that the people of the Ottawa Valley must answer, and must answer positively if they are to pass on to the next generation a river of which the whole valley, and indeed all of Canada, can be justly proud – tamed of its natural turbulence for 'the use and convenience of man' through the power that it generates, but still beautiful beyond description; a waterway steeped in history, the original gateway to the continent of North America, and still a river the waters of which can be enjoyed by all despite the diverse uses to which they are put in the service of man – waters still the home and refuge of wildlife innumerable, waters that can well be called 'liquid history.'

Then and only then will Ottawa Valley people of today be able to echo (despite their Victorian cadences) words spoken a century and a quarter ago about our valley by another of the lovers of the Ottawa, Thomas Coltrin Keefer:

When opened up it will be second to no other part of Canada in the healthy character of its climate, the fertility of its innumerable and well watered valleys, the transparent purity of its trout filled lakes and gravelly brooks; or in the magnificent panorama which is presented by mountain, flood and plain – decked out with ever-green and hardwood furring the sloping banks of her golden lakes, and affording under the influence of autumnal frost one of the most gorgeous spectacles under the sun. Nor can the day be far distant when those valleys will be filled with their teeming thousands, and the sheep and cattle on a thousand hills shall every where indicate peace and progress – the happy homes of a people whose mission it is to wage war only upon the rugged soil and gloomy forest, to cause the now silent valleys to shout and sing, and to make the wilderness blossom like a rose.

# APPENDIX

# SIR GEORGE SIMPSON'S ACCOUNT OF THE OTTAWA WATERWAY

(reprinted from his
*Narrative of a Journey Round the World
during the years 1841–1842*,
published in London in 1847 by Henry Colborn,
pages 14–27 of the first of the two volumes)

When all was ready, the passengers embarked, the centre of each canoe being appropriated to their accommodation. In the first canoe the two noblemen and myself took our seats; and the second contained Colonel Oldfield, Mr Bainbrigge, our Russian companion, and Mr Hopkins.* At ten minutes before eleven, the men struck up one of their hereditary ditties, and off we went amid the cheers and adieus of our assembled friends.

As the wind was high, the waves of the St Lawrence rather resembled those of the sea than of a river, while, borne on the biting gale, the snow drifted heavily in our faces. At Point Clare, where we dined, we luckily obtained the shelter of a roof, through the politeness of Mr Charlebois, whose wife proved to be an old friend of mine, being a daughter of Mr Dease, the northern discoverer, one of the gentlemen who had accompanied me across the Atlantic. At St Anne's rapid, on the Ottawa, we neither sang our evening hymn nor bribed the lady patroness with shirts, caps, etc., for a propitious journey: – but proceeded.

In the Lake of the Two Mountains we found our heavy canoes, now three days out from Lachine, still wind-bound; and, after bidding them good bye with our lighter craft and stronger crews, we reached the Hudson's Bay Company's establishment about half-past six. On approach-

*The two noblemen were Earl Caledon and Earl Musgrove, who were going to the Canadian prairies to shoot buffalo. The Russian companion was identified only as 'a gentleman in the service of the Russian American Company en route from Petersburg to Sitke.' Mr Hopkins was Edward Hopkins, the governor's secretary.

ing the land, we were saluted by the one cannon of the fort, while Mr MacTavish waited on the wharf to give us a hearty welcome; and, on reaching the house, we were kindly received by his lady. After being resuscitated by warm fires and an excellent supper, we spread our bedding on the floor.

Being trammelled by a roof, we indulged ourselves to the unusually late hour of half-past two; and even then we lost a little time in searching for some of our men, who, according to custom in such cases, were out of the way. In consequence of the height of the water, the forests along the bank appeared to grow out of a lake. At the foot of the Long Sault, a succession of rapids of about twelve miles in length, we breakfasted. Soon afterwards, we reached the Lock of Carillon, the first of a series of artificial works, erected by Government to avoid the rapids in question; passing through the whole, without delay or expense, as part and parcel of Colonel Oldfield's suite. In the lake above Grenville, into which these works conducted us, we met a steamer gliding so gently and silently along, that she might almost be supposed to have gone astray on these once secluded waters.

Next morning, after toiling for six hours, we breakfasted at eight, with the wet ground for our table, and with rain, in place of milk, to cool our tea. By one in the afternoon, while attempting to pass close under the falls of the Rideau, we were swept into the middle of the river by the violence of the current, our gunwales being covered by the foam that floated on the water. These Falls are about fifty feet in height and three hundred in breadth, being at the time we saw them more magnificent than usual by reason of the high state of the waters. It is from their resemblance to a curtain that they are distinguished as the Rideau; and they also give this name to the river that feeds them, which again lends the same appellation to the canal that connects the Ottawa with Lake Ontario.

Through a wide and smooth reach of the stream we came in an hour to the Chaudière rapids, forming the lowest of a series of impediments which extends upwards to the lake of the same name. Between the Rideau and the Chaudière there is a remarkable contrast. The former is a mere fall of water from one level to another, but the latter presents a desperate struggle of the majestic Ottawa, leaping, with a roar of thunder, from ledge to ledge and from rock to rock, till at last, wearied, as it were, with its buffetings, it sinks exhausted into the placid pool below.

At the outlet of the canal, which is situated between the Rideau and the Chaudière, stands Bytown, named after my late much valued friend, Colonel By of the Engineers; while on the opposite bank the ground above the Chaudière is occupied by the once flourishing village of Hull, the creation of an enterprising backwoodsman of New England, named Wright.

Up to Chaudière Lake the canoes were sent perfectly light by water, while the baggage and passengers were conveyed on wheels to the prettily situated village of Aylmer. Being here rejoined by our little squadron, we encamped up the lake on the grounds of my friend General Lloyd, from whose hospitable mansion our teatable, if the bottom of a tent could be deemed such, was provided, not for the first time in my voyaging experience, with the luxuries of milk and cream.

Here the bull-frogs serenaded us all night, to our infinite annoyance. Soon after sunrise, we made a portage round Les Chutes des Chats into the rapids which terminate the lake of the same name. In the course of the day, we had heavy work with a succession of difficult portages, breakfasting on the first, and meeting on the second my trusty half-breed guide Bernard, who now came into my canoe, while Morin was transferred to the other. The last of the series, the Grand Calumet, we were obliged to leave for next morning's amusement, though it was only half a mile distant.

Our encampment would have formed a rich and varied subject for a painter's brush. The tents were pitched in a small clump of pines, while round a blazing fire the passengers were collected amid a medley of boxes, barrels, pots, cloaks, etc; and to the left, on a rock above the foaming rapids, were lying the canoes; the men flitting athwart their own separate fire as actively as if they had enjoyed a holiday, and anxiously watching a huge cauldron that was suspended over the flames by three poles. The foreground consisted of two or three magnificent trees on a slight eminence; and the background was formed by dense woods and a gleaming lake.

It was six in the morning before we left the Grand Calumet behind us; and thence we proceeded without farther impediment to Fort Coulonge, distant about two hundred and ten miles from Montreal. Some of us had looked forward to this place with a good deal of interest, as a short halt would here be necessary in order to transact business and receive supplies. In addition to Mr Siveright, who was in charge of the establishment, I here met Mr Cameron, another of the Company's officers, who had come all the way from his own station of Lake Temis-cameng to wait my arrival. As the latter gentleman accompanied us, on our departure, with his canoe and five men, our party now became quite formidable, mustering forty persons in all. After making portages at several rapids, and among them the justly admired Culle Butte, racing round the base of a rocky hill in a very narrow channel, we encamped for the night at the entrance of Lac des Allumettes.

In the morning – the morning, be it observed, of the 9th of May – the water was crusted with ice thick enough to require the aid of poles in order to break a path for the canoes. After touching at the Company's post on the borders of the lake, we halted at five, being three hours earlier than usual, for breakfast, that the sun might do our work for us by melting away our icy barrier. We soon stumbled on another obstacle in the shape of a boom placed athwart the river by the lumberers of the neighbourhood ...

These lumberers may be considered as the pioneers of that commerce, which cannot fail ere long to find its way up this noble river, abounding, as it does, in every conceivable requisite for trade and agriculture, such as water-power, abundance of timber, good climate, and a variety of soil, sandy, stony, and rich. The scenery is generally picturesque, here rising in lofty rocks, and there clothed with forests to the water's edge; and the whole, being now deserted by its ancient lords, is left free to the civilizing influences of the axe and the plough.

In the course of this day and the next, we made several portages, reaching, about five in the afternoon, the point at which the Matawa flows into the Ottawa from the south-west. This spot might be considered as the first grand hinge in our route. We were here to leave the magnificent stream, on which we had accomplished the entire distance of nearly four hundred miles; for even at Lachine, and still farther down, the two great rivers of Canada, the Ottawa with its earthy yellow, and the St Lawrence with its lakeborn blue, are nearly as distinct from each other as when rushing to their confluence down their respective channels. At this place was a small post belonging to the Company, where we left Mr Bainbrigge to await the arrival of a small canoe, which I had ordered to follow us from Fort Coulonge to secure the retreat of Colonel Oldfield; and, as soon as his little vessel arrived, he was to follow, and, if possible, to overtake us.

At one of the rapids below Matawa, the heavy canoes, which came up a few days after ourselves, lost a very valuable chest of medicines, – one of the very few accidents which could be imputed to the carelessness of a voyageur during the long course of my experience. This morning, however, we were reminded that serious disasters had occurred and might occur again, for we breakfasted near two crosses, that had been placed over the bodies of two men, who were drowned, while running the adjacent rapid ...

To return to our voyage up the Matawa, I could not help remarking the influence of the state of the weather on a traveller's estimate of scenery. Under our sunny sky, the winding banks, wooded, in every bay and on every point, down to the waters' edge, were charmingly doubled, as it were, in the smooth and transparent stream; while Captain Back, under the horrors of a heavy shower, described this as the most dismal spot on the face of the earth, as a fit residence only for the demon of despair. Rain, be it observed, is a comparative trifle, while one enjoys the shelter of an oil-cloth in the canoe. The misery hardly begins to be felt, till you are deposited, with all your seams exposed to the weather, on the long grass, though even this stage has the merit of being far less wretched than that of forcing your way among the dripping branches. Here, for the event is worth noting, we encountered the first attack of the musquitoes.

Next day, we made eleven portages, crossing the height of land and reaching a feeder of Lake Nipissing. The only portage worthy of special notice was that of the Falls of Lake Talon, where a large body of water rushes through a narrow opening in the rocks from a height of about fifty feet. Separated from the boiling cauldron, into which the torrent throws itself by a projecting ledge, a silent pool, forming a kind of gloomy recess, carries the canoes to the foot of a rock so smooth and steep as to be almost impracticable to novices. This declivity and a narrow platform at the top constitute the portage. This spot furnishes a striking proof that the waters of this country must once have occupied a much higher level. The platform must have been part of the bed of the stream; the declivity must have formed a section of the Fall; and the dark and stagnant recess must have been a foaming whirlpool. Many other portages on the route present similar features, though perhaps in an inferior degree. We had now got fairly into the region of the fur-traders, beyond the ken alike of the farmer and the lumberer; and we here discovered the traces of beaver in the pieces of willow, which had been barked by this extraordinary animal.

To make the day's work with our eleven portages still harder, we did not encamp till after ten at night, while the closing division of our toil consisted of a swamp of about three quarters of a mile in length, the tract being, on the whole, the wettest and heaviest on our journey. Our resting-place was bad – the ground damp, the water muddy, the frogs obstreperous, and the snakes familiar. In spite, however, of all these trifles, fatigue was as good as an opiate; and in sound sleep we soon forgot the troubles of the day.

After indulging in the morning till half-past two, we reached Lake Nipissing at daybreak. Here I left Colonel Oldfield, instructing Mr Cameron, at the same time, to remain with him till Mr Bainbrigge should arrive. After seeing them safely planted by the side of a glorious fire, we bade them adieu. In less, however, than half an hour our progress was arrested by a field of ice; and having worked our way through it to the shore with difficulty, we cleared our ground, pitched our tents, and resigned ourselves to our fate.

After the fatigues of yesterday, our men, delighted with the godsend, soon fell asleep on the bare ground, even without the trouble of a wish, while we ourselves, besides making up all arrears of shaving, washing, dressing, etc.; killed time with eating, drinking, chatting, and strolling. From a native family in the neighbourhood we purchased some fish for a few biscuits; and we soon found that the biscuits might have been saved, for we succeeded in spearing twenty or thirty dorey, averaging two pounds each. Having attempted in the afternoon to find a path for our canoes, we were obliged to encamp for the night with a gain of only three quarters of a mile.

Making way next morning, we breakfasted on the portage between Lake Nipissing and its outlet, French River. On this stream we saw a few savages, who, though poorly clad, appeared to be faring well. Here we ran our first rapids; and in the afternoon we made a portage at the Récollet Fall, which, throwing itself from a slanting ledge of rocks almost in the direction of the river's breadth, leaves hardly room enough for a canoe to pass between the vortex at its foot and the perpendicular wall of the opposite bank. As we had the current in our favour, and were but little impeded by portages, we made our best march today, viz.: ninety-five miles. Encamping for the night, within a short distance of Lake Huron, we heard, for the first time, our little friend the whip-poor-will, a sure harbinger of warm weather; and a pair of these favourites of the voyageur serenaded us all night with their cheerful cry, which so closely imitates the name, that one is often inclined to suspect some person of imitating it.

Next morning we descended to Lake Huron through some remarkable rapids, which, in form and breadth, bear a close resemblance to canals cut in the solid rock. In one of these we were nearly snagged, after a fashion unknown on the Mississippi. While running down in gallant style, we perceived, by the dim twilight, a tree bridging the narrow current so as to form a complete barrier. The paddles were immediately backed; and a few blows from an axe quickly cleared our passage.

Before sunrise we entered Lake Huron, having now before us, with the single exception of Sault Sainte Marie, seven or eight hundred miles of still water to the head of Lake Superior.

We dined on an island celebrated for a stone which, when struck, emits a musical or metallic sound; and about eight in the evening we reached the Company's establishment, taking the name of La Cloche from the natural bell just mentioned. The northern shore of Lake Huron consists of rocky hills, dotted with stunted trees, chiefly pines; and the adjacent waters are closely studded with islands, varying from ten feet in diameter to many miles in length. Though the whole of this neighbourhood may be deemed an almost hopeless desert, yet the southern side of the lake is more fertile, as are also the Manitoulin Islands. These more promising districts are pretty well peopled either by Europeans or by Indians.

Next day, being the 16th of the month, and the thirteenth from Lachine, we reached the Sault Sainte Marie about five in the afternoon.

# REFERENCES IN TEXT

Notes on the text are provided below for the use of readers wishing to refer to the sources of information in the text. Lines are numbered from the top of each page except where 'E' is added; in these cases, numbering is from the last line on the page. When the reference is to one of the books listed in the Select Bibliography, only the name of the author is given. In the case of a journal article, the name of the journal is provided.

| *Page* | *Line* | CHAPTER ONE: THE WATERWAY |
|---|---|---|
| 3 | 2 | *Shanty, Forest and River Life in the Backwoods of Canada.* Montreal, 1883, p. 339. |
| 3 | 2E | Hampson, N. *History as an Art.* University of Newcastle on Tyne, 1968, p. 18. |
| 6 | 1 | Wallace, W.S., p. 35. |
| 6 | 21 | Innis, H.A., p. 262. |

CHAPTER TWO: THE SETTING

| | | |
|---|---|---|
| 23 | 4E | The *Report on Hydrology and Regulation of the Ottawa River*, by the Ottawa River Engineering Board (Canada, Ontario and Quebec), Ottawa, June 1965, together with its separate appendices, gives complete information on the Ottawa River. |
| 17 | 23 | Gold, L.W., and G.P. Williams. 'An Unusual Ice Formation in the Ottawa River,' *Jour of Glaciology*, vol. 4 (June 1963), pp. 569–73. |
| 19 | 4 | Keefer, T.C. *The Ottawa* (with lecture on *Montreal*). Montreal, 1854, p. 33 et seq. |
| 20 | 7 | Quoted in Kenyon and Turnbull, p. 42 (reprinted by permission). |

| *Page* | *Line* | |
|---|---|---|
| 29 | 17 | Logan, W.E. *Field Notes for 1845* (esp. Thursday 2 October) indexed as Book 1969, Public Archives of Canada. |

CHAPTER THREE: CANOES ON THE OTTAWA

| | | |
|---|---|---|
| 35 | 11E | Parkman, *Pioneers* (1865), p. 390 et seq. of 15th ed. (1879). |
| 37 | 11E | Coutlee, C.R. 'Historical notes on the Ottawa Valley,' an appendix to *Georgian Bay Ship Canal* Sessional Paper No. 19A, 8–9 Edward VII, Ottawa, 1909, pp. 504–44. |
| 38 | 15 | This is the view of G.R. Rigby and Helen Lambart in an unpublished paper, '*A New Site for Dollard at Carillon*,' 24 August 1961; see summary in A. Palmer, '*Water Covers Long Sault Site but Dollard site argument goes on*,' *Gazette*, Montreal, 13 March 1962. |
| 40 | 12 | Kenyon and Turnbull, p. 40 et seq. |
| 41 | 15 | Angus, p. 186. |
| 42 | 5 | Coutlee, 'Historical notes ...,' p. 506. |
| 42 | 11 | Bond (*Beaver* article, 1966), p. 6. |
| 43 | 15 | Quoted in Eccles, p. 68. |
| 47 | 1 | Neatby, p. 72. |
| 47 | 13E | Long, J. *Voyages and Travels of an Indian Interpreter and Trader etc* ... London, 1791, pp. 74, 75. |
| 48 | 7 | Innis, p. 193. |
| 49 | 10 | Quoted in Innis, p. 213, *et seq.* |
| 50 | 4E | Quoted in De Voto, p. 309. |
| 59 | 17 | *The Voyageurs and Their Songs.* 12-inch mono. disk, with 24-page booklet by T.C. Blegen. Minnesota Historical Society, St. Paul, Minn., 1966. |
| 60 | 16 | De Voto, p. 309. |
| 61 | 4 | Quoted in Lamb, p. 82 et seq. |
| 61 | 12 | Pond's Diary is printed in full in *Five Fur Traders of the Northwest*, edited by C.M. Gates. St. Paul, 1965, see p. 29. |
| 62 | 12 | Quoted in Wallace, p. 268. |
| 64 | 11E | See *Beaver* articles by Nute, Galbraith, and Tessendorf. Also see Morton, A.S. *Sir George Simpson: Overseas Governor of the Hudson's Bay Company.* Oregon Historical Society, 1944. |
| 66 | 8 | Quoted in Tessendorf, p. 40. |
| 66 | 18 | Collard, E.A. 'At Lachine,' *Gazette*, Montreal, 21 February 1970. |
| 68 | 15 | Simpson, Sir G. *Narrative of a Journey round the World during the years 1841 and 1842.* 2 vols., London, 1847. |
| 71 | 9 | Collard, E.A. 'The Canoes of Lachine,' *Gazette*, Montreal, 8 July 1964. |

CHAPTER FOUR: TRAVELLERS' TALES

| | | |
|---|---|---|
| 72 | 5 | Biggar, p. 262. |
| 72 | 4E | Biggar, p. 262. |
| 73 | 14 | Biggar, p. 301. |
| 73 | 1E | Quoted in Parkman, *Jesuits* ... (1867), p. 142 of 14th ed., 1880. |
| 74 | 1E | Quoted in Kenyon and Turnbull, p. 42 et seq. (reprinted by permission). |

| Page | Line | |
|---|---|---|
| 76 | 17E | Henry, A. *Travels and Adventures in Canada and the Indian Territories between the years 1760 and 1776*. 2 vols., New York, 1809; vol. I, p. 13, et seq. |
| 76 | 3E | Innis, Mary Q. (ed.). *Mrs. Simcoe's Diary*. Toronto, 1965, p. 66. |
| 77 | 15 | Langton, H.H. (ed.). *Travels in the Interior inhabited Parts of North America in the years 1791 and 1792* by Patrick Campbell. Champlain Society, Toronto, 1937, p. 122. |
| 77 | 3E | Tyrrell, J.B. (ed.). *David Thompson's Narrative of His Explorations in Western America 1784–1812*, Champlain Society, Toronto, 1916, p. 559. |
| 79 | 9 | Landmann, Colonel. *Adventures and Recollections*. 2 vols. London 1852; vol I, p. 289 et seq.; vol. II, p. 168. |
| 81 | 10 | Bertrand mentions this translation which was traced to Mr Josephson with the aid of Miss M. Millar of Kingston; used by permission of Mr Josephson. |
| 82 | 10E | Garry, Francis N.A. (ed.). 'Diary of Nicholas Garry, Deputy Governor of the Hudson's Bay Company from 1822 to 1835.' *Trans. Royal Soc. of Canada*, 2nd series, VI, 1900, Sec. II, p. 75 et seq. |
| 86 | 1E | Nute, Grace L. 'Journey for Frances,' *The Beaver*, outfit 284 (Winter 1953), pp. 50–54; and (Spring 1954) pp. 12–17; and outfit 285 (Summer 1954), pp. 12–18. |
| 89 | 21 | Bigsby, J.J. *The Shoe and Canoe*. 2 vols., London 1835. Vol. I, p. 132 et seq., and p. 163. |
| 91 | 21 | Wallace, W.S. (ed.). *John McLean's Notes of a Twenty-Five Years Service in the Hudson's Bay Territory* Champlain Society, Toronto, 1932 p. 115 et seq. |
| 92 | 14 | Back, G. *Narrative of the Arctic Land Expedition to the North of the Great Fish River*. London 1836, p. 32 et seq. |
| 93 | 15E | Stanley, G.F.G. (ed.). *In Search of the Magnetic North* by J.H. Lefroy. Toronto, 1955, p. 6 et seq. |
| 95 | 5 | Quoted in Barclay (Beaver article). |
| 95 | 3E | 'His Lordship Goes Voyaging,' *The Beaver*, outfit 275 (June 1944), pp. 10–13. |
| 96 | 17 | Ballantyne, R.M. *Hudson Bay or Everyday Life in the Wilds of North America*. London, 1905, p. 280 et seq. See also E. Quayle. *Ballantyne the Brave*. London, 1967. |
| 98 | 4 | Trollope, A. *North America*. 2 vols., London, 1862, vol. I, p. 99 et seq. |
| 99 | 3 | Bouchette, J. *The British Dominions in North America.* 2 vols., London, 1832, vol. II, p. 83. |

CHAPTER FIVE: LUMBERING ON THE OTTAWA

| 102 | 22 | Bouchette, J. *A Topographic Dictionary of the Province of Lower Canada*. London, 1832, pages not numbered but from section headed 'Hull.' |
| 104 | 12 | Garvey, M. *The History of Killaloe Station*. Pembroke, 1967, p. 19. |
| 108 | 8 | Whitton, p. 132. |

| Page | Line | |
|---|---|---|
| 118 | 19 | Information from Mr E. Zwicker, Ottawa. |
| 119 | 17 | Miller, H. *Canada's Historic First Iron Castings*. Inf. Circ. 10209 of Mines Branch, Dept. of Energy, Mines and Resources, Ottawa, 1968; see esp. Chap. II. See also C.J. Warrington and G.T. Newbold, *Chemical Canada*. Ottawa, 1970, p. 5. See also Hughson and Bond, p. 14. |
| 120 | 4 | Gourlay, p. 7. |
| 123 | 7E | Fleming, S. *Condition of the Ottawa River*. Ottawa, 1895; copy in Archives of Queen's University. |
| 125 | 14 | Borrett, G.T. *Letters from Canada and the United States*. London, 1865, p. 39. |
| 127 | 2 | Stacey, C.P. (ed.). *Records of the Nile Voyageurs 1884–1885*. Champlain Society, Toronto, 1959. |
| 127 | 13E | Lee-Whiting (article in *Can. Geog. Jour.* 1970); see also 'Loggers' Famous Pointer still Going Strong,' by the same author, *Ottawa Citizen*, 2 April 1966. |
| 128 | 6 | Lee-Whiting (article in *Can. Geog. Jour.* 1968). |
| 128 | 5E | Dreskin, N. 'Axe-maker to the World,' *Canadian Weekly* (*Gazette*), Montreal, 7–13 August 1965. |
| 129 | 16 | Metcalfe, J.C. 'A Century of Bootmaking for Valley Lumberjacks,' *Ottawa Journal*, 6 Sept. 1969. |

## CHAPTER SIX: CANALS AND STEAMBOATS

| | | |
|---|---|---|
| 134 | 5 | Public Records Office, London, W.01/553. |
| 134 | 2E | Stacey, C.P. 'The War of 1812 in Canadian History,' *Ont. History* (Papers and Records O.H.S.) vol. 50, 1958, p. 153. |
| 135 | 10E | Stacey, C.P. 'An American Plan for a Canadian Campaign,' *American Hist. Review*, vol. 46 (Jan. 1941), pp. 348–58. |
| 138 | 7 | Public Archives of Canada. Vol. C39 (1817–1821), p. 53 et seq. |
| 139 | 18E | PAC Vol. C39, p. 78. |
| 142 | 20 | PAC Vol. C51, p. 82. |
| 142 | 23 | PAC Vol. C51, p. 78. |
| 142 | 11E | PAC Vol. C40, p. 199. |
| 143 | 4E | PAC Vol. C51, p. 92. |
| 144 | 11 | PAC Vol. C55, p. 6 et seq. |
| 146 | 13 | Shepherd, R.L. 'Steam Navigation on the Ottawa River,' *Bulletin 13* (new series), *Can. Railroad Hist. Assoc.*, May 1940. |
| 147 | 3 | Morgan, H.R. 'Steam Navigation on the Ottawa River.' *Papers and Records* (*Ont. Hist. Soc.*), vol. 23, 1926, pp. 370–83. |
| 149 | 1 | Strothers, R. *Robert Henry Cowley (1859–1927)*. Toronto, 1935. |
| 161 | 12E | Legget, R.F. *Railroads of Canada*. Vancouver, 1973, p. 26. |
| 162 | 16 | *The Picturesque Rideau Route*. Toronto, 1900. |
| 163 | 2E | *Summary of Canal Statistics 1848–1936*. Dominion Bureau of Statistics, Ottawa, 1937, p. 24. |
| 164 | 15 | Shanley, W. *The Ottawa Survey*. Appendix 'C' to Annual Report of the Board of Commissioners of Public Works, Ottawa, 1856. |

| Page | Line | |
|---|---|---|
| 166 | 12E | From the Royal Archives, Windsor Castle, by gracious permission of H.M. The Queen. RA Add. El/ 4827 and 4839, Toronto, August 22, 1865. |
| 169 | 1 | Shanley, W. *Report on the Ottawa and French River Navigation Project.* Submitted to the Legislative Assembly of Canada, July 1858; reprinted Ottawa, 1900. |
| 169 | 9 | Clarke, T.C. *The Montreal, Ottawa and Georgian Bay Navigation.* Submitted to the Legislative Assembly of Canada in 1860; reprinted with a supplementary report, Ottawa, 1900. |
| 169 | 13E | Kingsford, W. *The Canadian Canals etc.* Toronto, 1865, p. 90. |
| 171 | 2 | *The Times* (London), 11 December 1905. |
| 171 | 19 | *Georgian Bay Ship Canal.* Sessional Paper no. 19a in vol. 10 of the *Sessional Papers* of the First Session of the Eleventh Parliament of the Dominion of Canada (8–9 Edw. VII), Ottawa, 1909. |
| 172 | 6E | *Official Report of Debates*: House of Commons, 17GV, 1926–1927, vol. II, p. 2096 et seq. |

CHAPTER SEVEN: SETTLEMENT ON THE OTTAWA

| | | |
|---|---|---|
| 178 | 5E | Cummins, Dorothy A. *Church and Community; a brief History of St. Mary's Church, Como, P.Q.* Rigaud, 1965, p. 4 et seq. |
| 179 | 8E | Quoted in E.A. Collard 'All Our Yesterdays,' *Gazette*, Montreal, 19 March 1966. |
| 180 | 14 | Rigby, G.R. *A History of Lachute.* Lachute, 1964, p. 6 et seq. |
| 181 | 22 | Graham, J. *The Water Highway of Argenteuil and its Centennial Anniversary.* Lachute, 1933. |
| 182 | 5 | *Treadwell Papers* in the Archives of Queen's University. |
| 183 | 16E | Higginson, Maria A., and Mrs J.T. Brock. *The Village of Hawkesbury 1808–1888.* Hawkesbury, 1961. See also W.H. Bradley. 'The Life of the Most Rev. C. Charles Hamilton,' *Jour. of the Can. Church Hist. Soc.* vol. 4 (Dec. 1961), pp. 1–15. |
| 185 | 13E | Roger, C. *Ottawa Past and Present.* Ottawa, 1871, p. 38. |
| 185 | 6E | Wade, M. *The French Canadians: 1760–1945.* Toronto, 1955, p. 281. |
| 186 | 13E | From information and family papers kindly provided by the late Dr. G.W. Dunning of Ottawa. |
| 187 | 11 | *Report of the Commission appointed to explore the country between the St. Maurice and the Ottawa in the year 1830.* Toronto, 1831. |
| 191 | 8E | PAC Vol. C75, p. 70. |
| 192 | 16E | PAC Vol. C42, p. 95 et seq. |
| 194 | 23 | PAC Vol. C59, p. 110. |
| 196 | 8 | Dilschneider, Donna. 'They Tripped Away,' *Ottawa Citizen*, 5 November 1964. |
| 196 | 20 | Hubbard, p. 22. |
| 196 | 11E | Dufferin, Countess of. *My Canadian Journal.* New York, 1891, entry for 7 June 1878. |
| 197 | 18E | J.T. Saywell (ed.). *The Canadian Journal of Lady Aberdeen.* Champlain Society, Toronto, 1960, p. 338 et seq. |

*Page* *Line*

198   1E   *The Pinhey Papers* in the Archives of Ontario. See also Gladys Blair, 'Horaceville,' *Ottawa Journal*, 21 and 28 November 1970.

200   20   Glazebrook, with supplementary information from the MacLaren papers in the Public Archives of Canada.

201   2E   See also Naylor, W.H., *History of the Church in Clarendon*. St. Johns, Que., 1919.

204   7   Quoted in Haydon, p. 246.

207   17E   Lee-Whiting, Brenda B. 'The Old Wooden Crosses of Wilno,' *Globe and Mail*, Toronto, 26 August 1972.

209   2   See Gérin-Lajoie (*Beaver* article). Also Pain, p. 69 et seq.

CHAPTER EIGHT: THE RIVER TODAY

210   3E   Ross, Edna. *John Kerr McMorine 1842–1912: Clergyman and Botanist*. Ottawa (?), 1969 (?).

212   19   McGee, G.H. *Birds, Botany, Geology*. Ottawa, 1968; 12-p. folder of the Ottawa Field Naturalists' Club.

212   23   Gillett, J.M. 'Botanizing on Haycock Island.' *Trail and Landscape*, vol. 2, no. 4, 1968, pp. 107–109.

213   12   Macdonald, Malcolm. *The Birds of Brewery Creek*. Toronto, 1947, p. 3 et seq.

216       Table based on information in *Report of Hydrology and Regulation of the Ottawa River* by Ottawa River Engineering Board (Canada, Ontario, Quebec), Ottawa, 1965 pp. 18–27, and *Water Quality and its Control on the Ottawa River* (Ottawa River Basin) 1971, vol I, p. 86.

220   12E   Palmer, A. 'On and Off the Record: Barge Floated thro' Rapids,' *Gazette*, Montreal, 23 April 1965.

221   6   Information from Mr. D.H. Farmer, Ottawa.

221   17E   'Ottawa Woman, 70, Paddles 100 Miles,' *Ottawa Journal*, 9 July 1967.

222   12   *Royal Commission on the Organization of Government* (The Glassco Commission) Ottawa, 1963, vol. 5, p. 36.

222   6E   'Island Sliced in Half Speeds Thurso Ferry,' *Ottawa Journal*, 1 August 1962.

223   4   Introduction to this 'forgotten' part of Ottawa River history was given to me by the late Mr Rowley Frith of Ottawa; Rev. S. Ivison guided me to the following books, copies of which were kindly loaned by Mr D. Kemp Edwards of Ottawa: McLaurin, C.C. *My Old Home Church*. Edmonton, 1937, p. 19 et seq., and Edwards, J. *Correspondence and Letters on Various Subjects by the late William Edwards of Clarence with a Sketch of his Life*. Peterborough, 1882.

228   20   *Museum of the Historical Society of Argenteuil County*. Carillon, 1938.

241   21   Fidler, p. 203.

244   9   Bedore, B.V. *The Broad Valley of the Ottawa*. Arnprior, n.d. (1961?).

245   2   The only reference I have seen to this incident and monument is Tassé, J., *La Vallée de l'Outouais*. Montreal, 1870, p. 30.

| Page | Line | |
|------|------|---|
| 245 | 10 | Gibson, J.A., and D.G.G. Kerr. *Sir Edmund Head, A Scholarly Governor*. Toronto, 1954. |
| 250 | 5 | 'Capital Catch,' *Ottawa Journal*, 8 July 1972. |
| 250 | 9 | Metcalfe, J.C. 'Minnows by the Millions,' *Ottawa Journal*, 27 June 1970. |
| 250 | 13 | *Water Quality and its Control on the Ottawa River* (Ottawa River Basin). Toronto and Quebec, vol. 1, 1971, p. 88. |
| 250 | 19E | For a useful summary see J. Carruthers, 'Ottawa River Fish not as Polluted as Ontario Government fears,' *Ottawa Journal*, 9 February 1973. |
| 250 | 10E | *Proceedings Ottawa River Conference* (June 12 and 13, 1970). Ottawa, 1970. |
| 251 | 18 | Information from Mr R.J. Brearley, London. |
| 252 | 17E | *Water Quality Report*, p. 3 et seq. |
| 255 | 16 | Keefer, T.C. *The Ottawa*. Montreal, 1854, p. 73. |

# SELECT BIBLIOGRAPHY

A number of the books consulted during the preparation of this volume, and which are today readily available either in bookstores or libraries, are listed below. I am much indebted to them, as the References clearly demonstrate, for secondary information or guidance to primary sources. It is hoped that readers will be assisted in further study of the Ottawa Waterway by some of these books.

Angus, J.B. *Old Quebec: in the Days Before Our Day*. Montreal, 1933.
Bertrand, J.P. *Highway of Destiny*. New York, 1959.
Biggar, H.P. (ed.). *Voyages du Sieur de Champlain*. Champlain Society, Toronto, 1925.
Bishop. M. *Champlain: The Life of Fortitude*. Toronto, 1965.
Bond, C.C.J. *City on the Ottawa*. Ottawa, 1961.
– *Early Days in the Ottawa Country*. Ottawa, 1967.
– *The Ottawa Country*. Ottawa, 1968.
Bourne, K. *Britain and the Balance of Power in North America: 1815–1905*. London, 1967.
Brault, L. *Ottawa, Old and New*. Ottawa, 1946.
Brebner, J.B. *Explorers of North America: 1492–1806*. London, 1933.
Brown, G.W. (ed.) *Dictionary of Canadian Biography*, vol. 1. Toronto, 1966.
Campbell, Marjorie W. *The North West Company*. Toronto, 1957.
De Voto, Bernard. *The Course of Empire*. Boston, 1952.
Eccles, W.J. *Canada under Louis XIV, 1665–1701*. Can. Cent. Series, Toronto, 1964.

Eggleston, W. *The Queen's Choice*. Ottawa, 1961.

Glazebrook, G.P. de T. *Life in Ontario*. Toronto, 1968.

Gray, J.M. *Lord Selkirk of Red River*. Toronto, 1963.

Gourlay, J.L. *A History of the Ottawa Valley*. Ottawa, 1896.

Greening, W.E. *The Ottawa*. Toronto, 1961.

Haydon, A. *Pioneer Sketches in the District of Bathurst*, vol. 1. Toronto, 1925.

Hubbard, R.H. *Rideau Hall*. Ottawa, 1967.

Hughson, J.W., and C.C.J. Bond. *Hurling Down the Pine*. Old Chelsea, Que., rev. ed. 1965.

Innis, H.A. *The Fur Trade in Canada*. Toronto, rev. ed. 1962.

Kennedy, C.C. *The Upper Ottawa Valley*. Pembroke, 1970.

Kenyon, W.G., and J.A Turnbull. *The Battle for James Bay, 1686*. Toronto, 1971.

Lamb, W. Kaye (ed.). *The Journals and Letters of Sir Alexander Mackenzie*. Toronto 1971.

Legget, R.F. *Rideau Waterway*. Toronto, rev. ed. 1972.

Lower, A.R.M. *The North American Assault on the Canadian Forest*. Toronto, 1938.

– *Great Britain's Woodyard 1763–1867*. Montreal, 1973.

McGill, Jean S. *A Pioneer History of the County of Lanark*. Toronto, 1968.

Morison, S.E. *The European Discovery of America: The Northern Voyages: A.D. 500–1600*. New York, 1971.

– *Samuel de Champlain: Father of New France*. Boston, 1972.

Morse, E.W. *Fur Trade Canoe Routes of Canada, Then and Now*. Ottawa, 1969.

Neatby, Hilda. *Quebec: The Revolutionary Age: 1760–1790*. Can. Cent. Series, Toronto, 1966.

Nute, Grace L. *The Voyageurs*. St. Paul, 1955.

O'Dwyer, W.C. *Highways of Destiny*. Pembroke, 1964.

Pain, S.A. *The Way North*. Toronto, 1964.

Parkman, F. *Pioneers of France in the New World*. Boston, 1865. Many later editions available.

– *The Jesuits in North America in the Seventeecth Century*. Boston, 1867. Many later editions available.

Price, Mrs. C., and C.C. Kennedy. *Notes on the History of Renfrew County, for the Centennial, 1961*. Pembroke, 1961.

Read, J.H.S., K. McNaught, and H.S. Crowe (eds.). *A Source Book of Canadian History*. Toronto, 1964.

Rich, E.E. *Montreal and the Fur Trade*. Montreal, 1966.

Saunders, Audrey. *Algonquin Story*. Toronto, 1963.

Stanley, G.F.G. *New France: the Last Phase, 1744–1760.* Can. Cent. Series, Toronto, 1968.

Wallace, W.S. (ed.). *Documents relating to the North West Company.* Champlain Society, Toronto, 1934.

Whitton, Charlotte. *A Hundred Years a'Fellin'.* Braeside, 1942.

*The Beaver* (quarterly, from Hudson's Bay House, Winnipeg) and the *Canadian Geographical Journal* (monthly, from 488 Wilbrod Street, Ottawa) are making valuable contributions to the recording of local Canadian history, as is well shown by the following lists of articles that relate to the Ottawa River and Valley:

From *The Beaver* (the annual volumes of which are called Outfits):

Barclay, R.G. 'Gray Nuns' Journey to Red River,' outfit 297 (Winter 1966), pp. 15–23.

Bond, C.C.J. 'The Hudson's Bay Company in the Ottawa Valley,' outfit 296 (Spring, 1966), pp. 4–21; reprints are entitled 'The Ottawa Valley and the Fur Traders.'

Galbraith, J.S. 'The Little Emperor,' outfit 291 (Summer, 1960), pp. 22–8.

Gérin-Lajoie, A. 'Fragments from a Journey,' outfit 300 (Winter 1969), pp. 24–31.

Gluek, A.C. 'The Minnesota Route,' outfit 286 (Spring, 1956), pp. 44–50.

Johnson, Alice M. 'Edward and Frances Hopkins of Montreal,' outfit 302 (Autumn 1971), pp. 4–19.

Nute, Grace L. 'Jehu of the Waterways,' outfit 291 (Summer, 1960), pp. 15–19.

Tessendorf, K.C. 'George Simpson: Canoe Executive,' outfit 301 (Summer 1970), pp. 39–41.

Van Kirk, Sylvia, 'Women and the Fur Trade,' outfit 303 (Winter 1972), pp. 4–21.

From the *Canadian Geographical Journal*:

Fidler, Vera. 'The Last of the Ottawa River Portages,' vol. 71 (Dec. 1965), pp. 202–203.

Lambart, Helen H., and G.R. Rigby. 'Submerged History of the Long Sault,' vol. 67 (Nov. 1963), pp. 147–57.

Lee-Whiting, Brenda B. 'The Opeongo Road: an Early Colonization Scheme,' vol. 74 (March, 1967), pp. 77–83.

– 'The Alligator – Unique Canadian Boat,' vol. 76 (Jan. 1968), pp. 30–33. vol. 76 (Jan. 1968), pp. 30–33.

Mallory, Edna S. 'Ottawa Lumber Era,' vol. 68 (Feb. 1964), pp. 61–73.

Morgan, R.J. 'The Georgian Bay Ship Canal,' vol. 78 (March, 1969), pp. 90–97.

Rigby, G.R., and R.F. Legget. 'Riddle of the Treadwell Trenches,' vol. 88 (March, 1974), pp. 38–42.

Wilson, C.P. 'Étienne Brulé and the Great Lakes,' vol. 66 (Feb. 1963), pp. 38–43.

# ACKNOWLEDGMENTS

The Ottawa River has fascinated me ever since I first paddled on its waters, now more than forty years ago. More recently, as I have found that so few of my younger friends realized the part that the Ottawa has played in the history of Canada, I hoped that I might be given time and opportunity to weave together the main strands of its story. *Ottawa Waterway* is the result. It could not have been written without most generous help from innumerable friends up and down the Valley, known and unknown, to some only of whom can I here record my debt.

The staffs of the following libraries and archives kindly assisted me in my searches for printed and documentary material: the Public Archives of Canada, the National Library of Canada, the Library of Parliament, the Ottawa Public Library; the libraries of Toronto, Queen's, and McGill Universities; the Central Reference Library of Metropolitan Toronto; the Archives of Ontario; the Library of Congress in Washington and the New York Public Library; and in London, England, the Public Records Office, the Ministry of Defence (Army) library, the Archives of the Hudson's Bay Company and of the United Society for the Propagation of the Gospel; and, for one special item, the Royal Archives at Windsor Castle.

The References and the Bibliography indicate clearly my indebtedness to the authors of many books and archival material but I wish to make special note of the courtesy of Drs W.A. Kenyon and J.R. Turnbull, and their publishers, Macmillans of Canada, for allowing me to quote passages from their recent translation of the journal of Chevalier de Troyes; of the Canadian Branch of the Oxford University Press for similar permission to quote from *Birds of Brewery Creek*; and of Helen Burgess, editor of *The*

*Beaver*, for use of the diary of Lady Simpson and other material which first appeared in the pages of that journal.

Chapter Six of this book is a summary of three draft chapters, two of which I hope to be able to use in preparing a more detailed account of the building of the Ottawa River Canals, when time permits. The late Dr Frank Forward and Dr Dorothy Forward were good enough to read the draft of the earlier chapter on the Georgian Bay Ship Canal, with which their father was closely associated when it was under active consideration. Dr C.P. Stacey not only read a similar draft chapter on the Ottawa River Canals but also favoured me with a copy of an early note of his own on this subject. Dr J.H. Jenkins and Mr D.D. Lockhart, of Ottawa, gave me the benefit of their expert knowledge in comments upon an early draft of Chapter Five on lumbering.

It is a measure of the way in which the writing of this book has repeatedly had to be put aside for more urgent duties that my thanks to three other friends must be expressed posthumously. The late Dr Charlotte Whitton, a great lady of the Valley, kindly took an interest in the concept of this book, her own *A Hundred Years a' Fellin'* being so useful a guide in the writing of Chapter Five; the late Mr. Rowley Frith took a lively interest in the slow development of work on this volume and guided me to the interesting but 'unknown' story of John Fox; and the late Dr G.W. Dunning told me of his own early days on the Ottawa, especially on a memorable evening just before he was so sadly stricken.

Three personal friends, real experts all on the Ottawa, have been of special assistance to me through their interest and directly through their own writings: Eric Morse, modern *voyageur* extraordinary, with his vivid writings on the old canoe routes and by his reading of an early draft (although I must make clear that he, as a lover of 'white waters,' in no way condones my account of engineering developments along the Ottawa); Clyde C. Kennedy with his informed writings about the upper part of the Valley and for giving me the idea of the diagram on page 24; and Courtney C.J. Bond with his invaluable writings about the 'Ottawa country.' I wish to pay special tribute to *Hurling Down the Pine* which Mr Bond wrote with Mr J.W. Hughson, a fine book about the Ottawa and its lumber trade.

Collecting the illustrations from which those which now appear in this book were selected has been in itself a pleasant and rewarding task. I confirm my appreciation to all to whom individual acknowledgment is made on pages ix to xi, adding my special thanks to the staff of the Picture Division of the Public Archives of Canada for their assistance. Dr Helen Wallis, Superintendent of the Map Room at the British Museum, introduced me to the Indian birchbark map (page 52) and allowed me to see the well-preserved original. The staff of the National Air Photo Library in Ottawa, and especially Mrs Heffernan, were most helpful – with their computer – in helping me to assemble the mosaic on pages 234 and 235 which is in such striking contrast with Champlain's map of 1616. Right Rev. W.J. Robinson, Bishop of Ottawa, gave permission for the reproduction of the coat of arms of his see; Dr D.J. McLaren, Director of the Geological Survey of Canada, similarly permitted me to share with readers one of Sir William Logan's sketches, from one of his field books carefully preserved down the years by the Survey and now in the safe keeping of the Public Archives. My friend and former colleague, J. Douglas Scott, transformed my rough sketch maps into the drawings which now illustrate the text.

To go further involves the risk of making invidious distinctions but I must take the risk, with a general assurance of appreciation to the many friends whom I cannot mention, by recording my thanks for special help received from: Miss Alice Johnson, Dr K. Bourne, Major John Hancock and Dr G.R. Rigby, all in England; Dr E.A. Collard of Montreal, Dr J.A. Gibson of St Catharines, Frank Nobbs, Hudson Heights, and Dr George Glazebrook of Toronto; and in Ottawa Mr Esmund Butler, Dr W.E. Collins, Messrs D. Kemp Edwards, D.H. Farmer, Thomas Fuller, G.B. Williams, W.F.H. Williamson, and E. Zwicker.

Only authors really know how much their books owe to their publishers. No author could have been better served than I have been by the University of Toronto Press, which has encouraged me during the writing, edited my manuscript, and guided the production.

Finally, I am once again indebted to my wife for her patience and understanding as this book has taken so much time that should have been hers. Fortunately, she shares my love of the Ottawa. Together we have explored its beauties and its storied history. Together, for in so many ways this is a joint effort, we share them with all who read these pages.

ROBERT LEGGET
Ottawa
28 February 1975

# INDEX

(P indicates that the item is pictured in an illustration)